IMAGES
of America

THE PORTLAND AREA
1869–1939

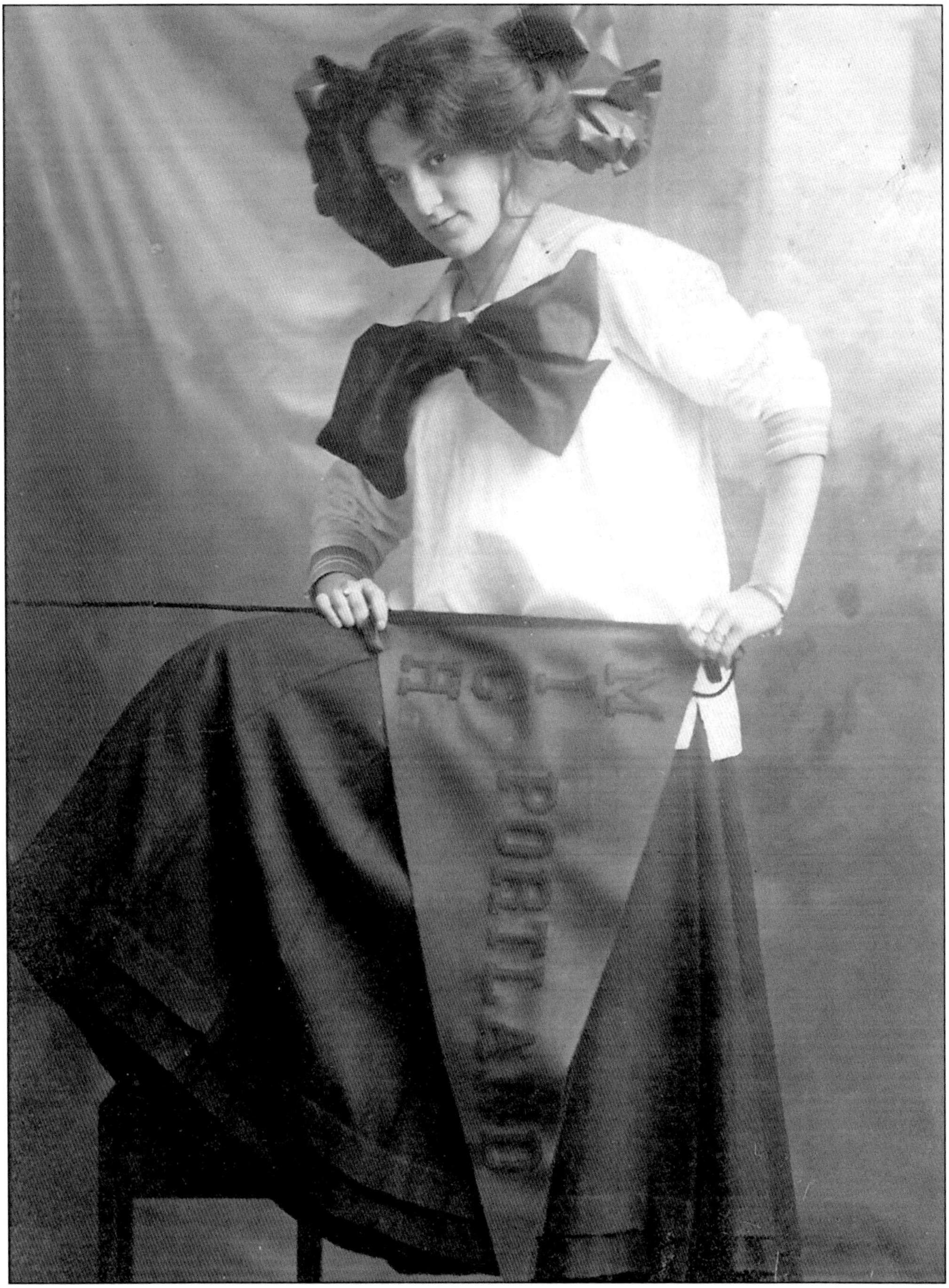

Rose Sulpizio with Portland Pennant. In this George Van Horn photographic postcard, Rose Sulpizio holds a "Portland, Mich." pennant. Rose was the daughter of Italian immigrants. Her father, Alphonso, came to America in 1890 and her mother arrived two years later. Rose was born in 1895. Rose's father owned and operated a candy shop on Kent Street. He eventually sold the shop to Santino Guidi and it became Candyland, a Portland favorite for many years. (Courtesy of the Portland Area Historical Society.)

IMAGES
of America

THE PORTLAND AREA
1869–1939

Mark D. Neese
on behalf of the Portland Area Historical Society

ARCADIA
PUBLISHING

ISBN 978-0-7385-3413-8

Published by Arcadia Publishing
Charleston, South Carolina

Printed in the United States of America

Library of Congress Catalog Card Number: 2005925683

For all general information contact Arcadia Publishing at:
Telephone 843-853-2070
Fax 843-853-0044
E-mail sales@arcadiapublishing.com
For customer service and orders:
Toll-Free 1-888-313-2665

Visit us on the Internet at www.arcadiapublishing.com

Contents

ACKNOWLEDGMENTS

I wish to thank, first and foremost, the Portland Area Historical Society for supporting this project. I am particularly grateful that they entrusted me with their outstanding photographic collection, thus enabling me to scan them on my home computer. Many thanks also to the society's editorial committee, particularly William Davis, Anne Rademacher, Carol Tonkin, and Robert Torp-Smith, who took the time to look over the manuscript and offer their valuable suggestions. Thanks also go to Seymour Van Derske for his colorful and informative stories about his ancestors, the Dilleys and Goodwins.

I extend my thanks to Anne Rademacher, Rick Teachout, Robert Torp-Smith, and Carol Tonkin for loaning me their photographs and postcards. These excellent images greatly contributed to this book. I also wish to thank Rick Teachout for sharing information regarding his beautiful home, the former Edward Goodwin house.

I wish to thank Bradley Seal and Patricia Need, who, when a complete stranger knocked on their door one Sunday afternoon, graciously and enthusiastically gave him the grand tour of their home, the former George Allen house. Their kindness and insight was much appreciated. Thanks also to Kay Devlin for providing information regarding her home, the former Charles Maynard house.

I would be remiss if I did not thank my parents for instilling in me, at a young age, a love and appreciation of history.

Finally, I wish to thank my wife Lynda, for not only assisting with the research for this book, but putting up with me during the four months that I was completely absorbed by this project. Your love and support has meant everything to me.

INTRODUCTION

The area that became Portland, Michigan was first populated by Native Americans. The Chippewa and Pottawatomi were the original residents of the Grand River and Looking Glass River's confluence, while the first European Americans did not establish a settlement here until 1833.

In the early 1830s, Elisha Newman visited some friends residing in Ann Arbor, Michigan. He wanted to establish a homestead in a good, unsettled area of Michigan and asked his acquaintances if they knew of any favorable locations. One of Newman's Ann Arbor friends was Joseph Wood, a man who had helped survey Ionia County. Wood encouraged Newman to visit the area near the confluence of the Looking Glass and Grand Rivers. Newman traveled to the area and was impressed enough to enter the first land claim in what would later become Portland, Michigan. The year was 1833.

Although the first land claim belonged to Elisha Newman, the first actual settler of Portland was Philo Bogue. Bogue arrived in November of 1833, and established a trading post. In May of 1836, Elisha Newman and his family arrived. They immediately set to work exploiting the water power of the Looking Glass River by damming it and building the settlement's first sawmill. Soon after, the fledgling settlement had a flour mill as well. By 1846, the village was platted on both sides of the Grand River.

On March 30, 1869, Portland was incorporated as a village. By 1881, Portland boasted a variety of different industries. Among these were two flour mills (one on the Grand River and the other on the Looking Glass River), a wagon and carriage manufacturer, an agricultural implement manufacturer, a stave factory, a fanning-mill factory, and a woolen mill along the north bank of the Looking Glass River.

By the turn of the century and well into the first three decades of the 20th century, industry abounded on the banks of the Grand and Looking Glass Rivers. Such businesses as the Portland Milling Company, Portland Manufacturing Company, Ramsey-Alton, Ypsilanti Reed, Salant & Salant, and Barley-Earhart produced items as diverse as flour, washing machines, furniture, shirts, and automotive products. Meanwhile, a thriving commercial district had grown along Bridge and Kent Streets, with a variety of goods and services, a sparkling opera house, and a large, luxuriant hotel. Portland was definitely a community on the move.

This book focuses on the Portland area between the years 1869 and 1939. If the years 1833 through 1869 can be seen as Portland's "birth and childhood" years, then 1869 to 1939 must surely be the village's adolescence and young adulthood. These years, bookended by the

Civil War and World War II, were a time in which industrialization and rapid technological advances changed the face of both Portland and America. At the same time, it was a last gasp of innocence before the events of World War II thrust America into the Nuclear Age.

On a more mundane level, but one particularly germane to the Images of America series, the years between 1869 and 1939 were a time in which photography reached the masses. Between 1900 and 1920, photographic postcards were arguably at the height of their popularity. The photographs from the late 19th and early 20th century are of very high quality and, quite frankly, make this time period an enjoyable one to document.

This book should not be seen as a comprehensive history of the Portland area, but more as an informative historical photo album from a specific time period. The shape and appearance of this book were dictated by the photographs and images that could be found. Many important places, events, and people in the community's history are missing simply because no image was available.

The work of two photographers features prominently in this book. They are George Van Horn and Lorenzo Webber. Van Horn was a professional photographer who operated his own studio and published hundreds of photos in Portland newspapers. He was seemingly at every important local event in the late 19th and early 20th centuries. Van Horn's photography is by turns serious and whimsical. Lorenzo Webber was a successful Portland banker who, in the early 1890s, purchased his own camera. He is thought to be the first amateur photographer in the village. From the early to mid-1890s, Webber took hundreds of pictures of Portland townspeople at work and play. He frequently snapped photos of unsuspecting customers as they approached his bank, which was located on the northwest corner of Bridge and Kent Streets.

It was Lorenzo Webber's photographs, in fact, that inspired this project. In the autumn of 2003, I began work on my final project in Eastern Michigan University's historic preservation program. My subject was the history of Portland's Bridge and Kent Street four corners, and I happened to stumble upon the Portland Area Historical Society's excellent photograph collection at the Portland Library. When I saw Lorenzo Webber's amazing document of turn-of-the-century Portland life, I knew that those photographs deserved to be published in a book. Writing this book has truly been a dream fulfilled, and I am thrilled that the brilliant photographs of both Van Horn and Webber will reach the large audience they so richly deserve.

I have done my utmost to be as historically accurate as possible, and apply the same level of historiography that would be expected in an academic work. All information contained in these captions is based on some sort of oral or written documentation: mainly newspaper articles, United States census records, county histories, directories, or first-hand recollections. It is my sincere hope that this book will be enjoyed for years to come, and will do justice to those who settled and built Portland.

One

TRANSPORTATION

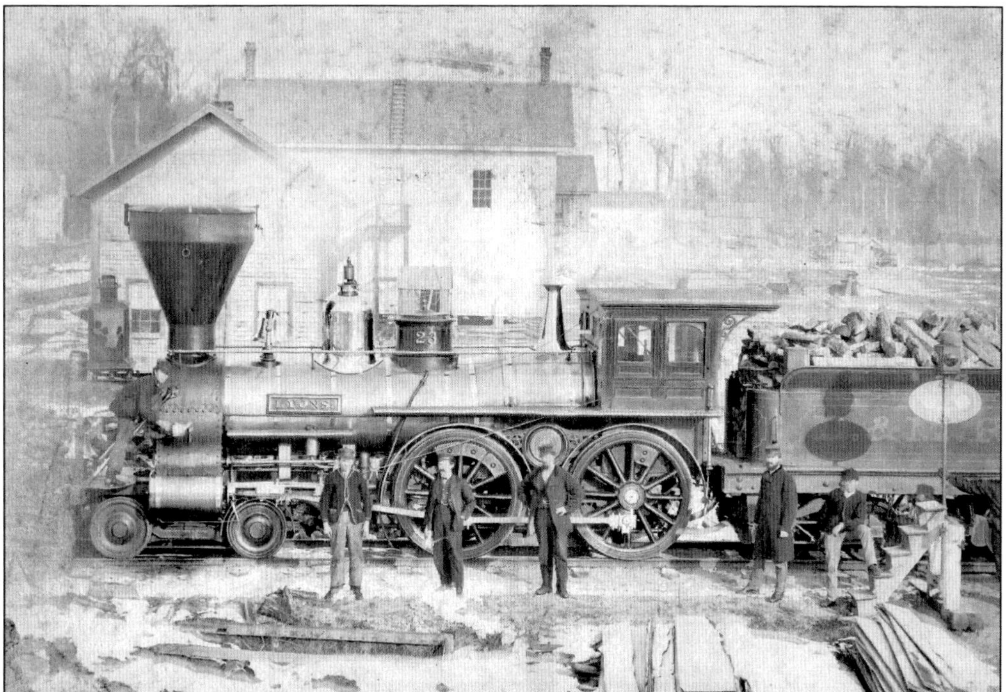

ONE OF THE FIRST TRAINS IN THE PORTLAND AREA. This wood-burning Detroit & Milwaukee Railroad steam locomotive probably arrived in the late autumn of 1869. The D&M Railroad ran through Muir, Ionia, and Saranac. (Courtesy of the Portland Area Historical Society.)

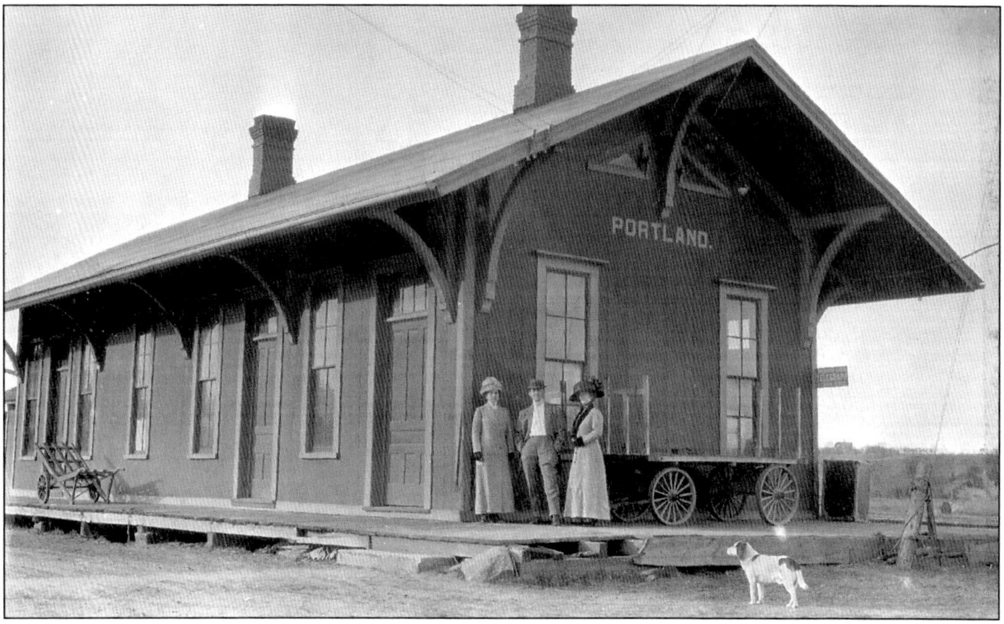

Waiting for the Afternoon Train. This sharply-dressed trio poses next to a baggage wagon as they wait for the morning train at the Portland depot, *c.* 1910. In the early 20th century, when this photograph was taken, there were five daily trains east to Danby, Eagle, Grand Ledge, and Lansing; and five daily trains west to Collins, Lyons, Ionia, and all points beyond. Note the sign on the right-hand side of the building that reads "Telegraph." (Courtesy of the Portland Area Historical Society.)

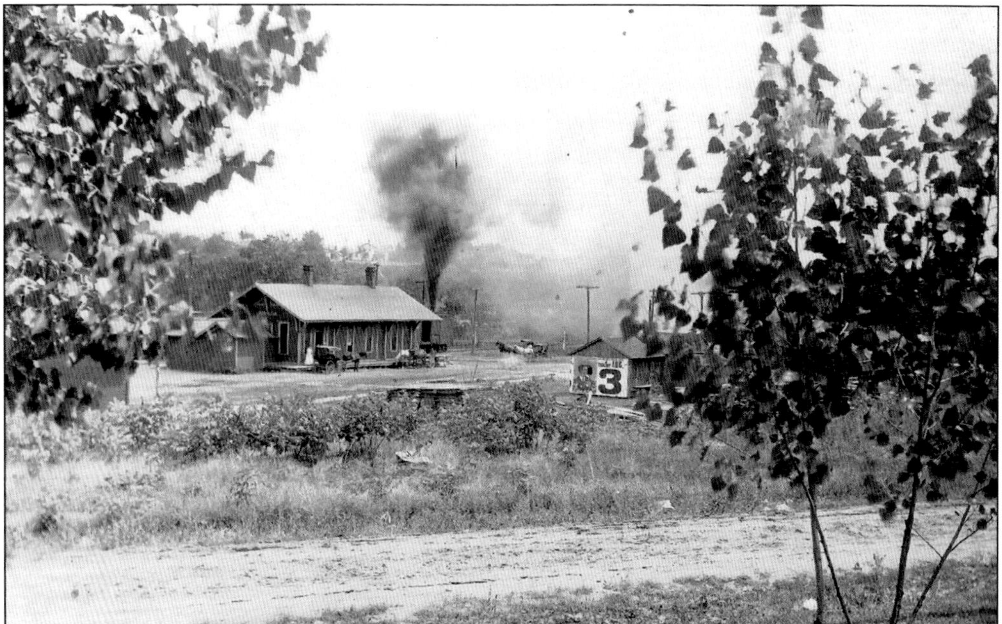

Portland Depot. This view faces east towards the Portland depot. The depot was located on the northwest edge of the village, near the present-day intersection of Water and Pleasant Streets. (Courtesy of Robert Torp-Smith.)

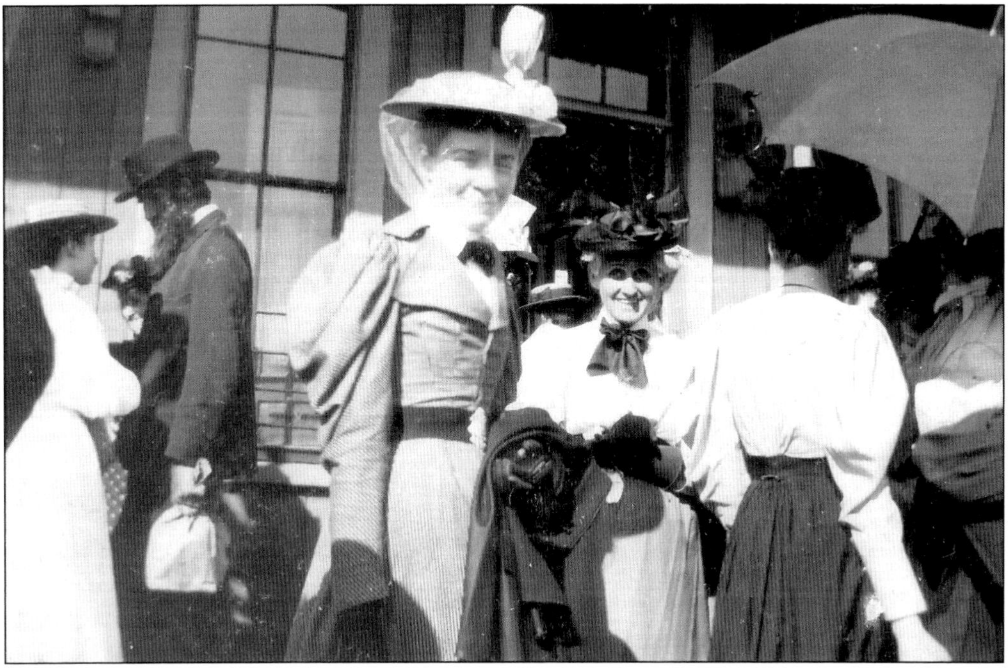

Excursion Group. Portland banker Lorenzo Webber took these photographs of an excursion group waiting for the train at the Portland depot, *c.* 1895. In the top photograph, the two women facing the camera are Mary White Buck and Mary E. Webber. Mrs. Buck was the wife of George Buck, a Portland-area farmer. Mrs. Webber was Lorenzo Webber's mother. In the second photograph, only the women near the front are identified. Beginning with the woman in black on the far left, they are: Italy Dey, Frances Reynolds, Meredith Smith, Christine Webber, Nettie Guilden, Lucy Whitlock, Minnie Jenkins, Gertrude Morehouse, Ethelyn Briggs, and Mary White Buck. (Courtesy of the Portland Area Historical Society.)

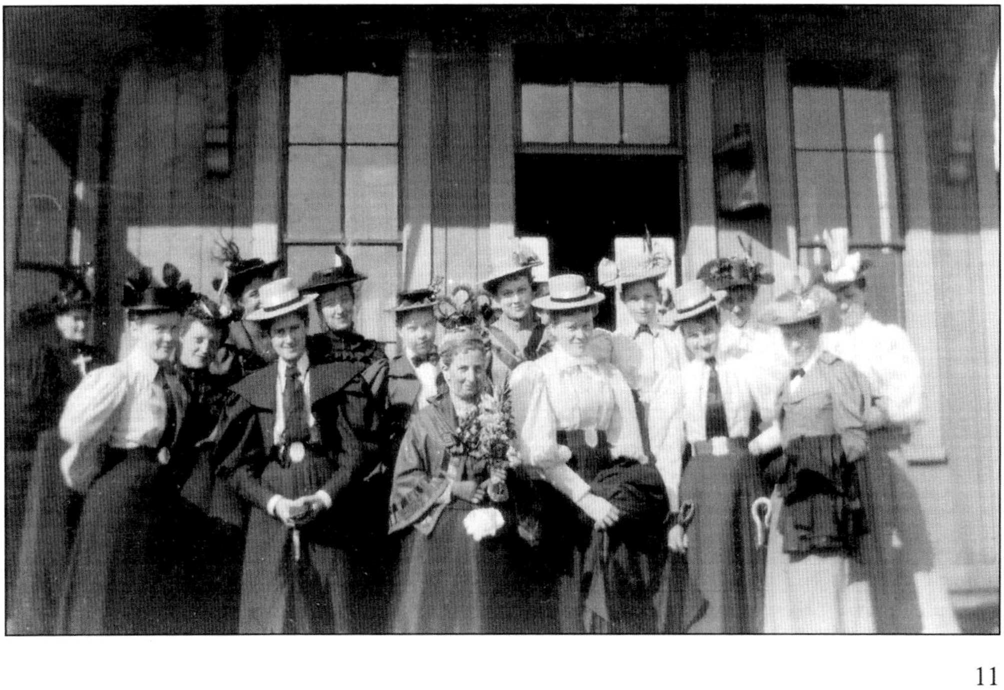

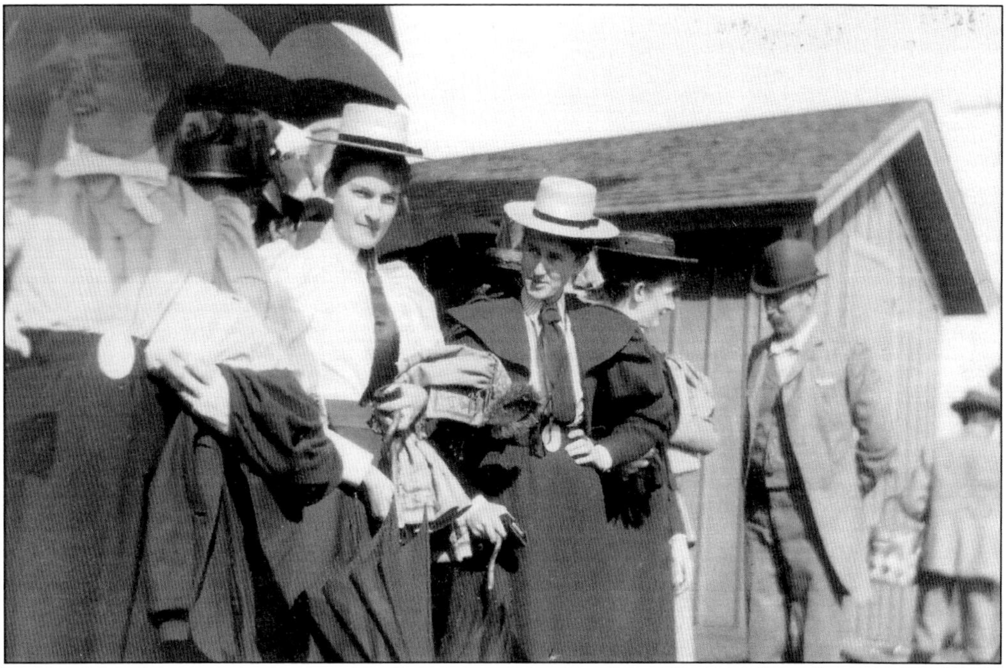

(*above*) **GATHERING IN FRONT OF DEPOT.** In the Victorian era, women were advised to avoid wearing laces and velvet because dust particles attached to the fabric. It was also considered in poor taste to wear elaborate or expensive jewelry while traveling. (Courtesy of the Portland Area Historical Society.)

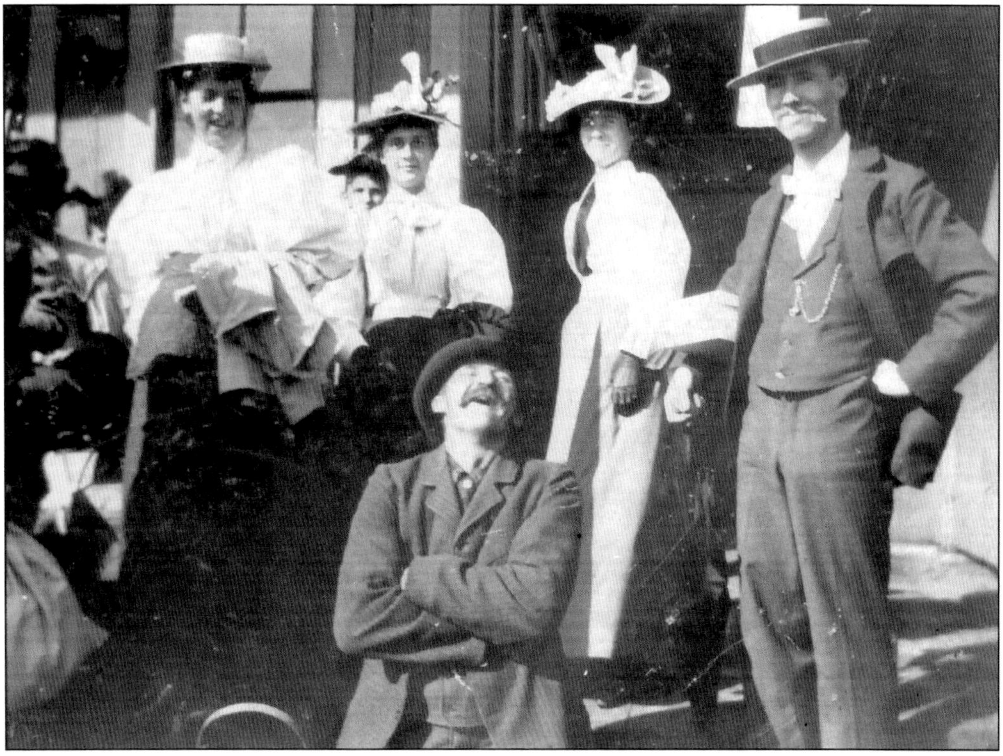

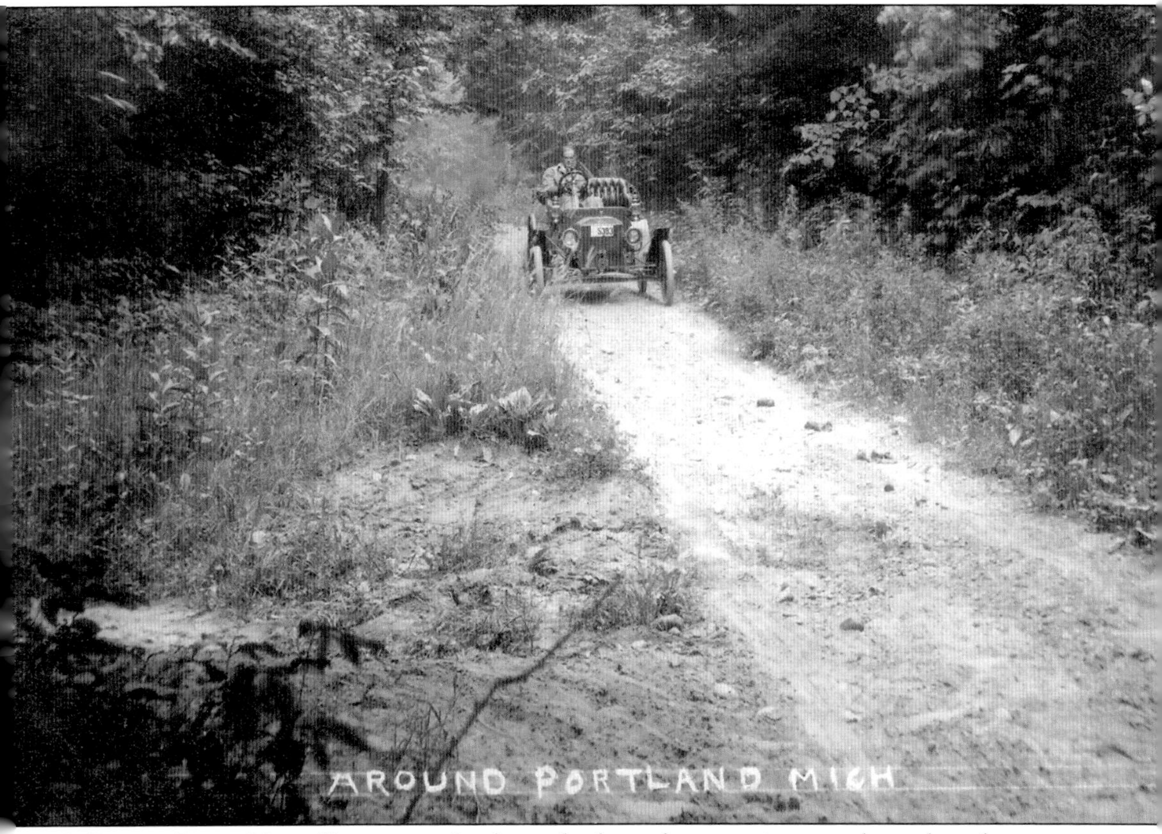

A ROUGH ROAD NEAR PORTLAND. In the early days of automotive travel, rural roads were narrow, bumpy, and altogether treacherous. This one-lane, rock-strewn trail outside of Portland is representative of typical rural road conditions *c.* 1910. It was at this time that the "Good Roads Movement" took hold in Michigan. Led by such people as Horatio Earle, who became the state's first highway department commissioner, the Good Roads Movement lobbied successfully for state and federal funding to both improve existing roads and build new ones. (Courtesy of the Portland Area Historical Society.)

(*opposite, bottom*) **LAUGHING AND WAITING FOR THE TRAIN.** This group, caught during a moment of jocularity, is waiting for the train to take them to Ottawa Beach on Lake Michigan. The photograph was taken on August 7, 1895. Pictured from left to right are Dora Webber, Nellie Guilford, Nora Lakin, and Eugene Smith. The man laughing in the front is identified on the back of the photograph as "Brooks the drayman." A drayman hauled freight to and from the depot and railroad freight house. (Courtesy of the Portland Area Historical Society.)

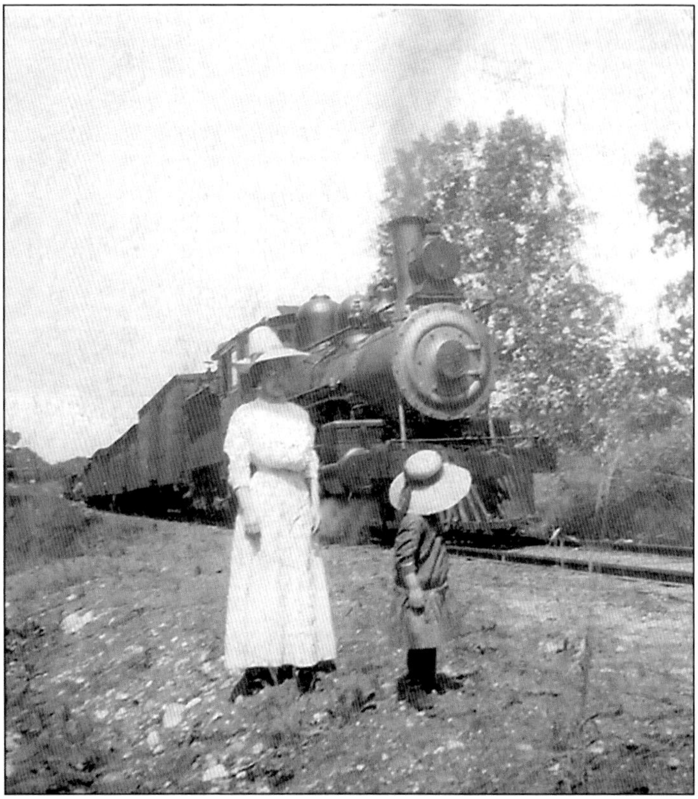

WATCHING THE TRAIN WEST OF TOWN. This photograph was taken on June 5, 1911. Myrtle Blackman and young Ernestine Vogt watch a train pass by west of Portland. (Courtesy of Carol Tonkin.)

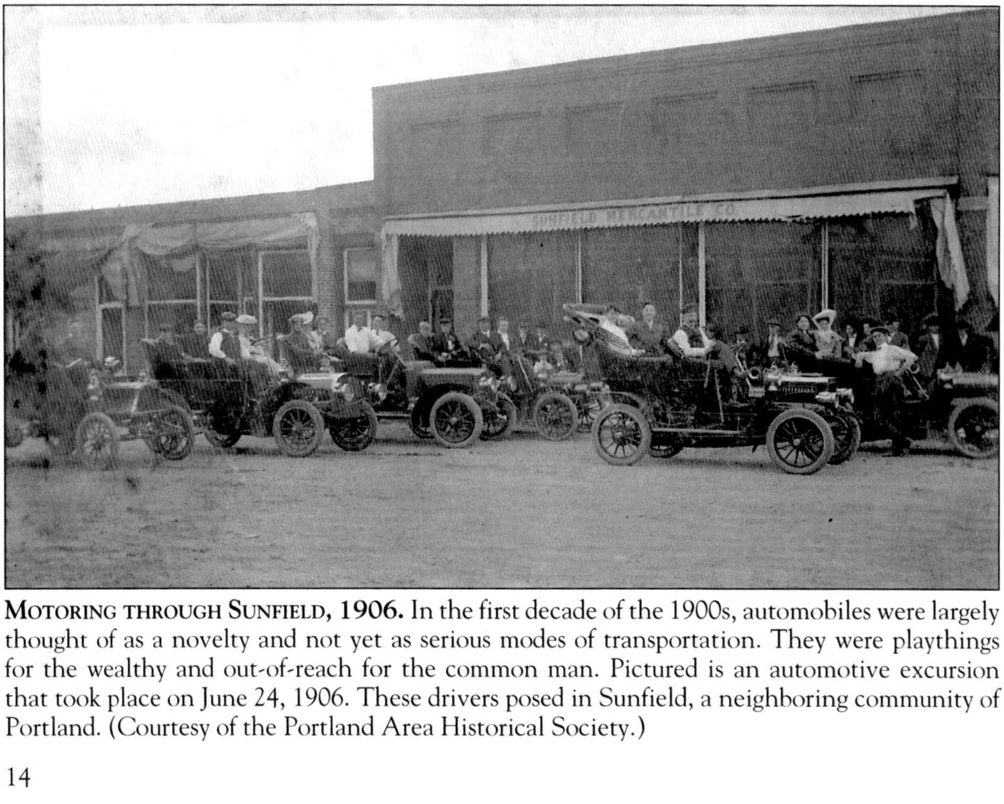

MOTORING THROUGH SUNFIELD, 1906. In the first decade of the 1900s, automobiles were largely thought of as a novelty and not yet as serious modes of transportation. They were playthings for the wealthy and out-of-reach for the common man. Pictured is an automotive excursion that took place on June 24, 1906. These drivers posed in Sunfield, a neighboring community of Portland. (Courtesy of the Portland Area Historical Society.)

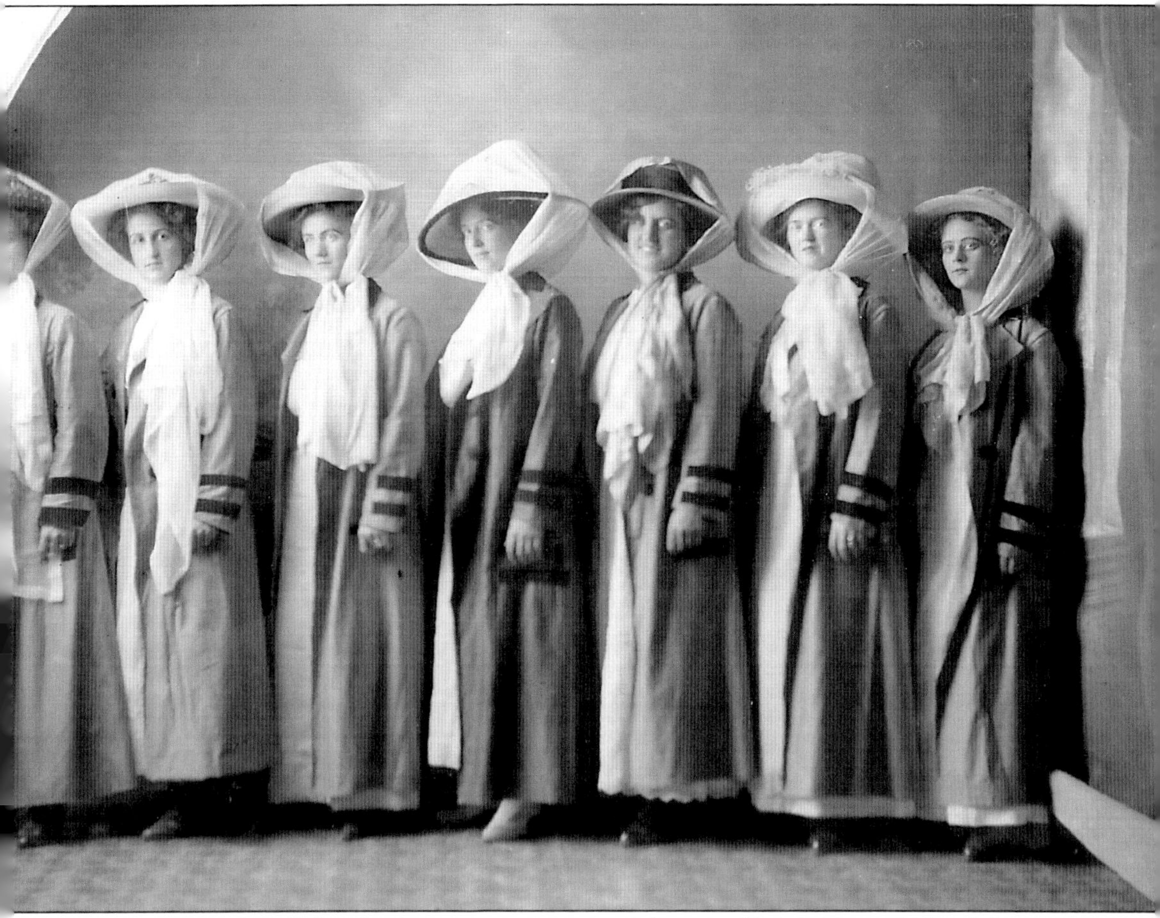

Chorus Girls. This all-female chorus group performed the song "In My Merry Oldsmobile," at a Portland benefit function. Nearby Lansing was the birthplace of Olds Motor Works. Ransom E. Olds manufactured his first automobile in 1897. By the first decade of the 20th century, touring around in autos had become a national craze. In 1905, songwriters Vincent Bryan and Gus Edwards tapped into this new American passion by writing "In My Merry Oldsmobile." The broad-brimmed hat and duster ensembles were worn in touring cars to protect dresses from dust and dirt. Pictured from left to right are as follows: Grace Jenkins Bates, Bessie Rowley Lehman, Loo McDougal McBride, Florence Fiero Stewart, Mabel Miller Clark, Sarah McCormick Rice, and Marjorie McKenny. (Courtesy of the Portland Area Historical Society.)

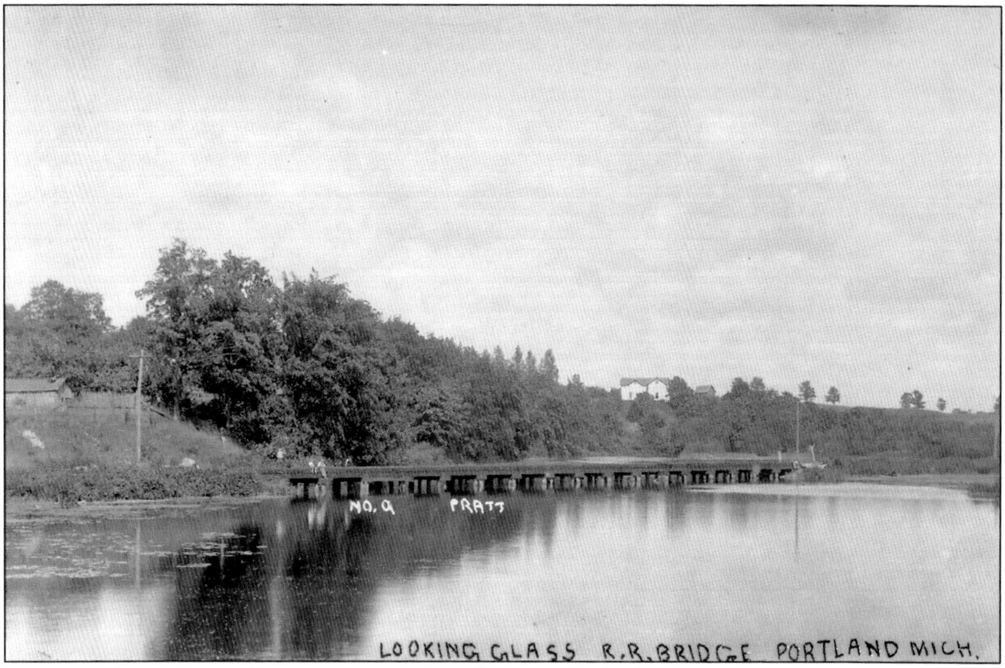

LOOKING GLASS RIVER RAILROAD BRIDGE. This view looks upriver towards the railroad bridge spanning the Looking Glass River, *c.* 1910. The bridge was located east of present-day Divine Highway. (Courtesy of Robert Torp-Smith.)

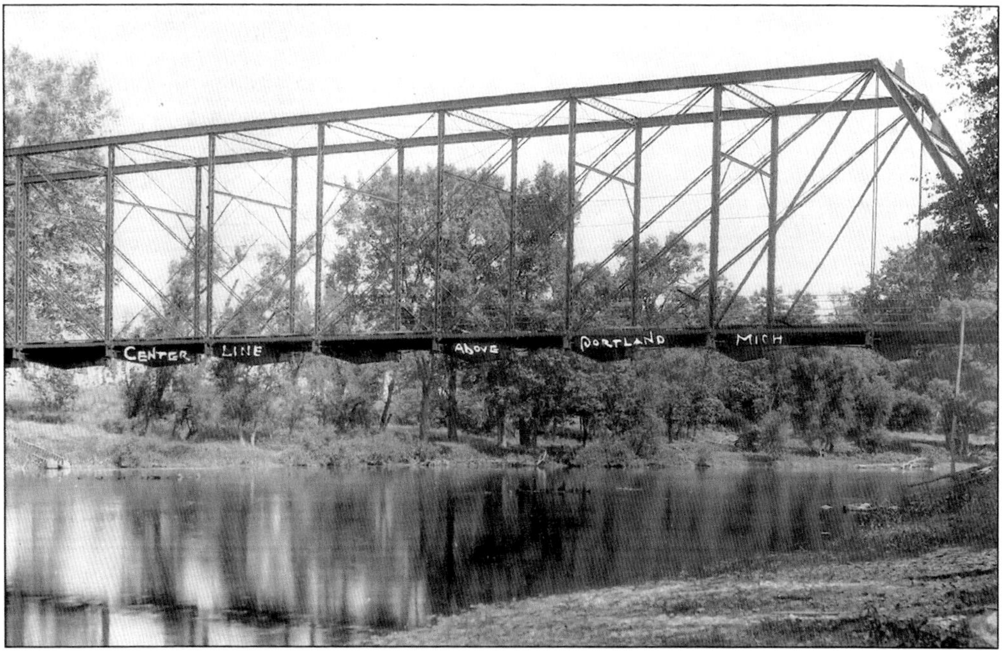

CENTER LINE BRIDGE. The center line bridge was about two miles south of Portland in Danby Township. The bridge was close to the intersection of both the north/south and east/west Danby Township centerlines. (Courtesy of Robert Torp-Smith.)

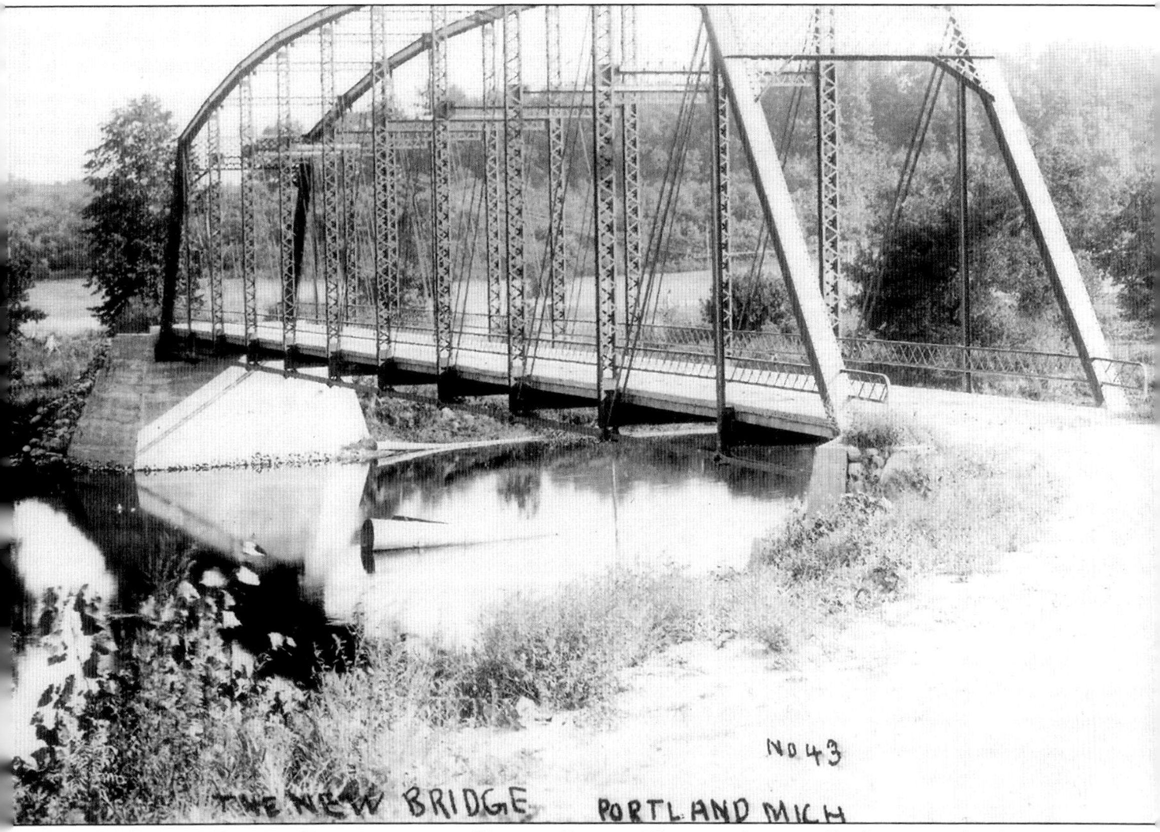

Kent Street Bridge Spanning the Grand River. This single-span Parker truss bridge is identified in this postcard as "the new bridge." The term "Parker" refers to the polygonal topchord that gives the bridge an arched appearance. Built in 1907 by the Wynkoop & Gormley firm of Toledo, Ohio, the bridge is one of only three existing Parker truss bridges identified in the Michigan Department of Transportation's historic bridge inventory. The bridge was relocated downriver and facilitates one of the crossings of the Portland pedestrian river trail. (Courtesy of Robert Torp-Smith.)

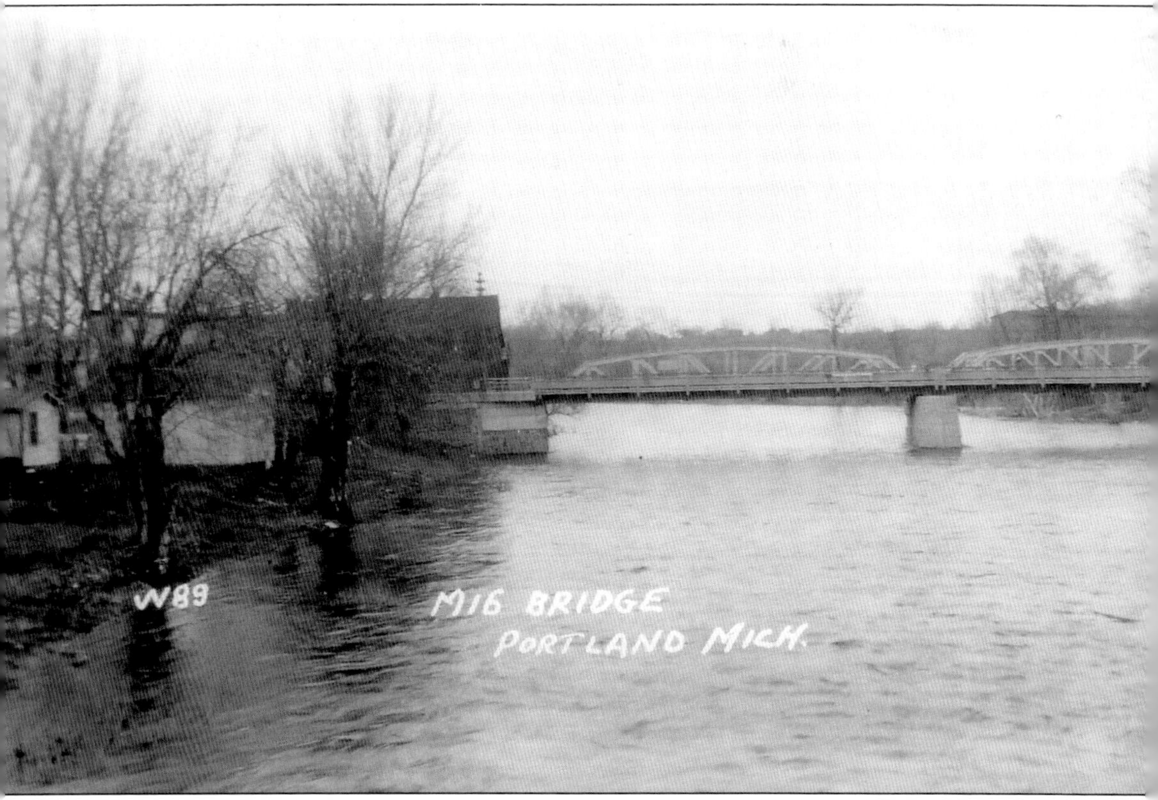

M-16 BRIDGE. This view looks downriver towards the M-16 (Grand River Road) Bridge crossing the Grand River. From 1918 to 1926, Grand River Road was designated as M-16, a state trunkline highway. The highway ran from Detroit, through Lansing, and all the way to Grand Haven. In 1926, the route was renamed US-16. (Courtesy of Robert Torp-Smith.)

Two

Business and Industry

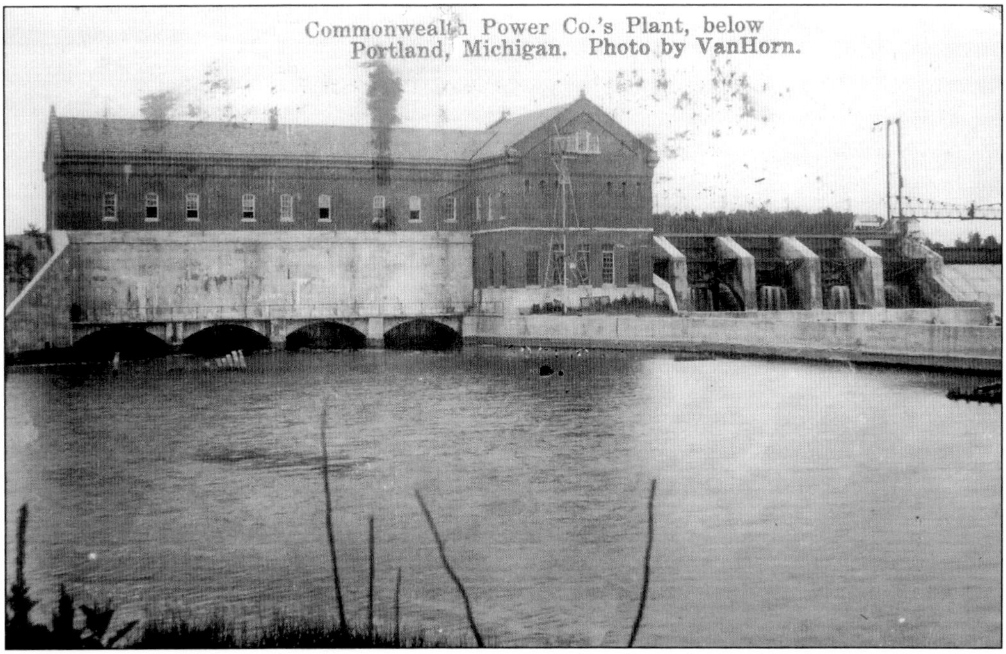

Commonwealth Power Company Plant, c. 1915. This dam is located in Lyons and was built in 1857. At that time, it served as a mill pond, as well as controlling the Grand River. It was rebuilt in 1870 and 1921, and converted to a hydro-electric power plant. The dam still stands to this day. (Courtesy of Robert Torp-Smith.)

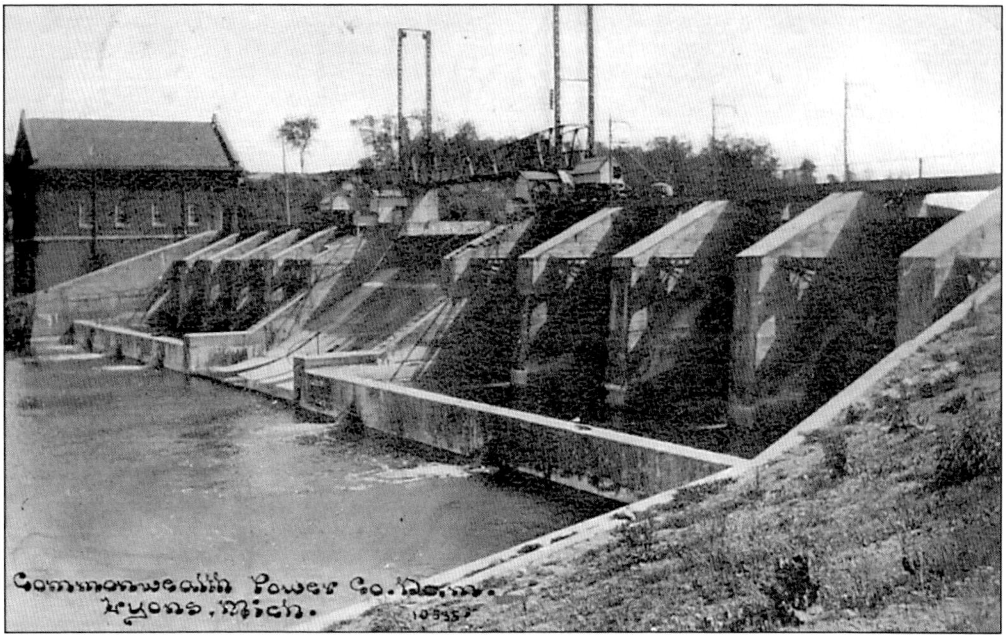

COMMONWEALTH POWER COMPANY DAM. This is another view of the Commonwealth Power Company Dam. (Courtesy of Robert Torp-Smith.)

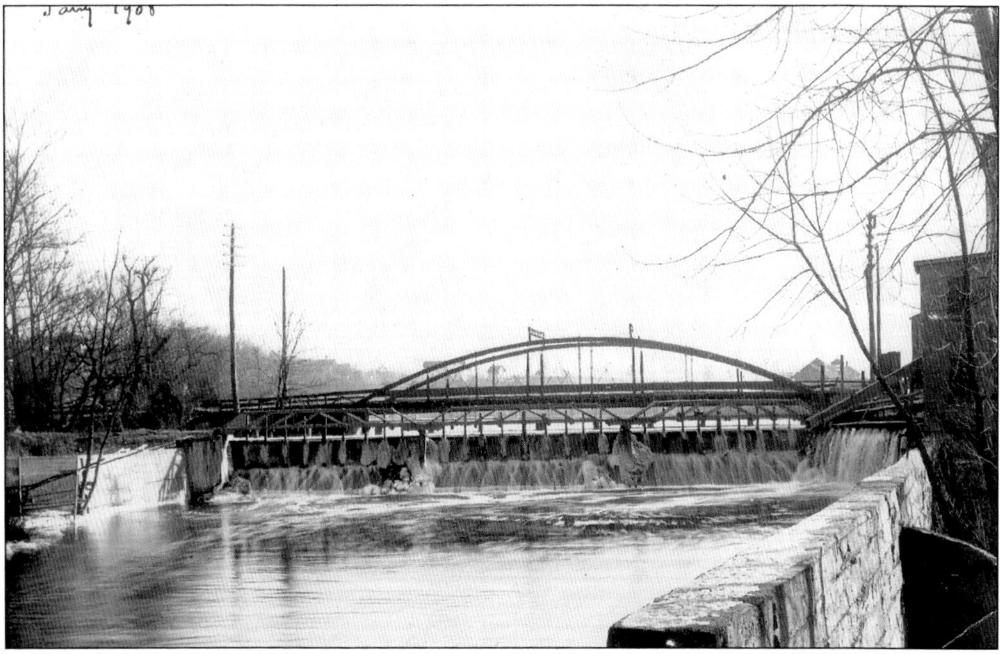

DAM ON THE LOOKING GLASS RIVER, 1908. This dam was located on the Looking Glass River near the Portland Milling Company. The shadowy building on the right is the mill itself. Portland's success as an industrial center relied on the ability to harness the river through the construction of dams. (Courtesy of Robert Torp-Smith.)

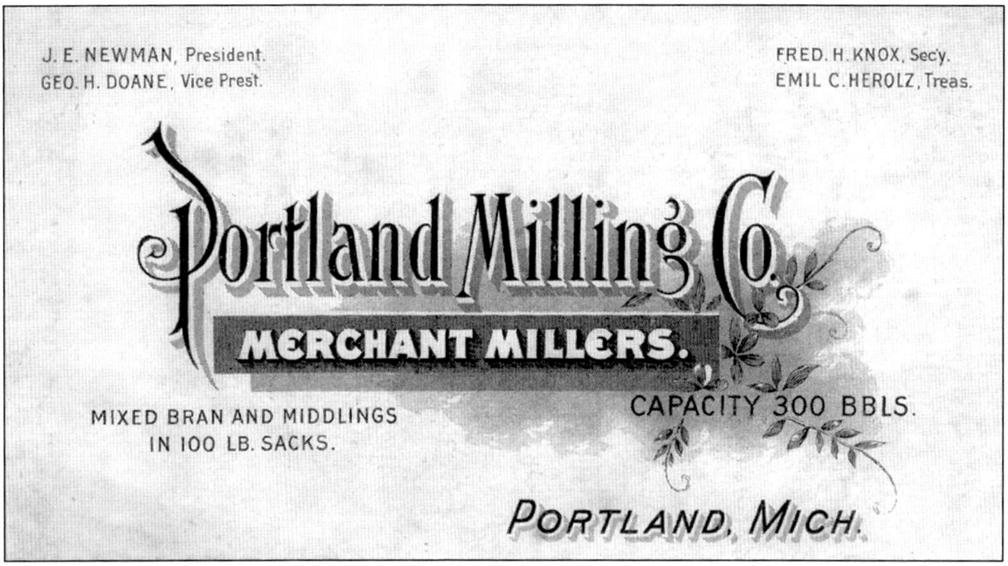

PORTLAND MILLING COMPANY. This is a business card for the Portland Milling Company. Portland Milling, located on the Looking Glass River, had the city's largest grain elevator and mill. When the Newman & Rice mill burned to the ground in February 1893, a new mill was soon under construction and completed in October. The company was reorganized and renamed the Portland Milling Company. They produced "Lily White" and other brands of flour. Some of the terminology on this business card may need translation for the laymen: The term "bbls" is an abbreviation for bushels, while "middling" refers to a co-product of the wheat milling process generally used as livestock feed. (Courtesy of the Portland Area Historical Society.)

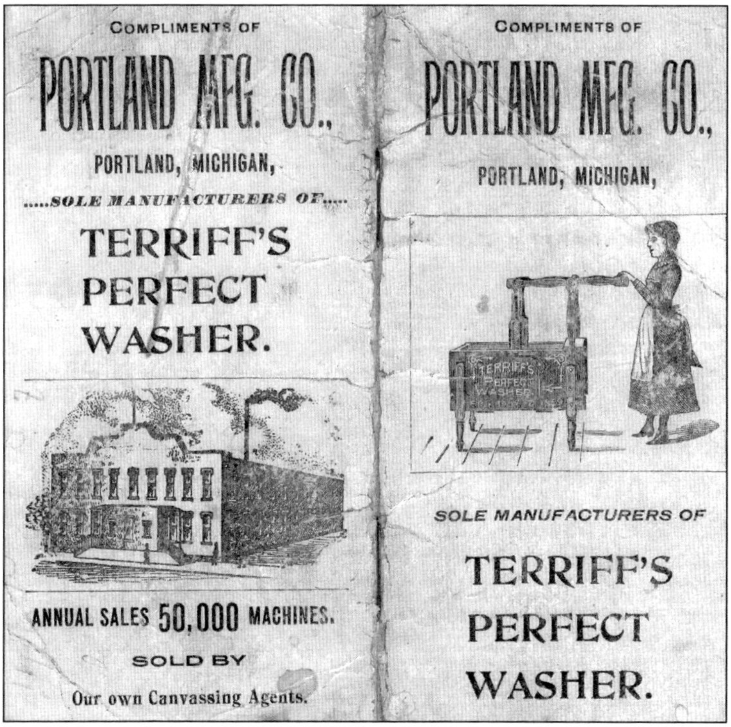

TERRIFF'S PERFECT WASHER. The Portland Manufacturing Company, makers of the Terriff's Perfect Washer washing machine, gave away this small memo book as a promotion for their machine. On the back cover is an illustration of the company's building on Kent Street, while on the front cover a young woman demonstrates how to operate the washer. (Courtesy of Richard Teachout.)

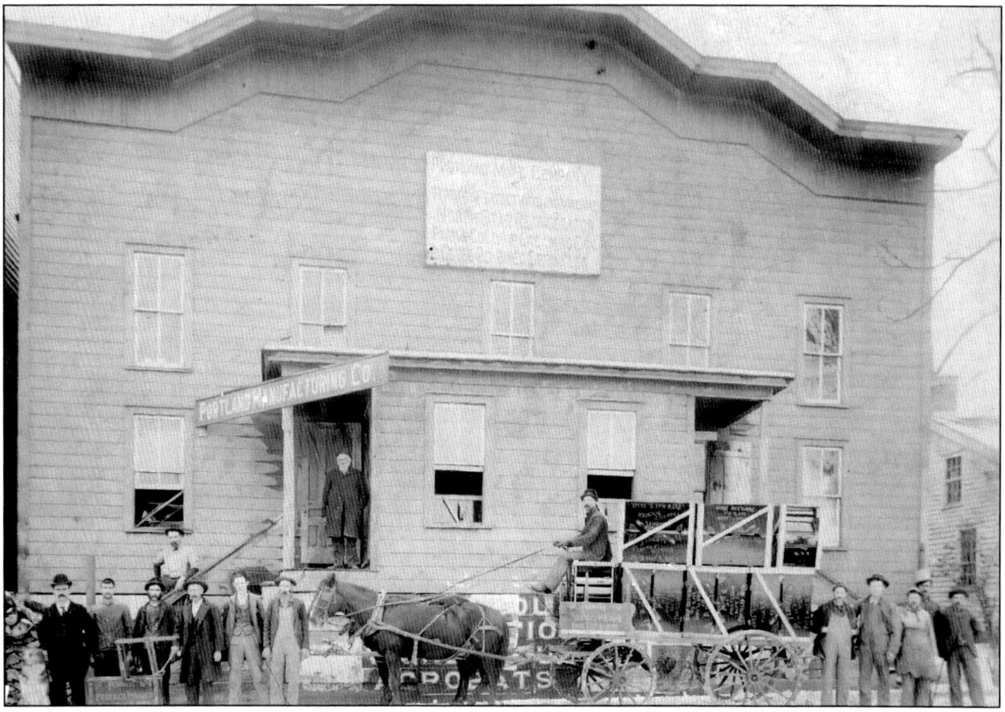

The Portland Manufacturing Company. The Portland Manufacturing Company washing machine warehouse was located at the current site of the Portland City Hall. A shipment of Terriff's Perfect Washers is loaded behind the warehouse building. The man in the dark suit on the far left is inventor, and company founder, W.W. Terriff. The sign on the building's façade reads, "Portland Manufacturing Co., Terriff Perfect Washing Machine. North Star Refrigerator. Park's Cold Air Cleaning Can. B. Globee Combined Sprinkler." (Courtesy of Richard Teachout.)

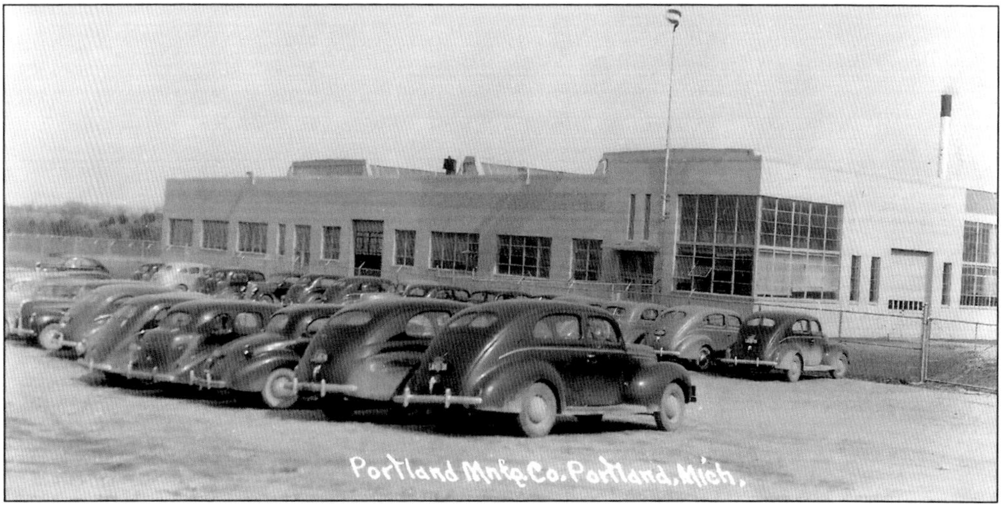

Portland Manufacturing Company, c. 1940. By the end of the 1930s, the Portland Manufacturing Company had become the Portland plant of the Holley Carburetor Company and was ready for a modern facility. In 1940, this building was constructed on Lyons Road on the northwest end of Portland. It was occupied by the company until 1953, when the factory was taken over by Thompson-Ramo-Woodlridge, Inc. (TRW, Inc.) (Courtesy of Robert Torp-Smith.)

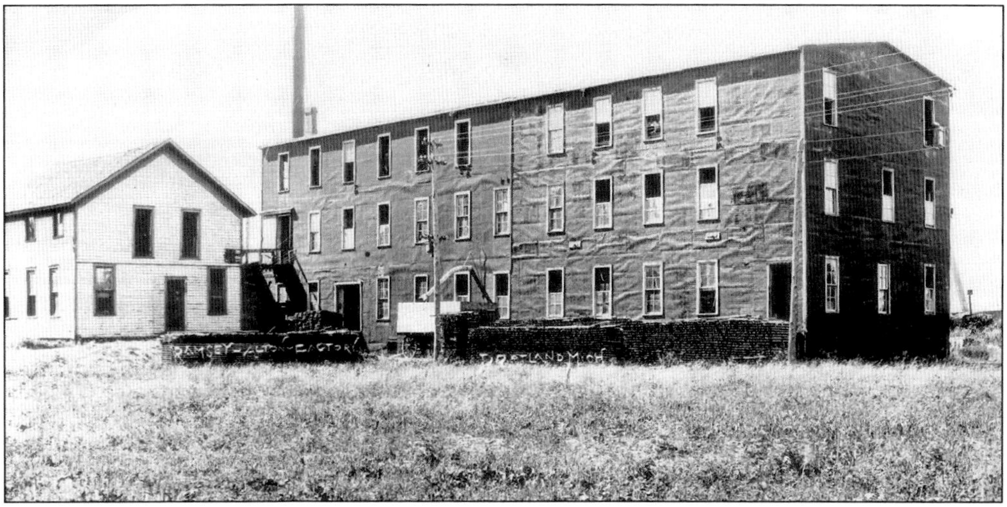

RAMSEY-ALTON FACTORY IN THE EARLY 1900S. The Ramsey-Alton Manufacturing Company built this factory in 1902. Ramsey-Alton was a furniture company that, in the early 1900s, specialized in their Oak Craft brand of Mission-style seat rockers, chairs, and settees. A 1912 company advertisement boasted, "The Ramsey-Alton Mfg. Co. have built up, within a very few years, not only a modern plant but have gathered together a body of skilled Craftsmen, who take as much real interest in the product of the shops as do those who have large interests at stake, enabling this concern to turn out a product which has and is receiving the very substantial approval of the furniture trade, not only in the states but in several foreign countries." (Courtesy of Robert Torp-Smith.)

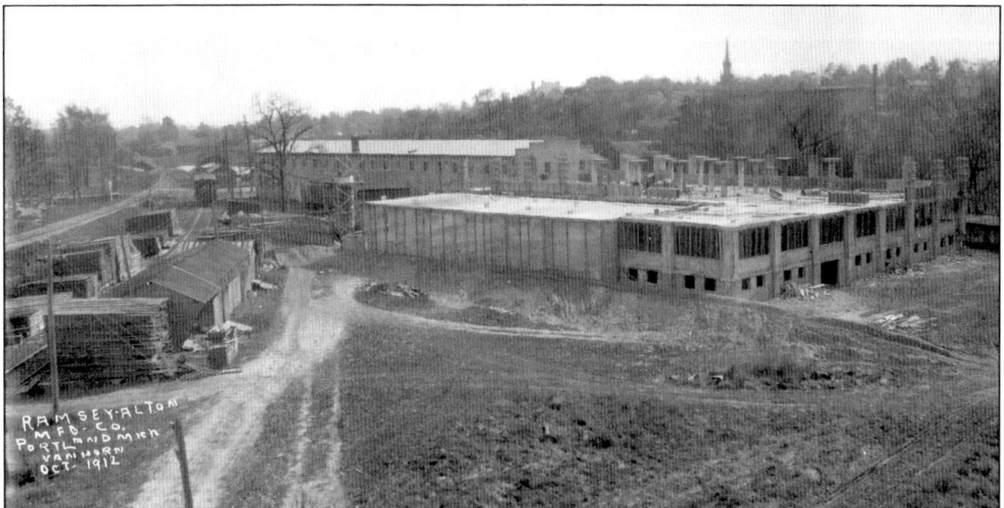

NEW RAMSEY-ALTON FACTORY UNDER CONTSTRUCTION, 1912. As this building neared completion in October 1912, Ramsey-Alton stated that "the plant as a whole is to be one of the most modern of its kind, built especially for the convenience and protection of the craftsmen employed therein and is to be equipped with all the improved machinery and tools necessary to the building of Oak Craft Furniture." By 1912, the Ramsey-Alton company had become a highly successful manufacturer of Arts and Crafts and Mission-style furniture and the demand for their products had necessitated the erection of this large new factory. The building was constructed adjacent to the 1908 storehouse. (Courtesy of the Portland Area Historical Society.)

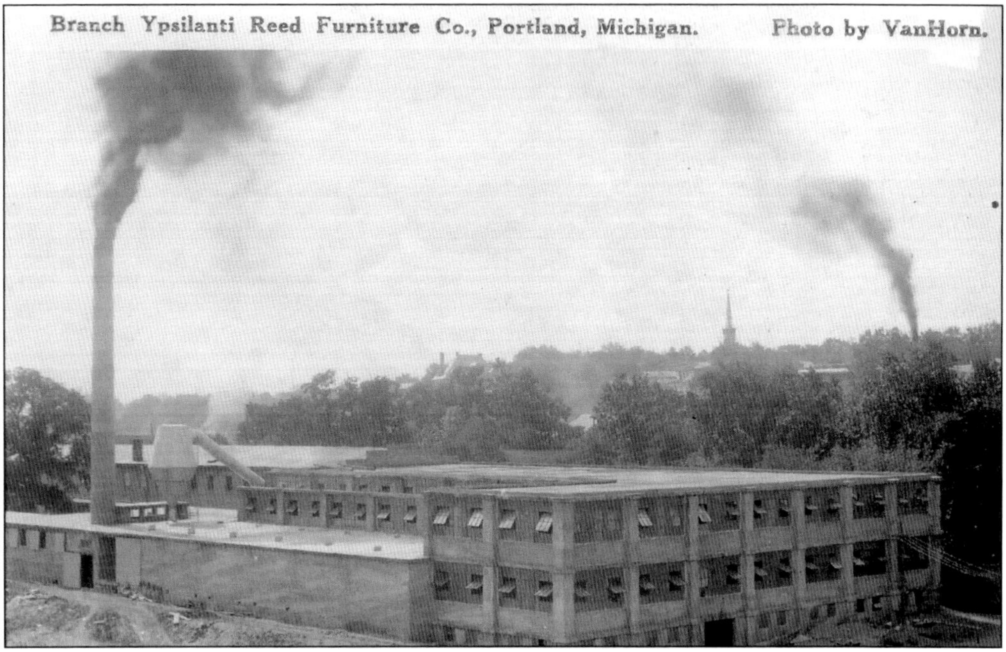

YPSILANTI REED FURNITURE COMPANY, C. 1920. In 1919, the Ypsilanti Reed Furniture Company moved a branch of its operation into the factory formerly occupied by the Ramsey-Alton Manufacturing Company. Ypsilanti Reed was headquartered in Ionia and manufactured various models of reed furniture. Its Portland factory employed approximately 400 people. (Courtesy of Anne Rademacher.)

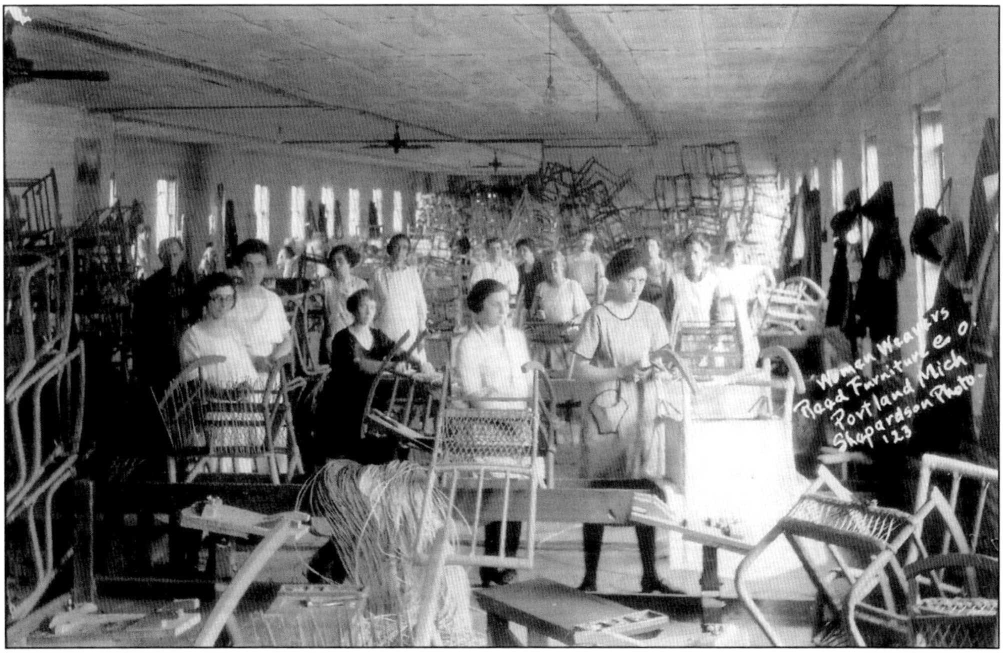

YPSILANTI REED FURNITURE COMPANY WORKERS. The women weavers of the Ypsilanti Reed Furniture Company took a break from work to pose for this 1923 photograph. (Courtesy of the Portland Area Historical Society.)

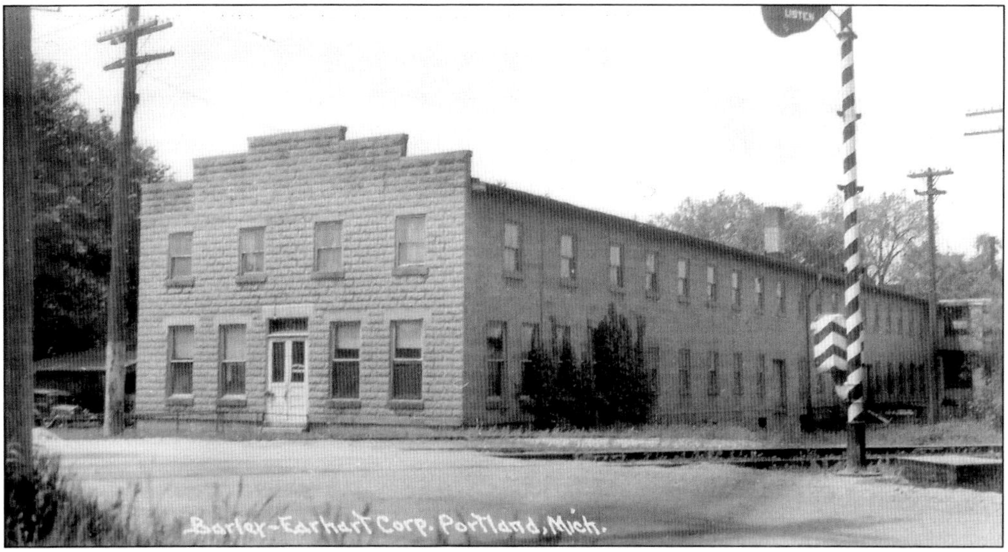

BARLEY EARHEART CORPORATION, C. 1938. In January 1938, the Barley-Earhart Corporation began operations in Portland in the building formerly occupied in previous years by the Ramsey-Alton Manufacturing Company, the Ypsilanti Reed Furniture Company, and the Salant & Salant shirt company. The building, originally used as a storehouse, was erected by Ramsey-Alton in 1908. It was known as the "Village Hall" because taxpayer money helped fund its construction. In order to make this expenditure legal, the building was officially designated as a village hall. (Courtesy of Robert Torp-Smith.)

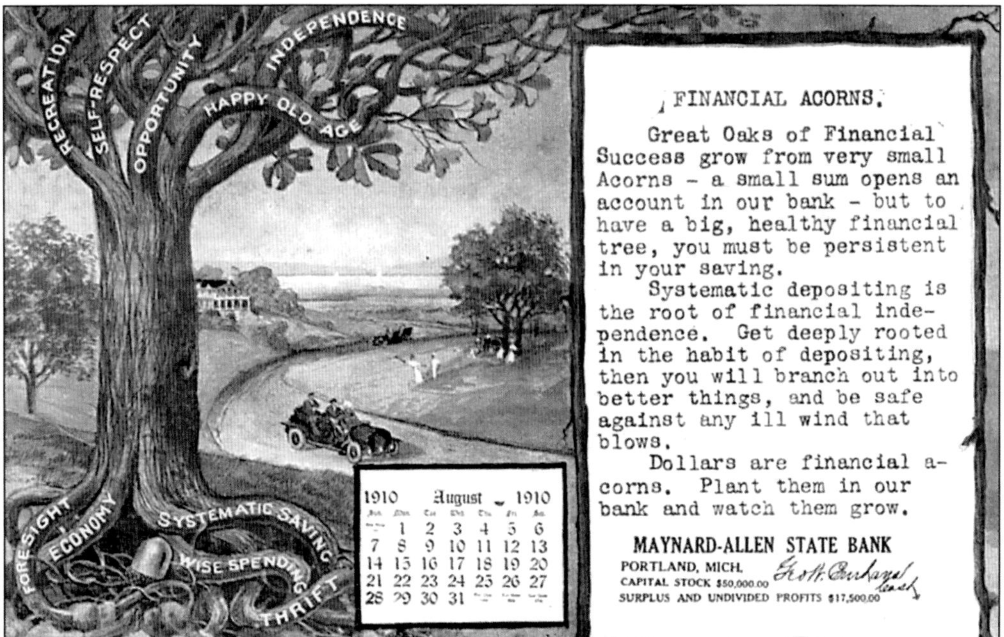

PROMOTIONAL POSTCARD FROM MAYNARD-ALLEN STATE BANK. Manly Cromkrite of Sebewa received this advertising postcard from the Maynard-Allen State Bank in early August 1910. The bank used creative symbolism on the front of the card to encourage the recipient to open up a savings account at the bank. (Courtesy of Robert Torp-Smith.)

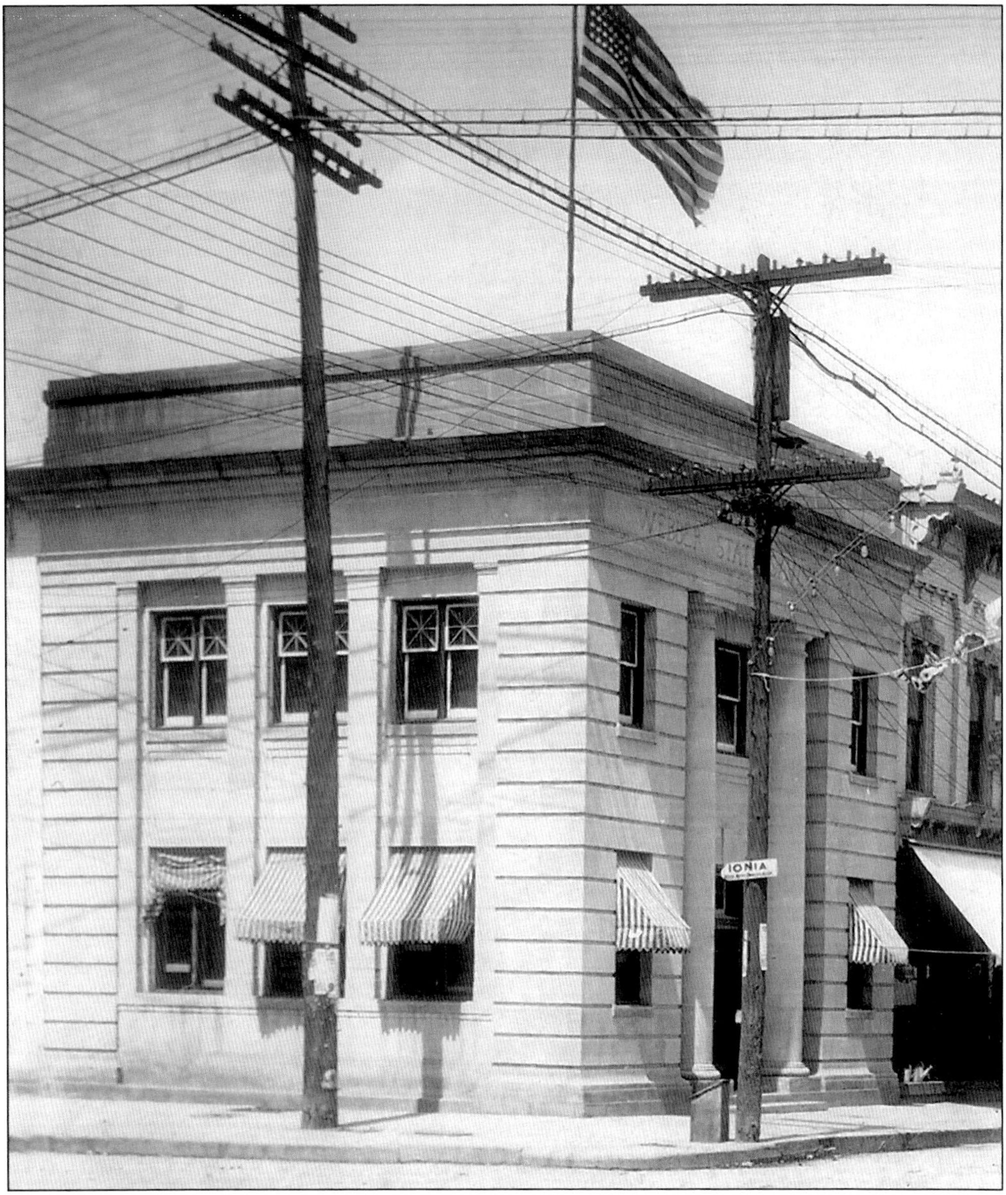

WEBBER STATE BANK, C. 1915. The Webber State Bank had a long history in Portland. Its origins can be traced back to Lorenzo Webber and his son John A. Webber, who came to Portland in the spring of 1870 from New York State. Upon settling in the community, they founded the L. Webber & Son Bank. For the first few years of its existence, the bank occupied a room in the back of another business until the Webbers purchased the northwest corner of Bridge and Kent. In 1884, Lorenzo Webber died and left the bank duties to his son, John A. The name of the business was changed to simply, "John A. Webber, banker." Seven years later, John A. Webber's son George, who had been assisting in the bank, died at the tender age of 19. John A. called upon his eldest son Lorenzo (named after his grandfather) to return to Portland from his studies at Harvard University. Lorenzo replaced George as his father's assistant and worked in the bank business for the next forty years. In 1931, the Webber State Savings Bank merged with the Maynard Allen State Bank. (Courtesy of Richard Teachout.)

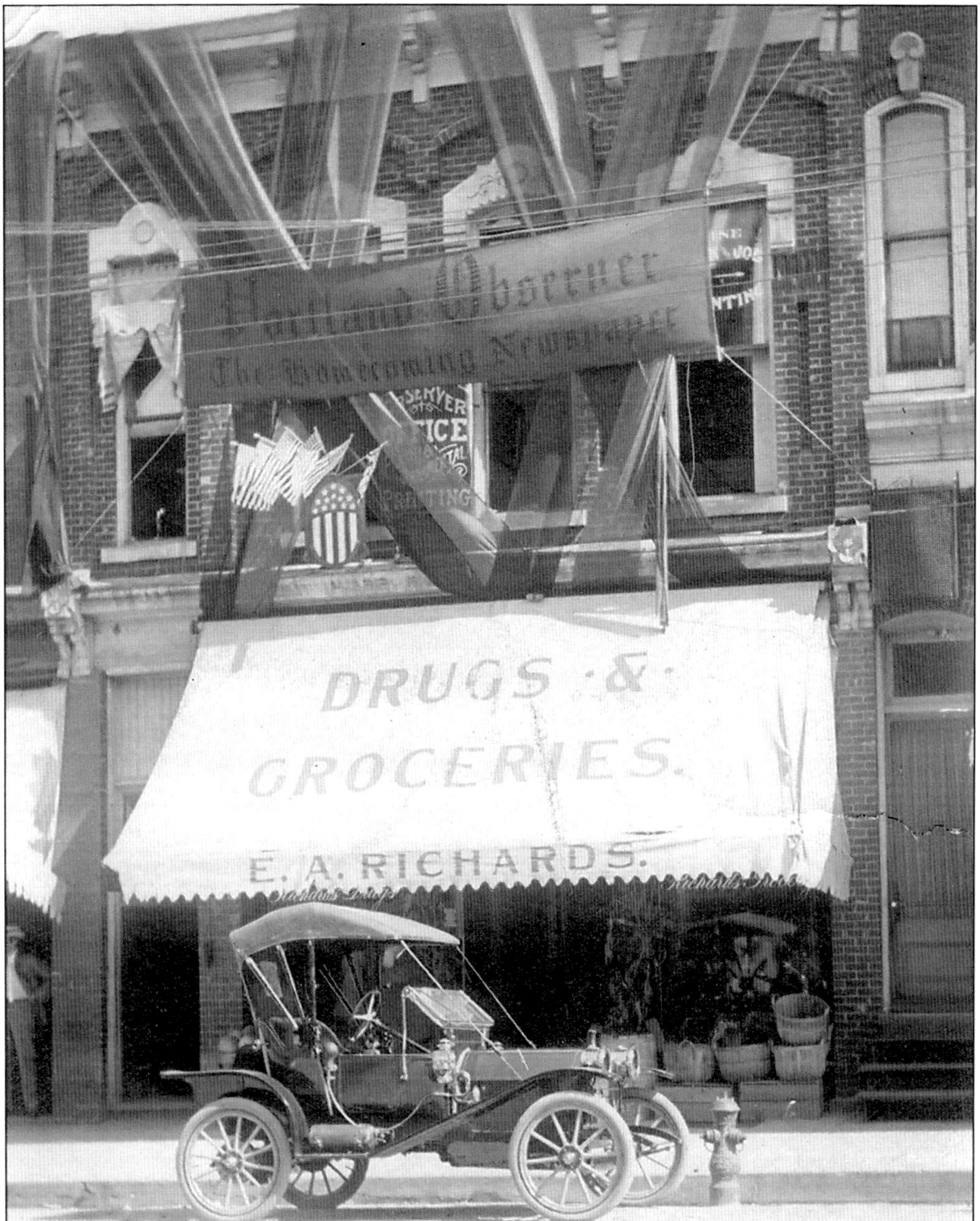

Two Businesses Decorated for the 1911 Homecoming. Behind this vintage automobile is E.A. Richards' drug store on the first floor, and the offices of the *Portland Observer* on the second floor. The occasion for the elaborate decoration was the Portland Homecoming celebration of 1911. E.A. Richards arrived in Portland in 1898, where he took over operation of the H.M. Gibbs drug and grocery store. A few years later he purchased the store, renamed it after himself, and operated the business until his death in 1926. His second floor neighbor, the *Portland Observer*, was established in 1867 as the *Portland Advertiser*. In 1870, the name was changed to the *Portland Observer*. In 1939, the newspaper consolidated with the *Portland Review* and became the *Portland Observer-Review*. (Courtesy of the Portland Area Historical Society.)

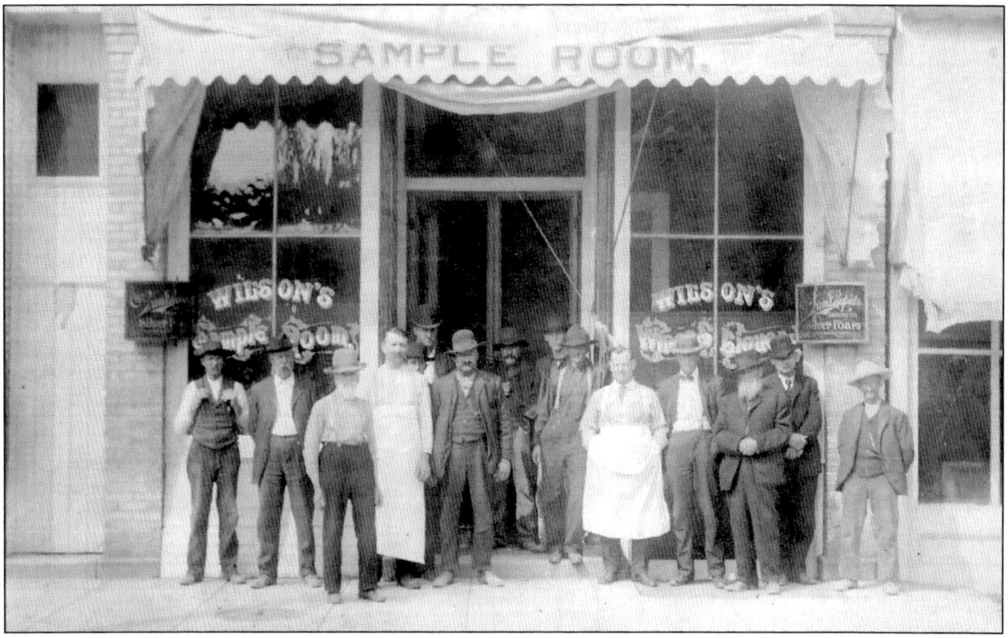

WILSON'S SAMPLE ROOM. A group of Portland residents stand in front of Wilson's Sample Room. Merchandise agents and traveling salesmen came to Portland and other communities to try and sell their goods. Sample rooms provided a space for these salesmen to display, sell, and take orders for their wares. (Courtesy of the Portland Area Historical Society.)

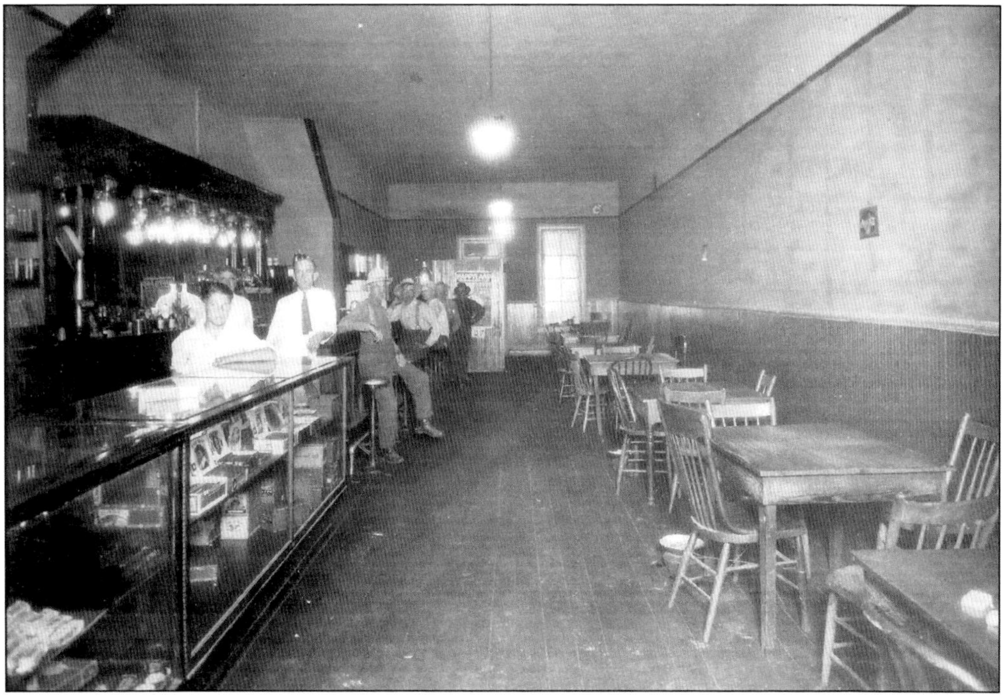

SLOW DAY AT A PORTLAND SALON, c. 1920s. In what appears to be the daylight hours, a half-dozen or so men gather around the bar of this establishment. The glass display case is full of cigars and spittoons are located between the tables. (Courtesy of the Portland Area Historical Society.)

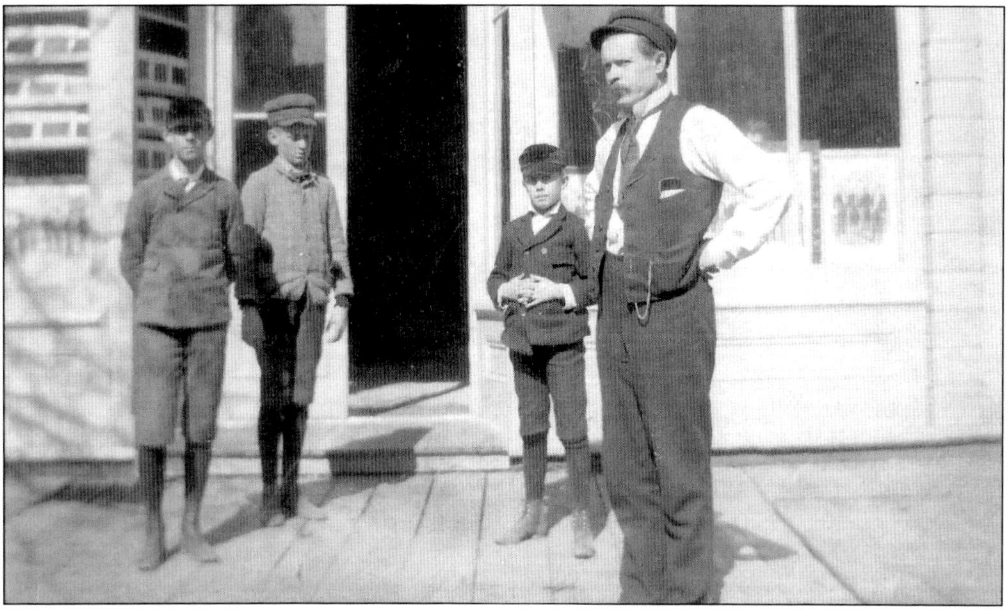

George Mahon, Tailor, April 1895. George Mahon stands in front of his tailoring shop with three local boys. The boy on the left is Lester Row and the boy on the right is Clarence Ward. The boy in the middle is unidentified. In his newspaper advertising, Mahon boasted the "newest styles, latest weaves, moderate prices, greatest fit." This photograph is another of the many that local banker Lorenzo Webber took that documented everyday life in 1890s Portland. (Courtesy of the Portland Area Historical Society.)

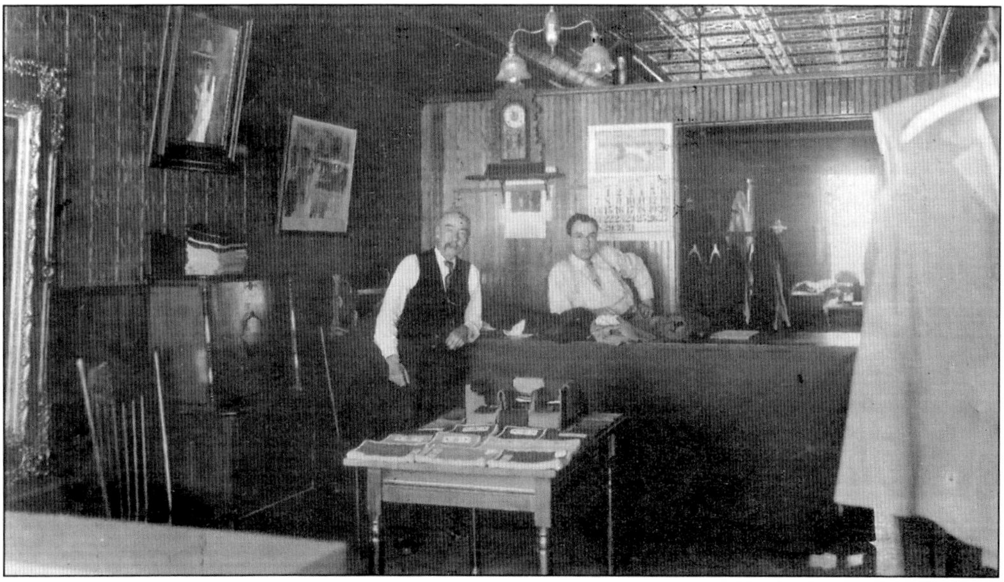

S. Wilton & Son, Tailors. Portland photographer George Van Horn created this promotional postcard, the back of which reads, "Compliments of S. Wilton & Son, Merchant Tailors." The Wiltons' store was located in the Alton Building on Kent Street. They specialized in mens' trousers, suits, and overcoats. Samuel Wilton was born in England in 1847 and immigrated to the United States in 1871. His sons George and Roy worked with him in the tailor shop. (Courtesy of Anne Rademacher.)

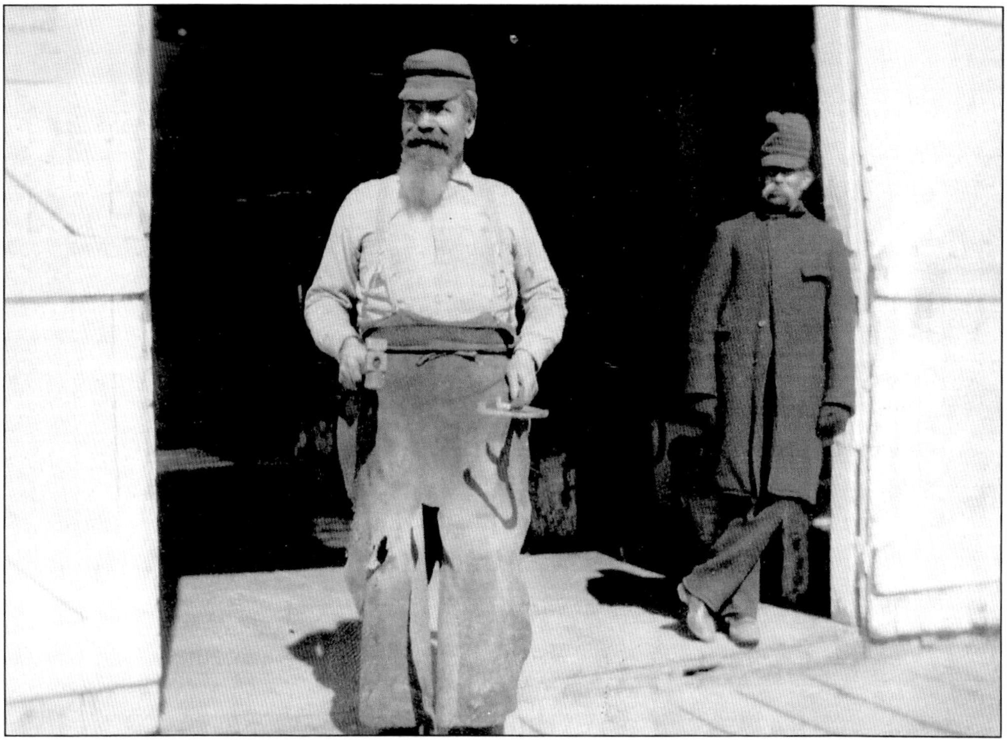

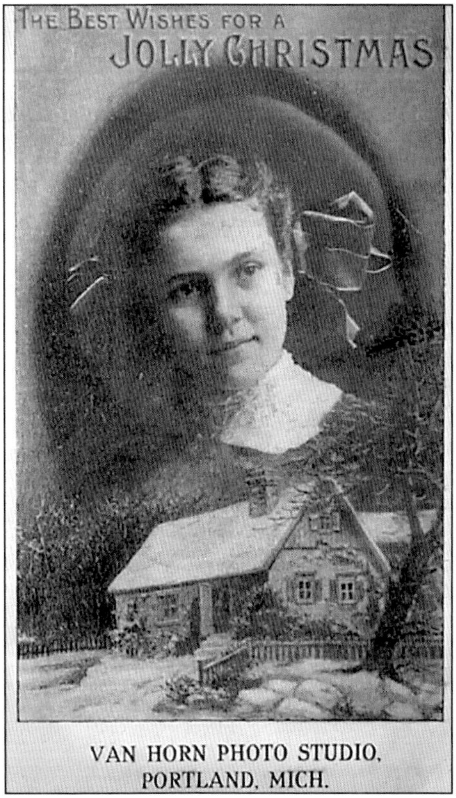

WILLIAM T. SMITH, BLACKSMITH, APRIL 1895. Like any other small industrial community of the 19th century, Portland relied on its independent skilled tradesmen as much as it did on the manufacturing plants and mills that dotted its two rivers. Here, blacksmith William T. Smith displays the tools of his trade as he holds a finished horseshoe. (Courtesy of the Portland Area Historical Society.)

VAN HORN CHRISTMAS POSTCARD. Portland photographer George Van Horn sent out this postcard wishing his customers a "jolly Christmas." George Van Horn was easily the most prolific Portland photographer in the late 19th and early 20th centuries. He created photographic postcards and portraits, and documented the important people and events of the community. His work was prominently featured in the pages of the local newspaper,the *Portland Observer*. (Courtesy of Anne Rademacher.)

Three

Kent Street and Downtown

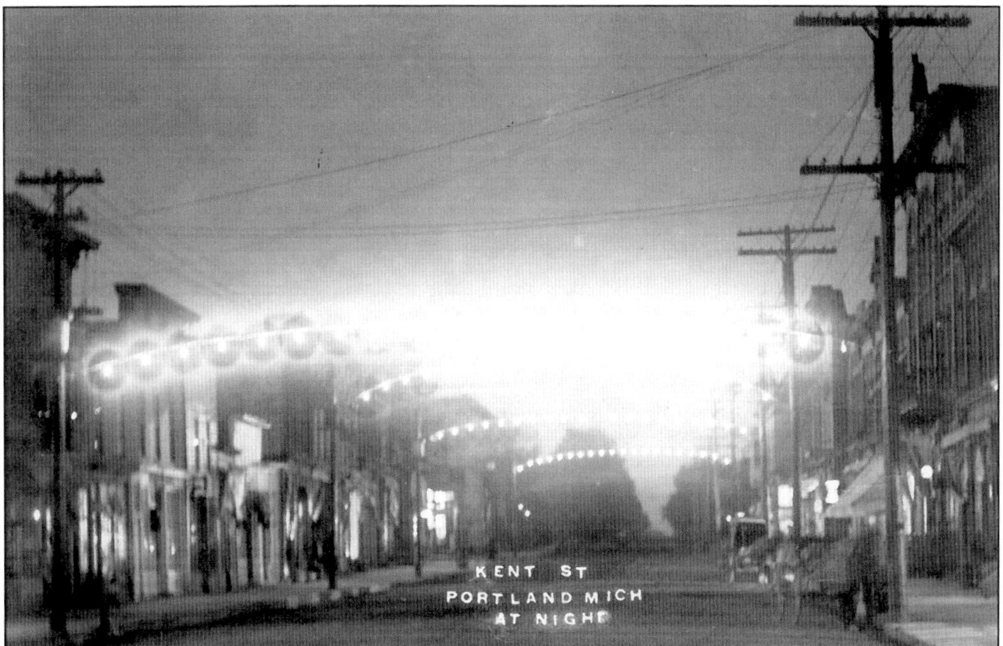

Kent Street at Night, c. 1910. Strings of electric lights illuminate downtown Portland. Downtown Portland had just recently been electrified when this photograph was taken. Kent Street, between Bridge Street and present-day Grand River Avenue, was the commercial, mercantile, and social hub of the village. (Courtesy of Robert Torp-Smith.)

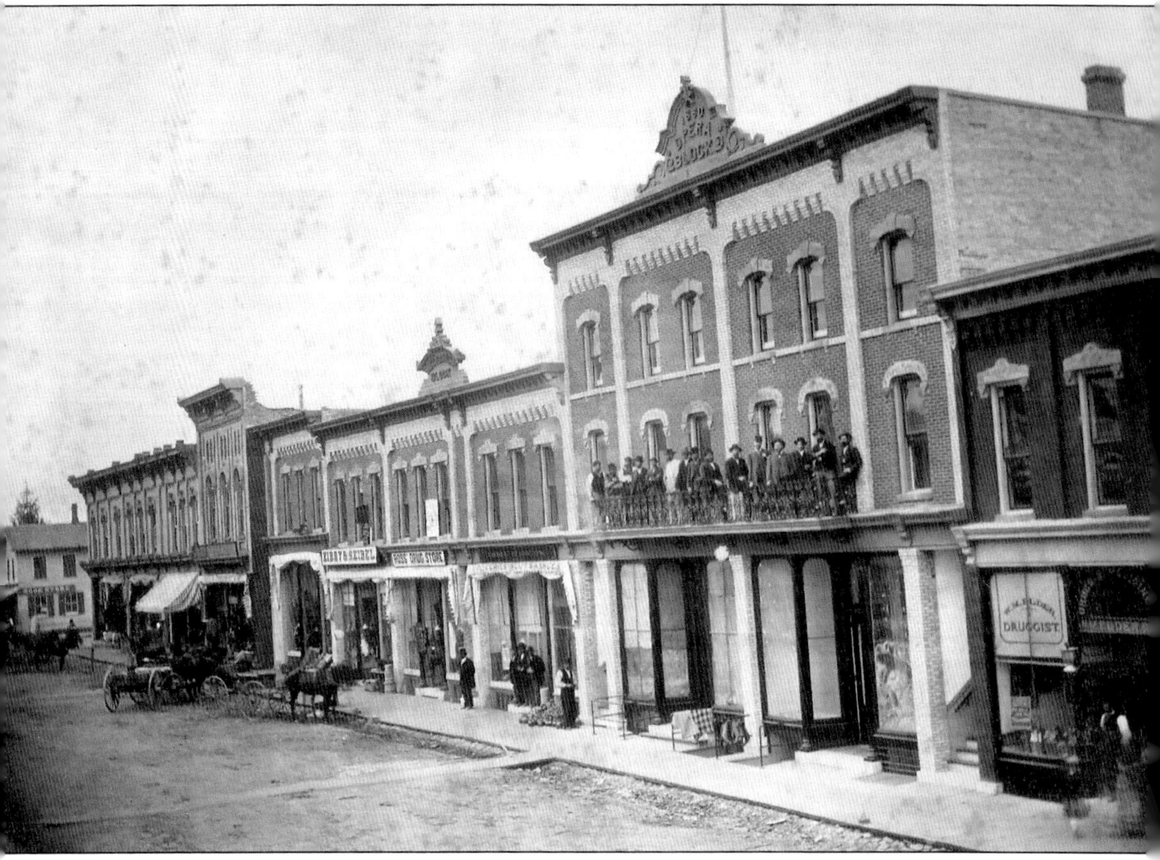

PORTLAND OPERA HOUSE. On February 25, 1880, the *Portland Observer* newspaper announced plans for the construction of a theater. They noted, "It is to be a hall suitable for Portland, even though the population should double or treble." The bustling village was in need of a grand opera house, if for no other reason than to relieve the community's churches from, "the use of their edifices for entertainments which are only suitable for a hall." One of the first events in the opera house, which took place on October 19, 1880, was a meeting of the Republican Party featuring a speech by former Michigan Governor Austin Blair. The opera house continued to be the premier entertainment and social venue in the village until the advent of movie houses during the World War I era precipitated its decline. (Courtesy of the Portland Area Historical Society.)

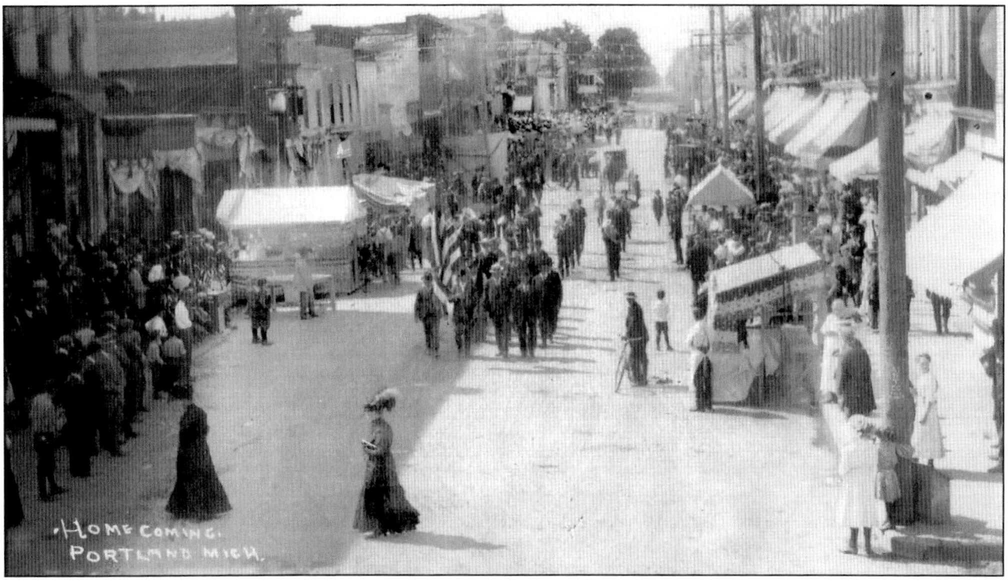

THE GAR LEADS THE 1911 HOMECOMING PARADE ON KENT STREET. Portland's first-ever Homecoming Festival was held from September 1–4, 1911. The village welcomed its sons and daughters for four days of parades, music, speeches, and other entertainment. The festival began in earnest on Friday evening, when a Professor Van Orman made an ascension and drop in a hot air balloon. From that point on, the homecoming was a rousing success. The only significant disappointment took place on Saturday afternoon when Senator William Alden Smith of Grand Rapids failed to appear at his scheduled speaking engagement. (Courtesy of Richard Teachout.)

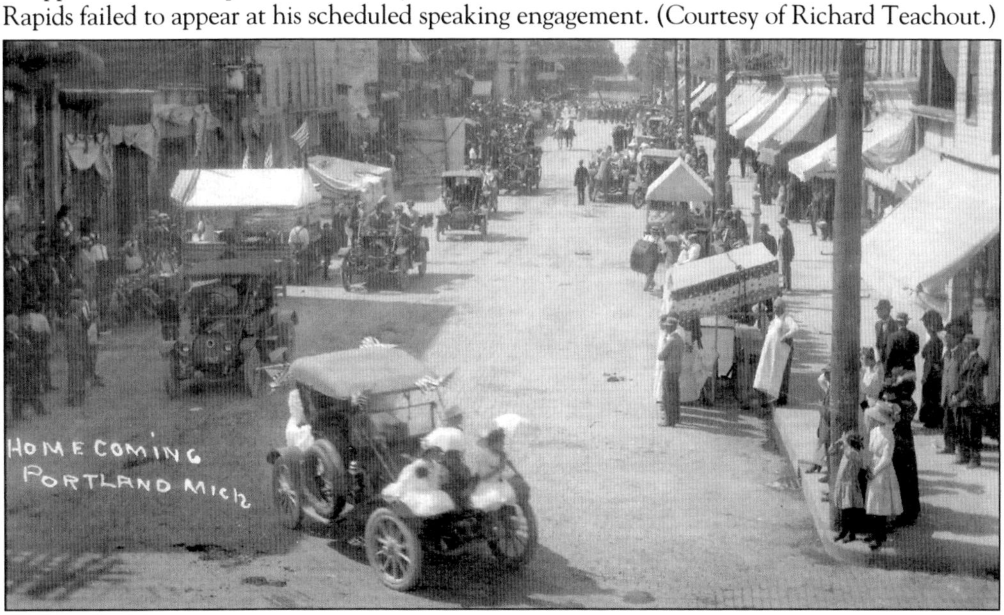

PORTLAND HOMECOMING, 1911. On Labor Day morning, September 4, 1911, this parade of automobiles made its way north along Kent Street. On this final day of Portland's Homecoming Festival, the automobile parade was followed by a second parade in which every manufacturing industry and almost every business was represented. Other festivities included a noontime ox roast and an afternoon baseball game between Portland and an all-female team called the Western Bloomer Girls. (Courtesy of Robert Torp-Smith.)

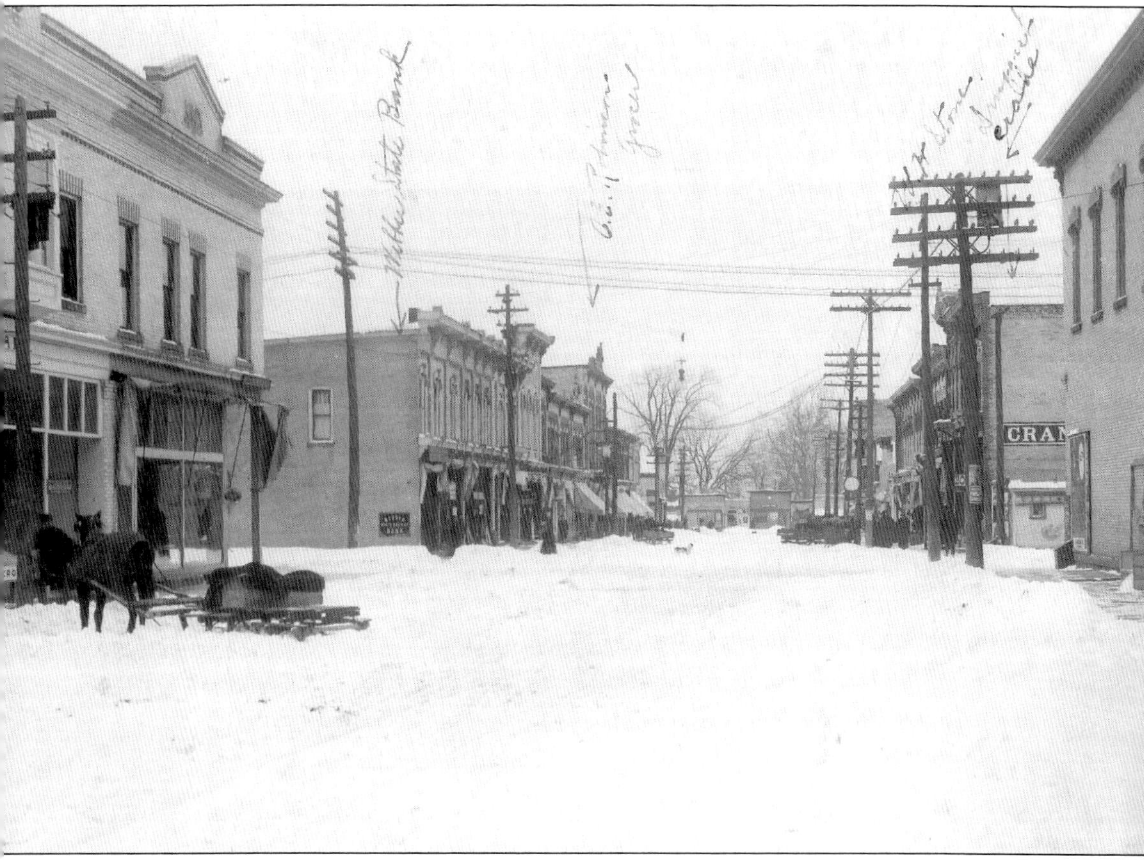

The Corner of Bridge and Kent Streets, c. 1910. The four corners of Bridge and Kent Streets on a particularly snowy winter day. This photograph was most likely taken in about 1910, since the Blanchard-Knox Block (currently known as the Kramer Building) was built in 1907 and the current classical revival façade of the Webber State Bank building was constructed in 1914. (Courtesy of the Portland Area Historical Society.)

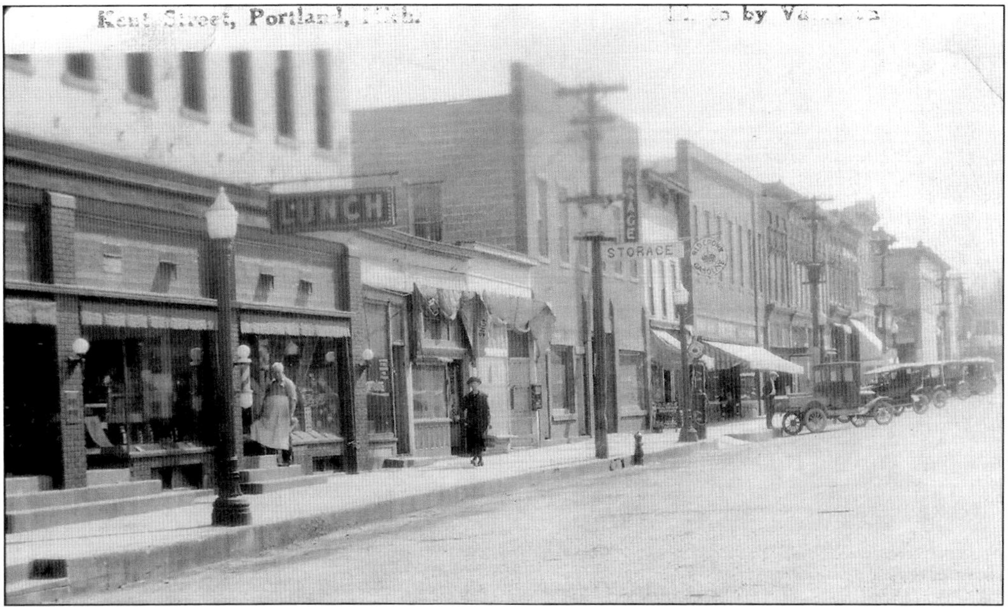

The East Side of Kent Street, c. 1920. The building with the "LUNCH" sign in front is the Hotel Divine. The globe of a Red Crown gasoline pump can be seen down the street. Red Crown was the brand name for Standard Oil Company's lowest octane gasoline. Before the proliferation of gas stations, this was a common sight along the main streets of America. Single building, multi-service gas stations became more prominent in the late 1920s and early 1930s. (Courtesy of the Portland Area Historical Society.)

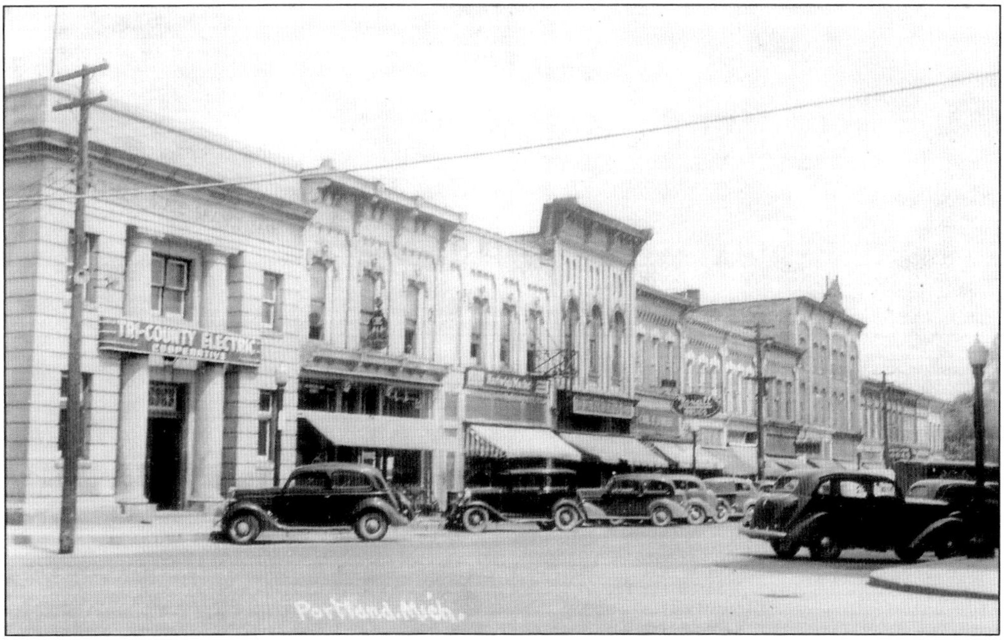

Kent and Bridge Street Intersection, Late 1930s. The Tri-County Electric Cooperative located in Portland in 1937 and set up its offices in the Webber State Bank building. It remained at this location until 1941, when a generating plant and new office facilities were completed. (Courtesy of Robert Torp-Smith.)

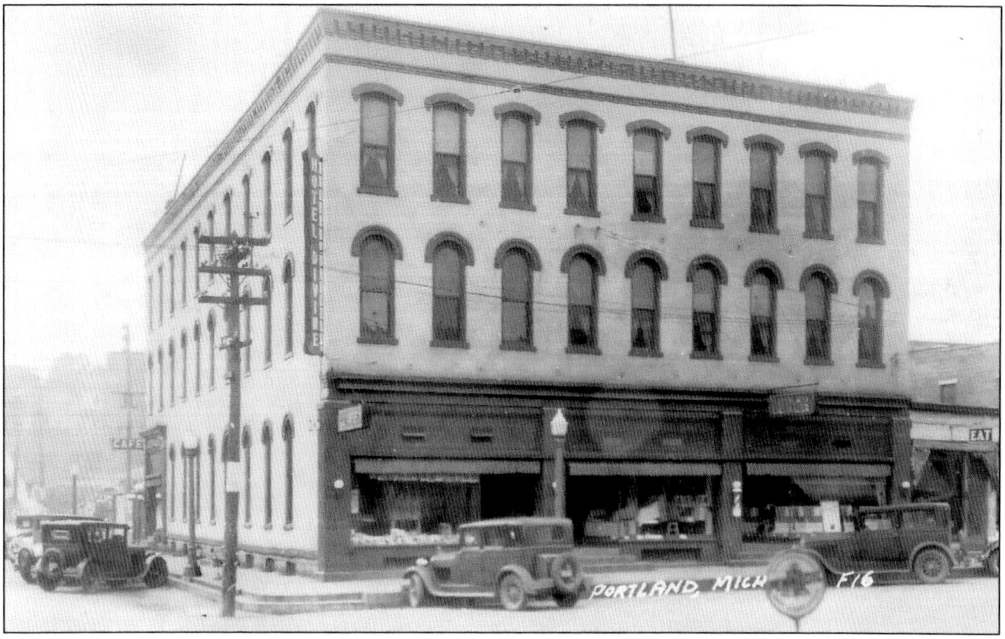

Hotel Divine. The Hotel Divine is shown in two photographs; the above image is from the 1920s and the below image is from around 1940. This Portland landmark stood on the northeast corner of Grand River and Kent Streets from the 1880s until 1975. Originally known as the Welch House, the name was changed to the Hotel Divine when Monroe Divine bought the establishment in the late 1890s. Monroe Divine operated the hotel until his death in 1909. Monroe's son, Chester, assumed the proprietorship and continued in this capacity until 1944, when he decided to retire and sell the hotel. During the years in which railroad travel dominated, and into the early years of automotive travel, the Hotel Divine was a popular halfway point for travelers making their way from Lansing to Grand Rapids. (Top photo courtesy of Anne Rademacher. Bottom photo courtesy of Robert Torp-Smith.)

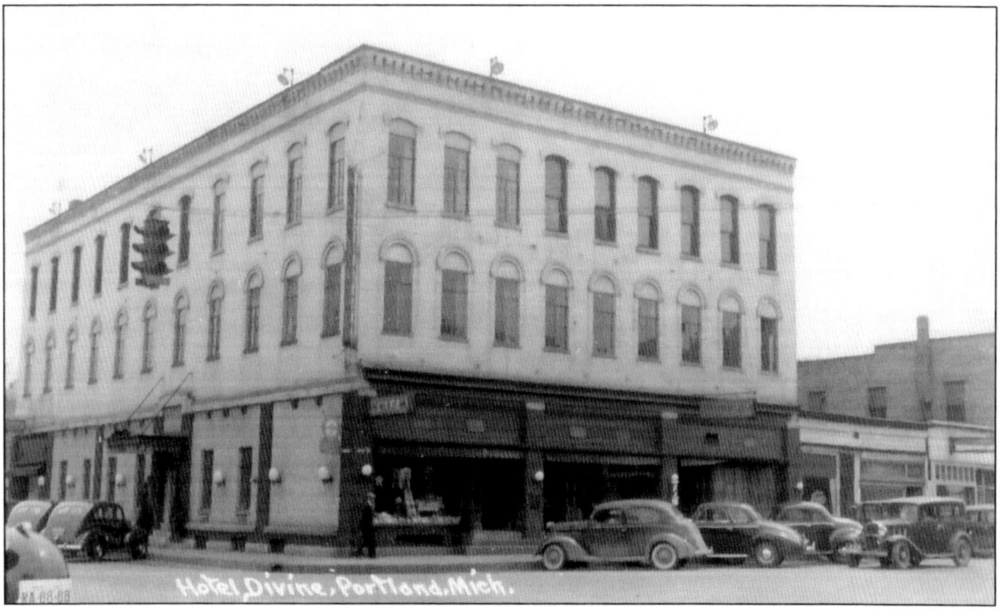

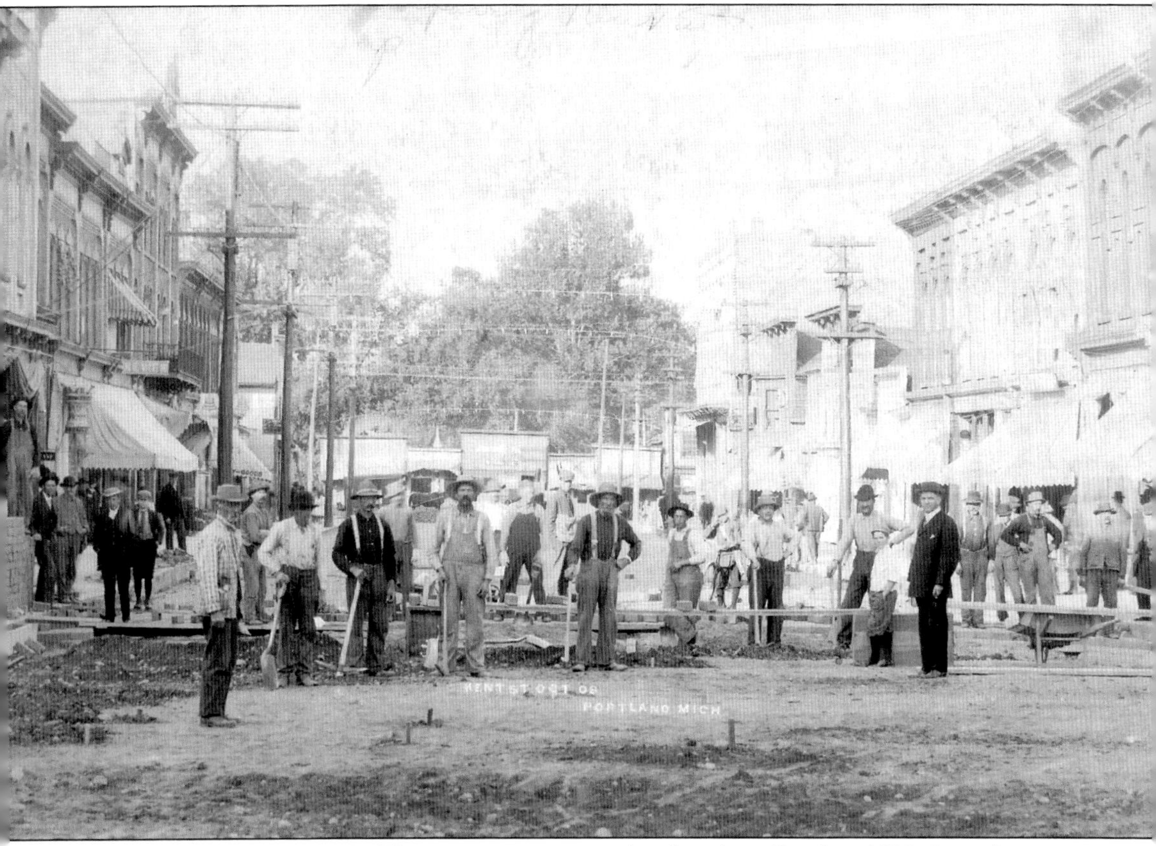

PAVING KENT STREET, 1909. This project was completed in late October 1909. In order to save money, the village hired an engineer to assist rather than accept the terms of a contractor. The lowest bid was $7,873.64 and the village managed to complete the job for less than $7,500. (Courtesy of the Portland Area Historical Society.)

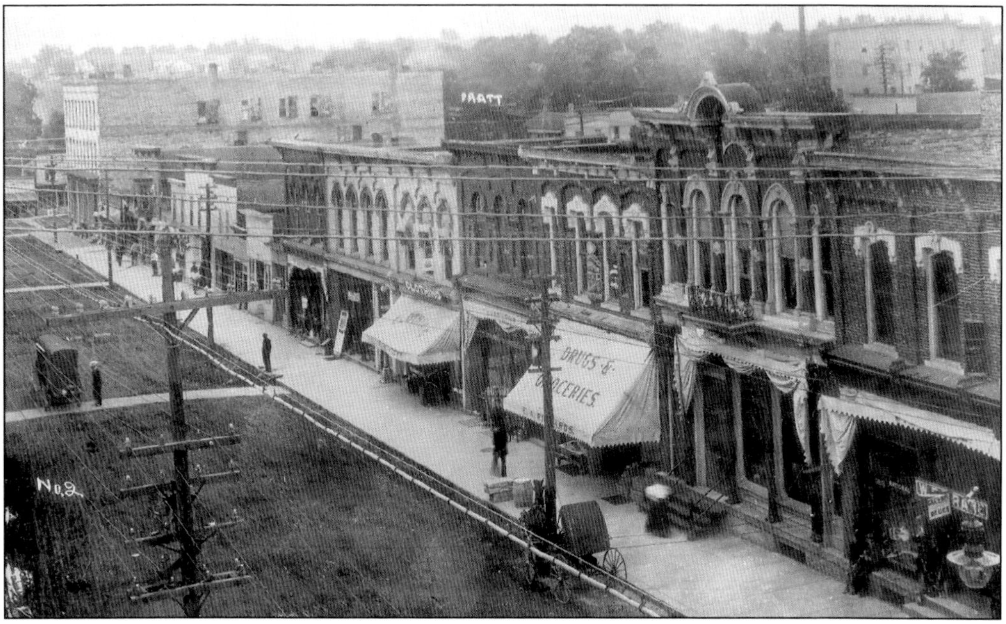

FACING NORTH ALONG THE EAST SIDE OF KENT STREET, EARLY 1900s. On the far left of the photograph is the Hotel Divine, and on the extreme right is Wallace D. Crane's drug store. Next to the drug store is the Maynard-Allen State Bank, and E.A. Richards' grocery store. The building in the upper right corner is the Portland Milling Company. Note the wood plank sidewalk and the telephone wires. (Courtesy of the Portland Area Historical Society.)

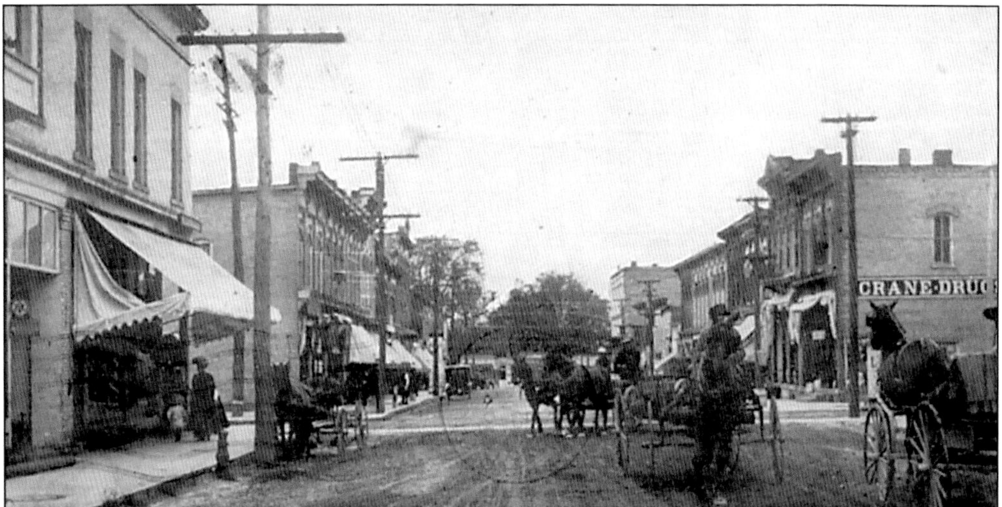

BUSY DAY ON KENT STREET, C. 1908. The Blanchard-Knox Block, in the left foreground, was completed in 1907. Kent Street was not paved until October 1909, so this dates the picture to around 1908. The Blanchard-Knox Block was occupied by the furniture and undertaking enterprise of Emory Blanchard. (It was not unusual for furniture stores to arrange and conduct funerals as a sideline business.) Blanchard had been in business for about 38 years before moving into the sparkling new Blanchard-Knox Block. For many years, he had occupied the first floor of the Opera House building. Unfortunately, Emory Blanchard was only able to enjoy this new building for seven years. He died on February 4, 1914. (Courtesy of Richard Teachout.)

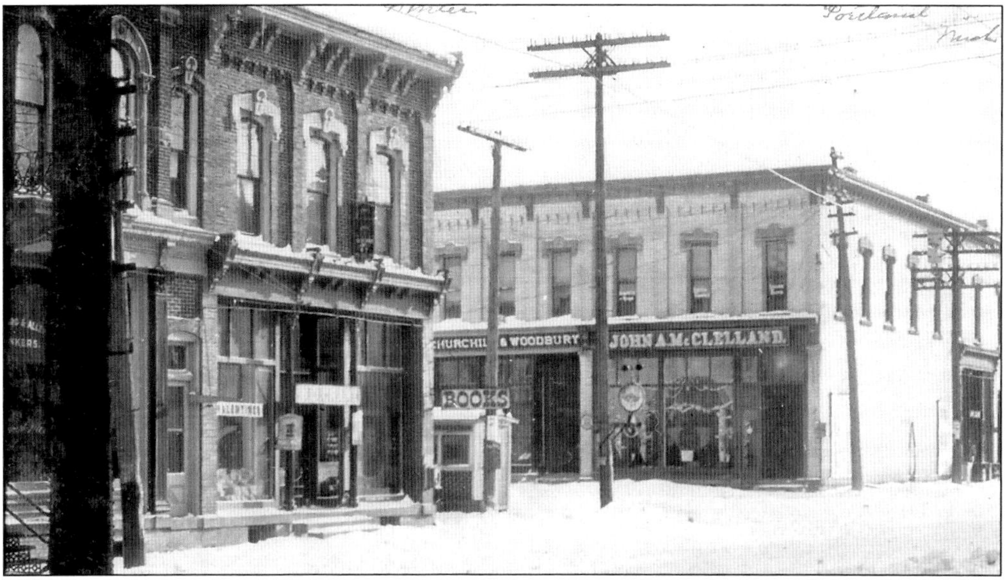

Facing Southeast towards the Corner of Bridge and Kent Streets, c. 1908. This photograph was taken on an extremely snowy day in downtown Portland. Wallace D. Crane's drug store displays valentines in the display window, so the picture was most likely taken in early to mid-February. The stores of Woodbury & Churchill and John A. McClelland are clearly visible on the southeast corner of Bridge and Kent Streets. Both businesses were Portland institutions whose existence spanned from the late 1800s well into the first half of the 1900s. (Courtesy of Robert Torp-Smith.)

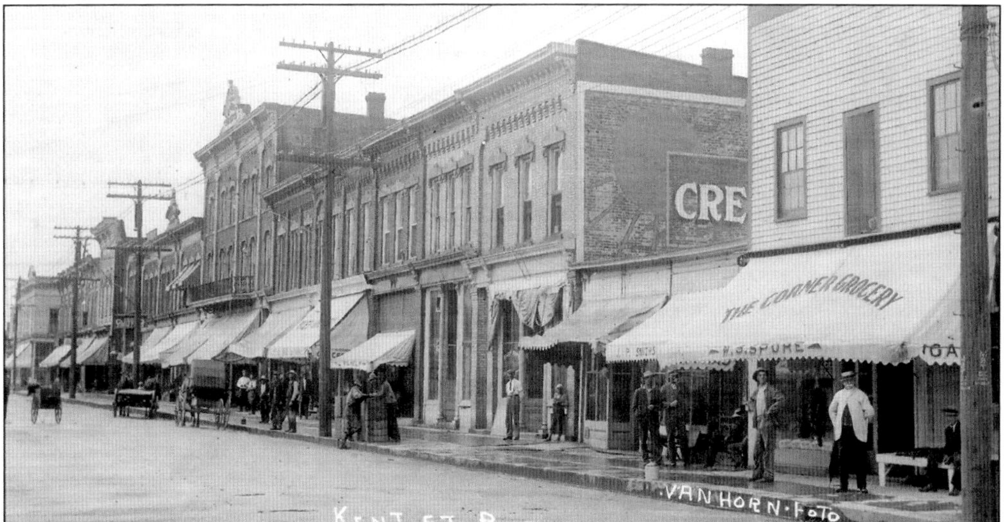

West Side of Kent Street, c. 1912. It appears to have been a rainy and wet day on Kent Street when George Van Horn snapped this photograph. In the foreground, on the northwest corner of Kent and James, is W.A. Spore's Corner Grocery. In January 1912, Spore bought the store from Floyd Martin. Spore placed special emphasis on the store's tea and coffee department and offered a special incentive for patrons to buy his tea. When a customer purchased one pound of tea, Spore presented him or her with a coupon. Eight coupons and $2.99 entitled the customer to a set of china. (Courtesy of Robert Torp-Smith.)

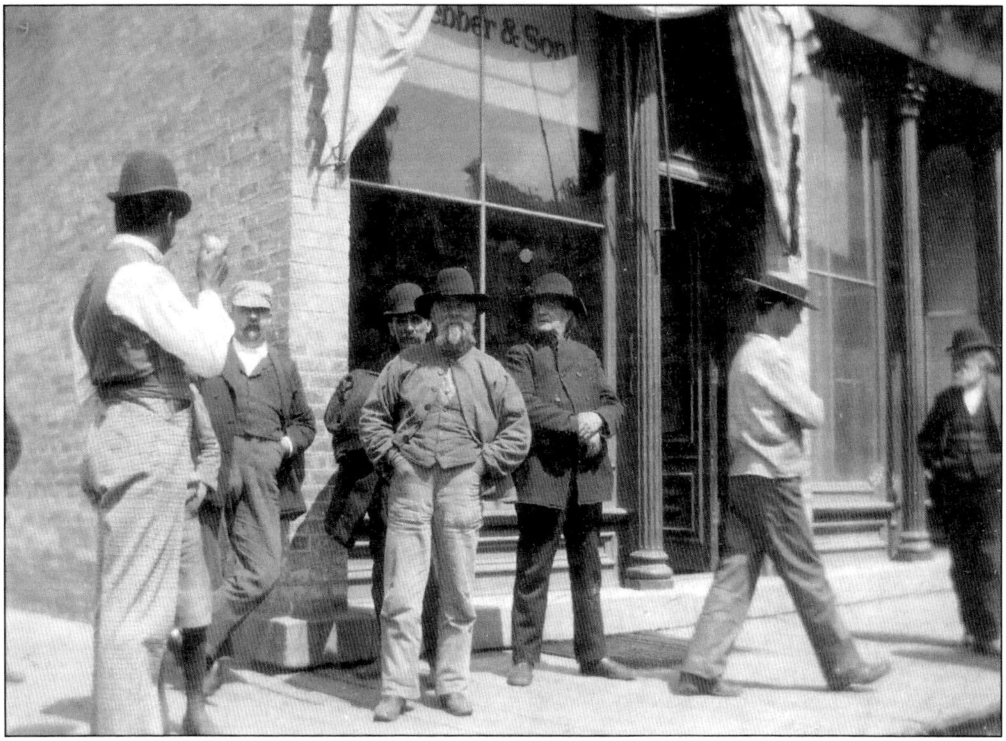

In Front of the Webber Bank, 1895. Several men mill about in front of the Webber State Savings Bank, which at this point was known as John A. Webber & Son. This is an excellent view of the bank's façade prior to its 1914 renovation. The bearded man in the middle with his hands in his pockets is Ira Southard. The men to his left are Pierce G. Cook (in the dark jacket with his arms folded), Bert Reynolds (wearing what appears to be a straw boater hat), and George R. Smith (walking towards Bert Reynolds). (Courtesy of the Portland Area Historical Society.)

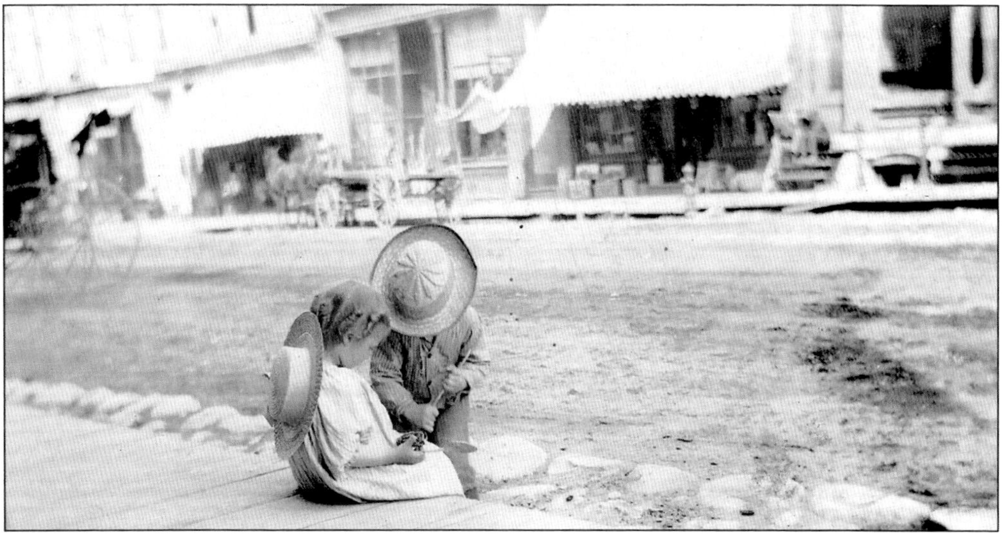

Children Playing on Kent Street, c. 1895. Lorenzo Webber's camera captured these two children playing on the wood plank sidewalk in front of his bank. (Courtesy of the Portland Area Historical Society.)

Four

City Views

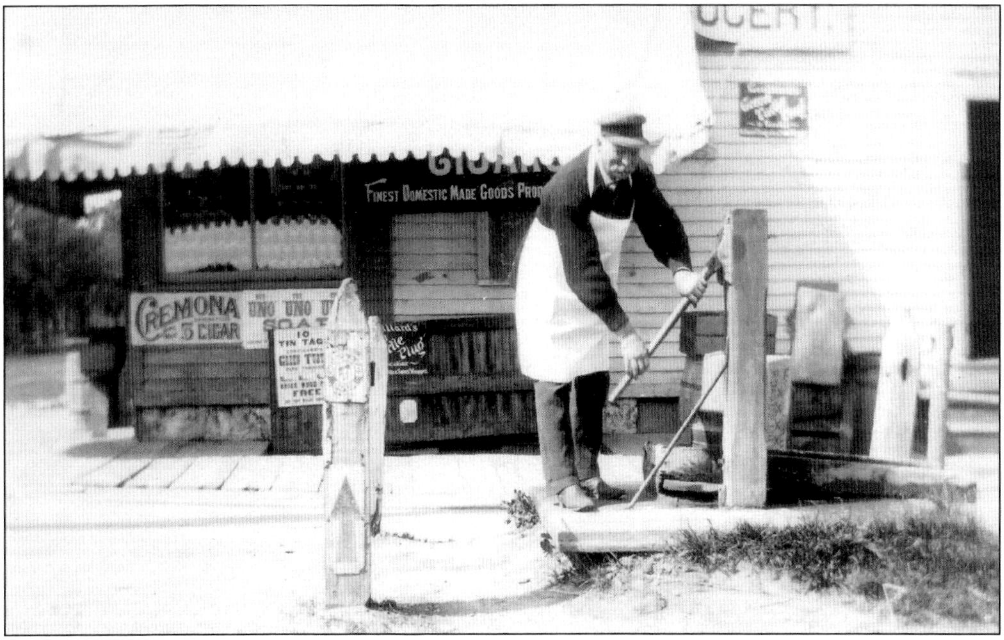

The Town Pump. The Portland town pump was located at the southwest corner of the Bridge and Kent Street intersection. Chained to the pump was a tin cup that was used for drinking by the entire community. Nineteenth-century residents of Portland shared most everything in order to survive, not the least of which was the drinking cup. After all, this was a time when running water was a luxury. Nearby, but not pictured in this photograph, were watering troughs for horses and for dogs. (Courtesy of the Portland Area Historical Society.)

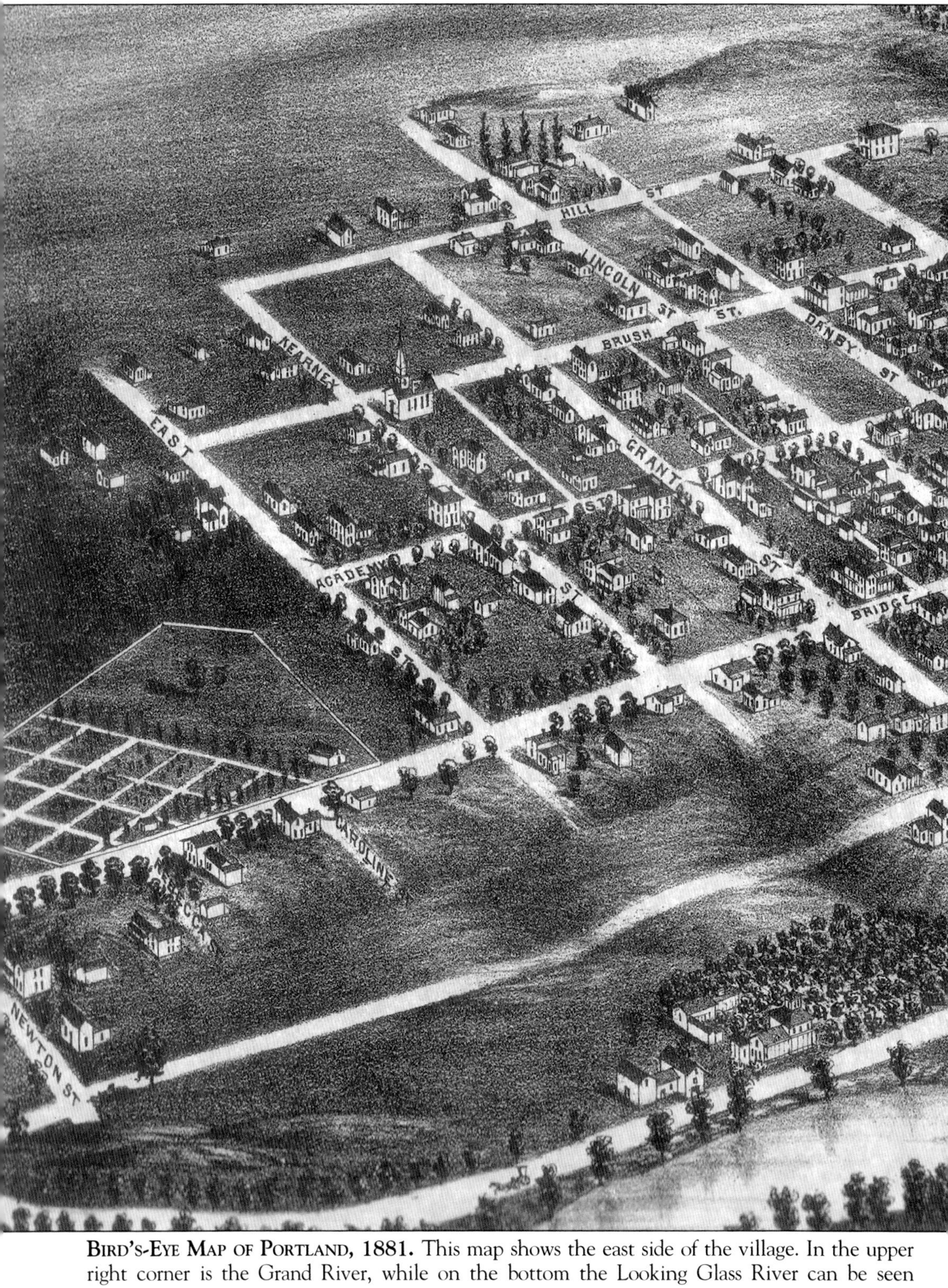

Bird's-Eye Map of Portland, 1881. This map shows the east side of the village. In the upper right corner is the Grand River, while on the bottom the Looking Glass River can be seen

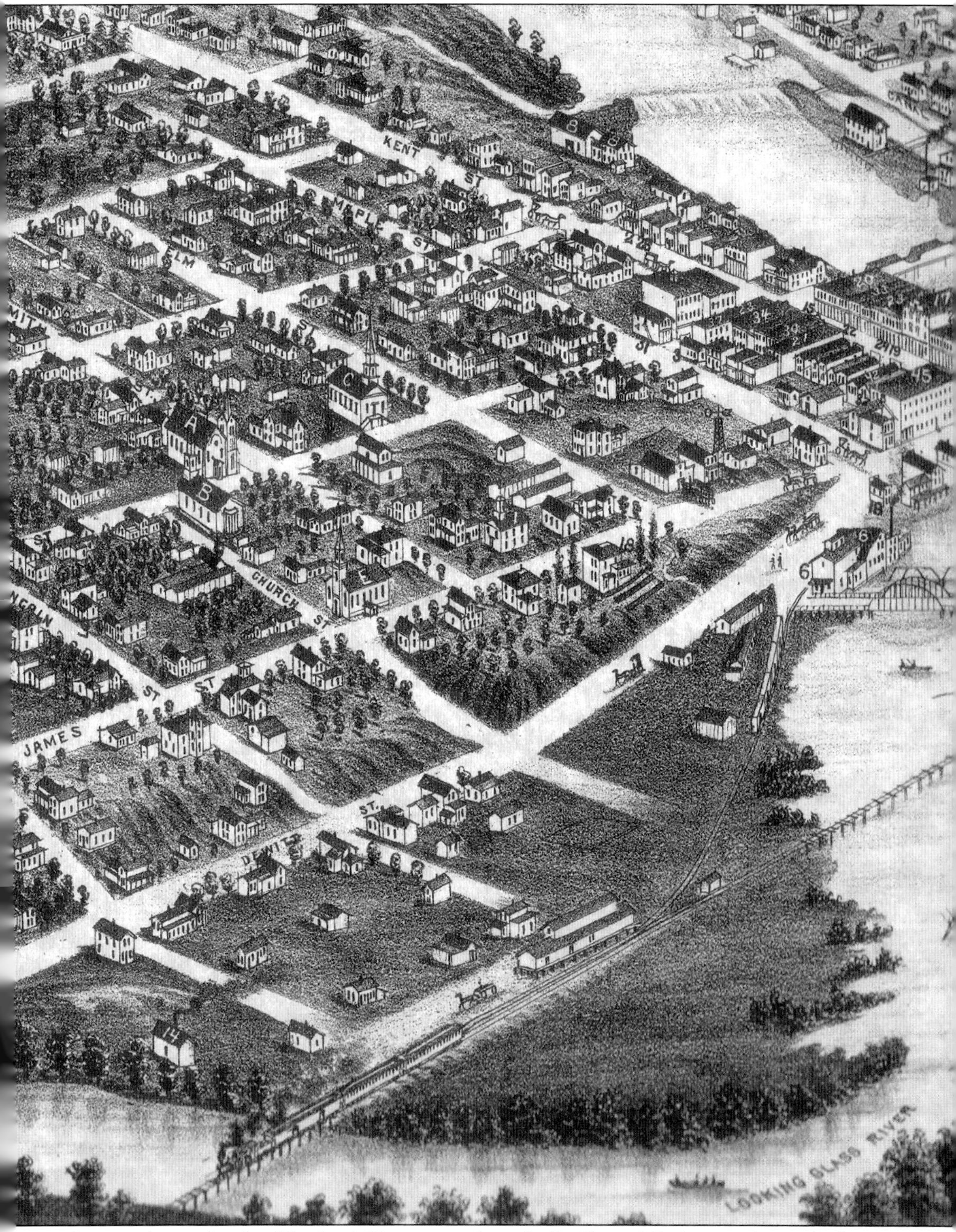

snaking on the north side of Portland. This map violates the "golden rule" of map making, which is that north should always be on the top. In this map's case, north is in the bottom right corner.

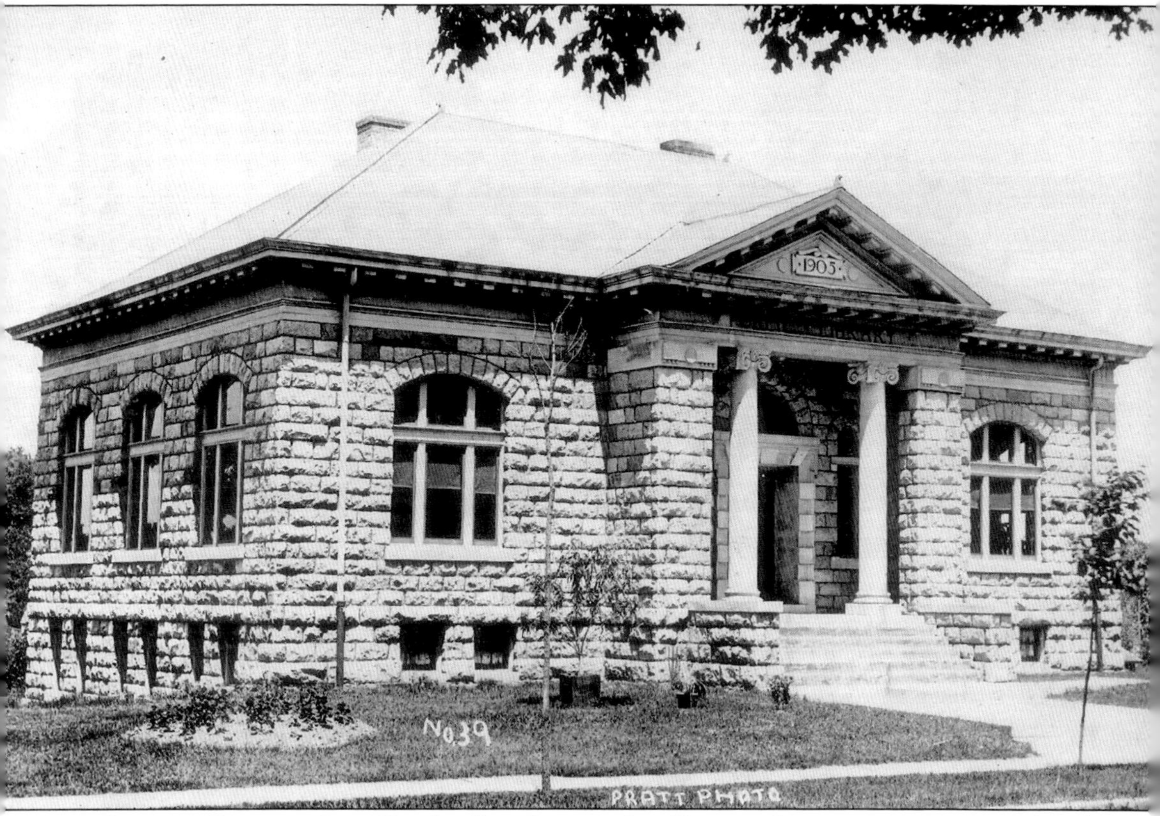

Carnegie Library. One of Portland's architectural and historical gems owes its existence largely to the vision of Mrs. Thomas Bandfield and the financial support of Andrew Carnegie. Mrs. Bandfield, a member of the Ladies Literary Club, wrote to the steel magnate and philanthropist. In her letter, she explained that the club wanted to buy a site for a library if Carnegie would finance the building. Carnegie agreed to furnish $10,000 if a site were provided and if taxpayers would provide no less than $1,000 to maintain it. The citizens of Portland voted in favor of raising the funds, and construction of the library commenced in July 1905. The dedication took place on June 8, 1906, and schools and stores were closed for the day so that people could attend the ceremony. University of Michigan president James B. Angell delivered the keynote speech. Andrew Carnegie's gift to Portland continues to serve the public to this day. (Courtesy of Robert Torp-Smith.)

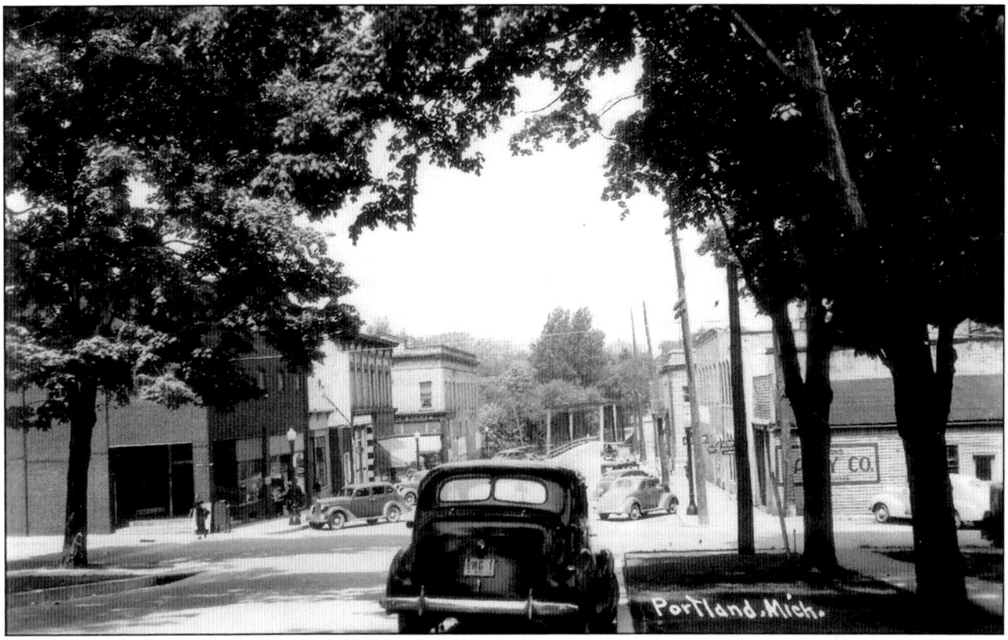

FACING WEST ALONG BRIDGE STREET. The four corners of Bridge and Kent Streets are just beyond this shady canopy of trees. The large brick building on the left, familiar to all Portland residents, is the Masonic Temple building. This edifice was built in 1925 and was designed specifically as a Masonic Temple. (Courtesy of Robert Torp-Smith.)

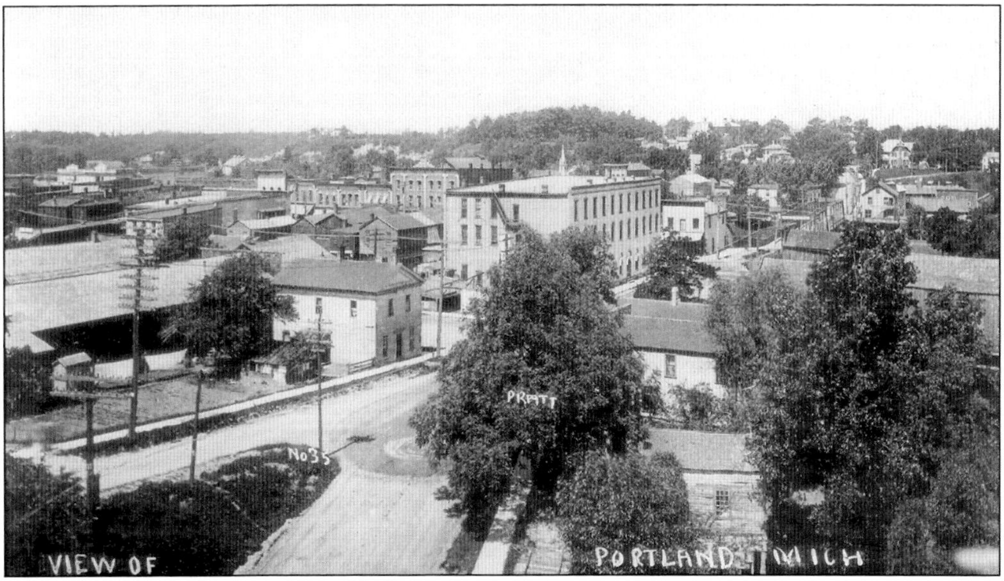

INTERSECTION OF JAMES AND DEWITT (PRESENT-DAY GRAND RIVER AVENUE). This photograph affords an excellent view of downtown Portland. The large three-story building in the center is the Hotel Divine. The Hamlin Building is the wood, gable-front structure on the southeast corner of James and Maple Streets. To the immediate left of the Hotel Divine, and a bit further in the distance, is the Portland Opera House. One can also discern the bluffs on the west side of the Grand River, visible above the rooflines of the businesses along Kent Street. (Courtesy of the Portland Area Historical Society.)

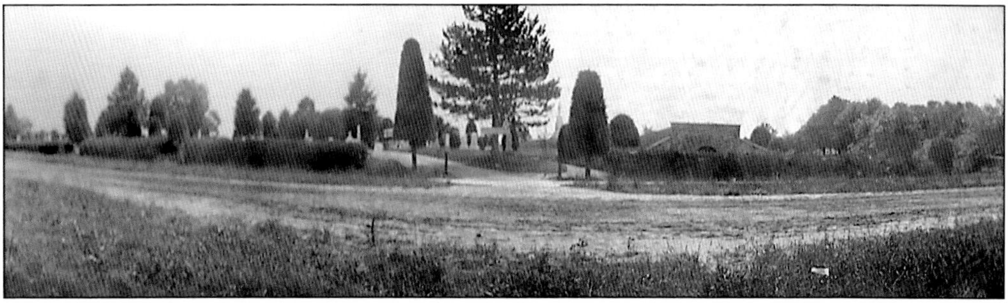

PORTLAND CEMETERY. Bridge Street resembled a country road when this photograph was taken of the Portland Cemetery entrance. The Civil War soldiers' monument can be seen in the distance. (Courtesy of Chuck Minkley.)

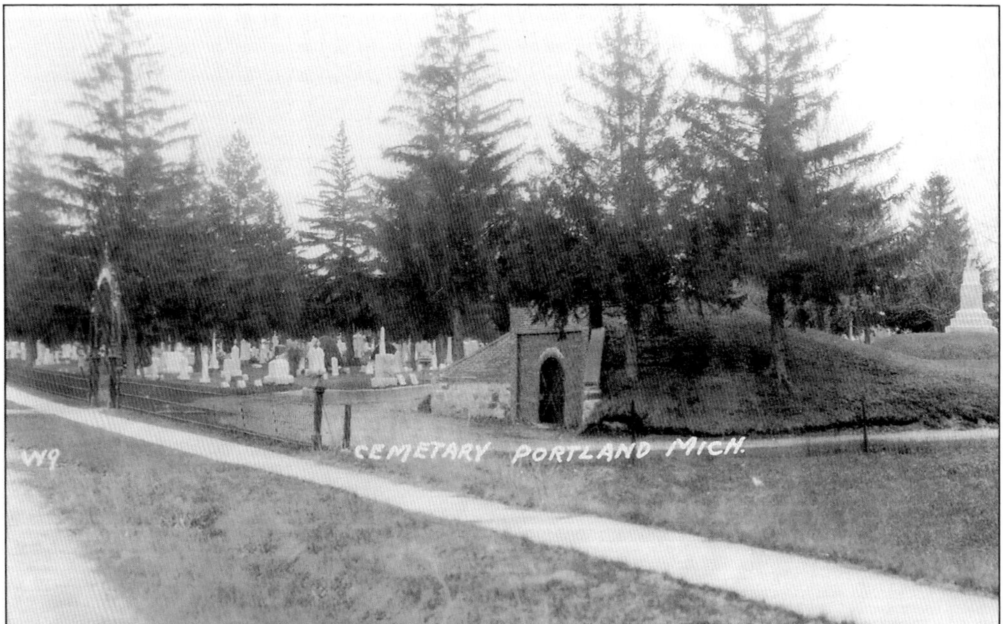

ANOTHER VIEW OF THE PORTLAND CEMETERY. This view faces east along Bridge Street towards the Portland Cemetery. The earth mound with the brick arched entrance was used to store caskets during the winter months. The Portland Cemetery dates all the way back to 1837, almost as long as the community has existed. The creation of the Portland Cemetery coincides with the rural cemetery movement that gained popularity in the 1830s and is best exemplified by the Mt. Auburn Cemetery in Cambridge, Massachusetts. New attitudes towards death influenced cemetery design. There was a move away from crowded and dingy graveyards towards arboreal, park-like cemeteries. (Courtesy of Robert Torp-Smith.)

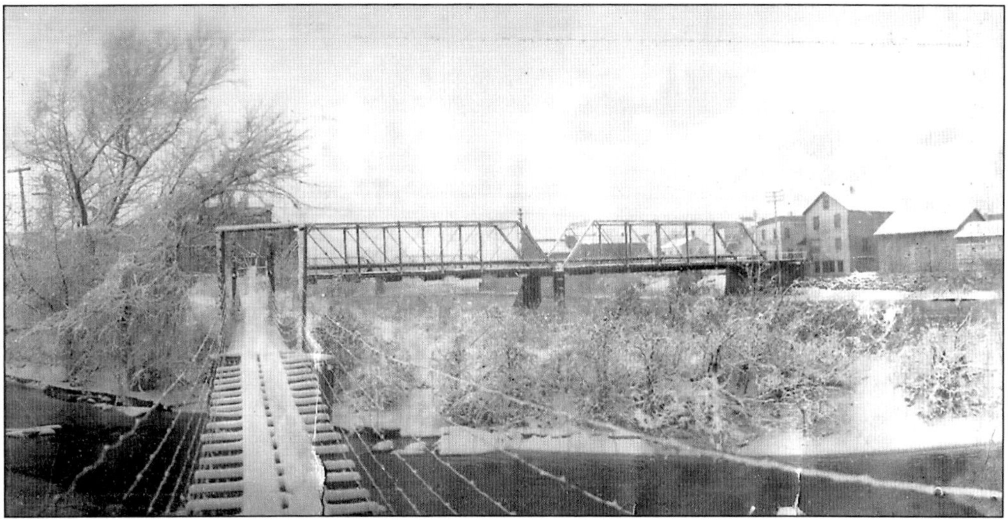

Swing Bridge. This is the swinging foot bridge over the mouth of the Looking Glass River. It was built as a convenience for the workers of the Ramsey Alton factory, and was also used by sports enthusiasts to reach Goodwin Park where baseball and football games were played. (Courtesy of the Portland Area Historical Society.)

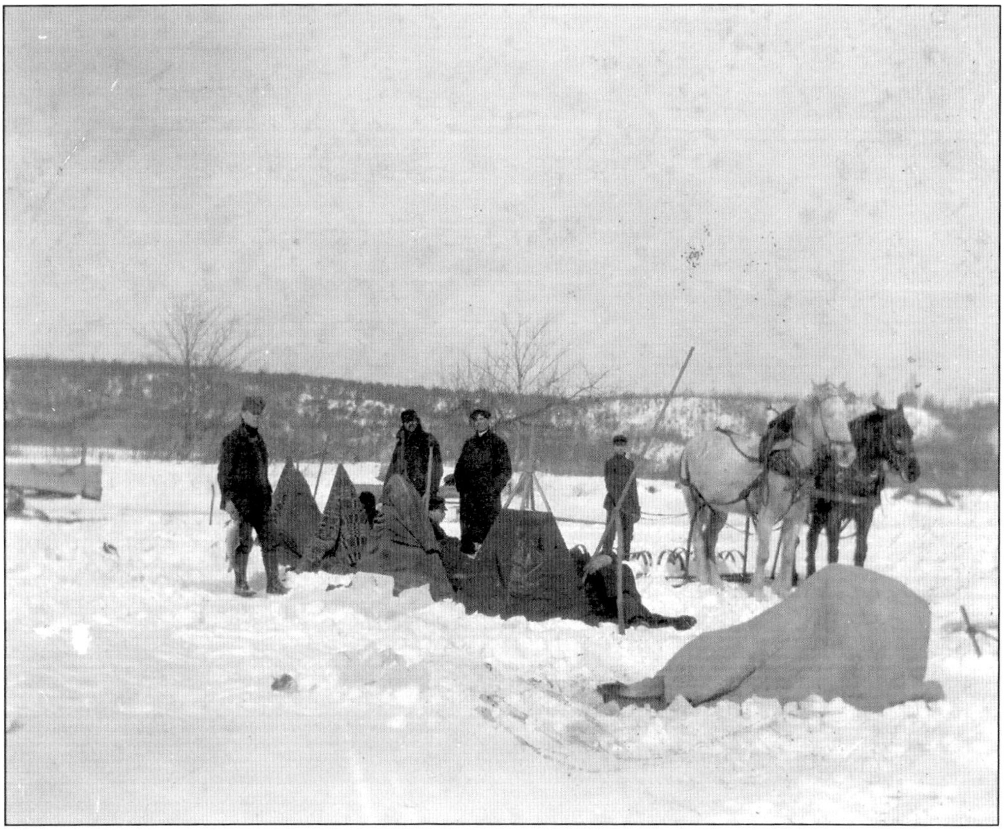

Ice Cutting on the Grand River. (Courtesy of the Portland Area Historical Society.)

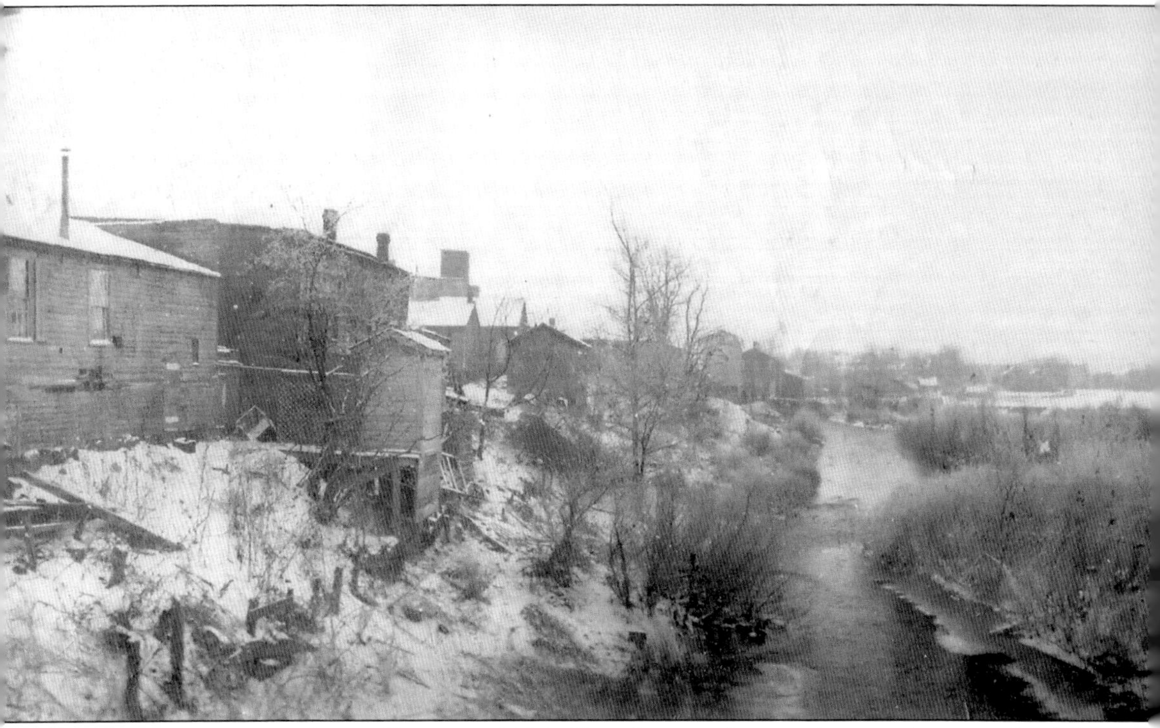

INDUSTRY ON THE GRAND RIVER, C. 1900. This photograph was taken on the east side of the Grand River near the Bridge Street Bridge. In fact, the bridge is visible on the extreme right of

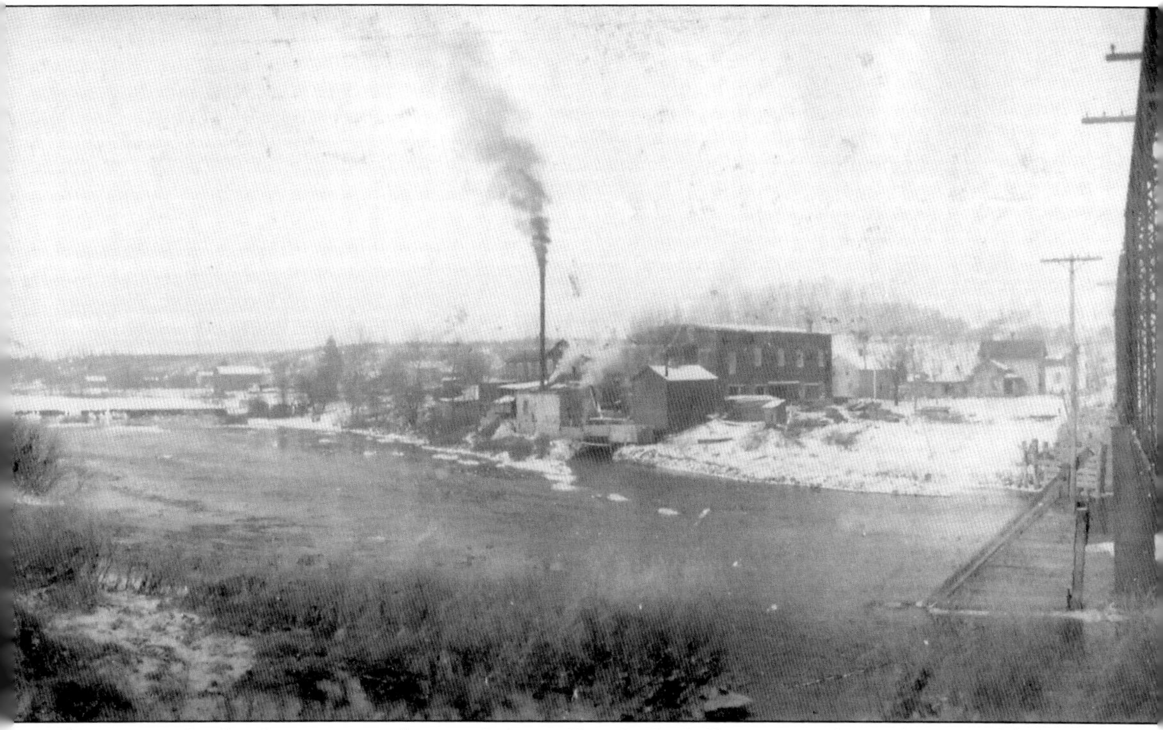

the picture. In the distance is a dam, and the mill with the billowing smokestack is most likely the Griffin & Campbell Sash Company. (Courtesy of the Portland Area Historical Society.)

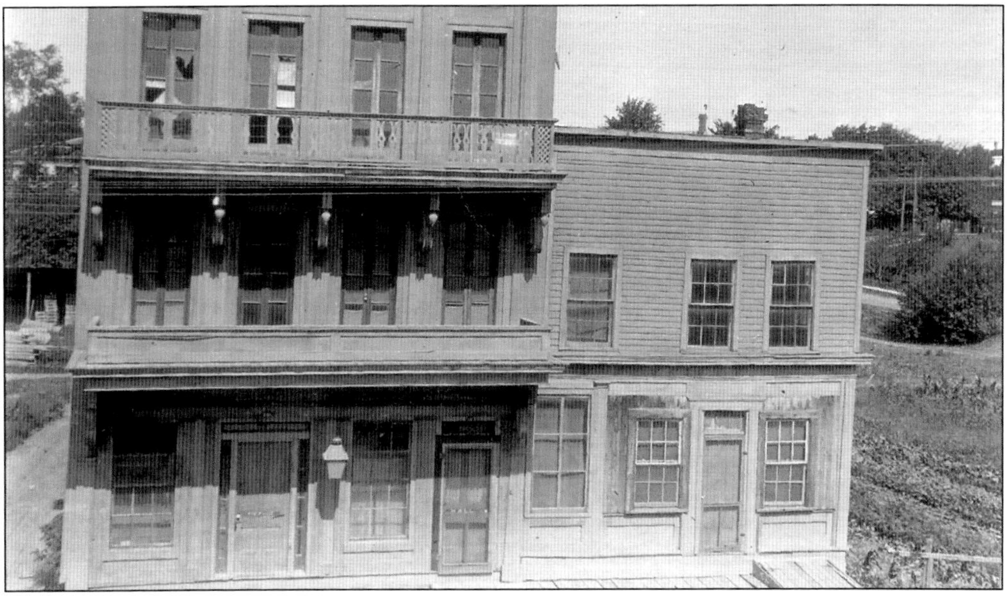

NATIONAL HOTEL. By the time this photograph was taken on September 15, 1907, the National Hotel had clearly seen better days. The hotel was located on the west side of Water Street, between Bridge Street and present-day Grand River Avenue. In the 1880s, it was known as the Richmond House. By the early 1890s, the name had been changed to the National Hotel. The establishment changed hands several times in that decade. The *Michigan State Gazetteer* lists Charles Groger as proprietor from 1893 to 1894, Frank Burhans in the years 1895 to 1896, and Becket Lewis in 1899. By the first decade of the 20th century, the National Hotel had closed. (Courtesy of Robert Torp-Smith.)

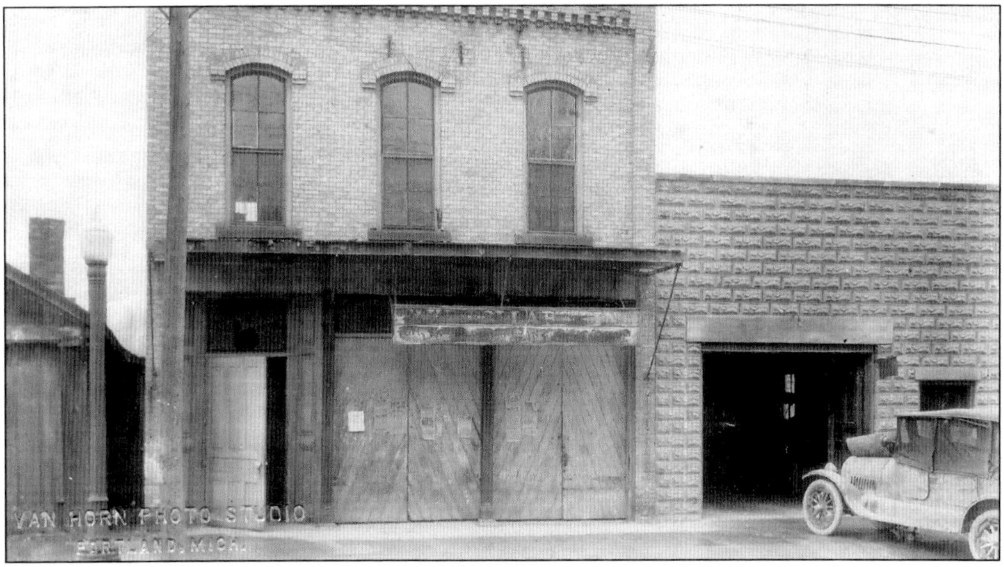

"FRONT VIEW, VILLAGE HALL." So states the caption written on the back of this George Van Horn photograph, which is dated April 3, 1919. The fliers that are tacked to the front of the building all relate to an upcoming election. One reads, "How to vote by mail," and another has the banner, "County Road Proposition," presumably with the proposition described in the text underneath. (Courtesy of the Portland Area Historical Society.)

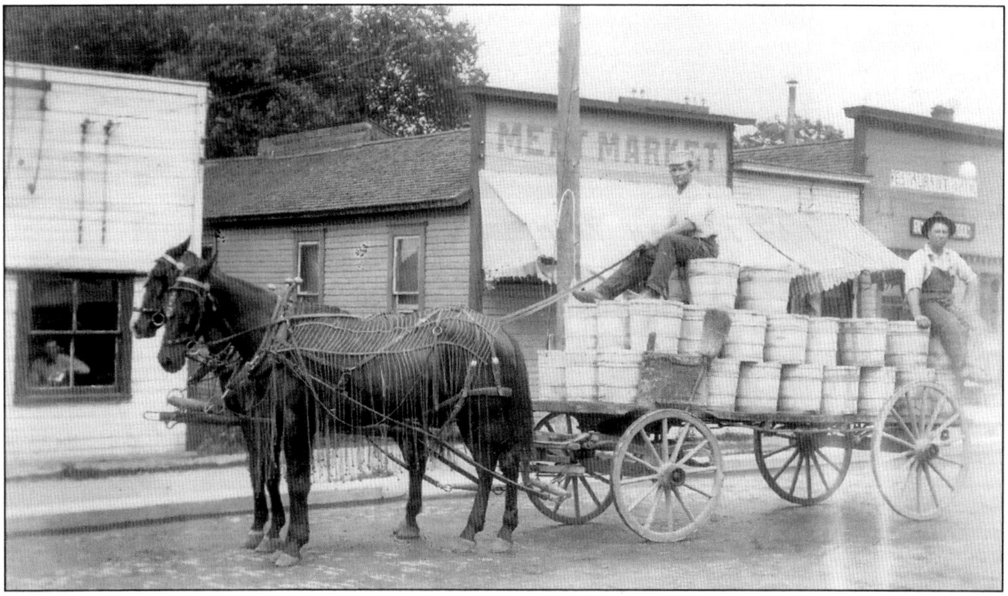

Delivery Men on Grand River Avenue (Formerly Dewitt Street), c. 1910. These men take a break to pose for George Van Horn's camera. The photograph was taken at the north end of Kent Street, where the businesses were still primarily built of wood with false fronts. (Courtesy of Robert Torp-Smith.)

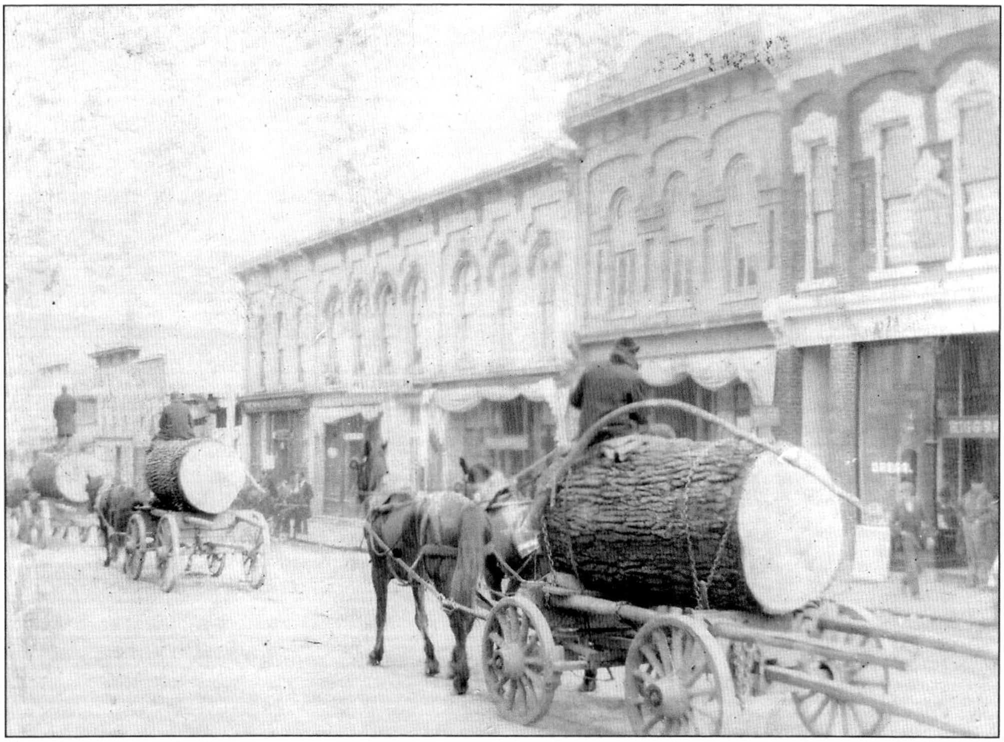

Hauling Logs down Kent Street, c. 1890s. With the many factories and mills along the Looking Glass and Grand Rivers, there are any number of places these large logs could have been headed. (Courtesy of the Portland Area Historical Society.)

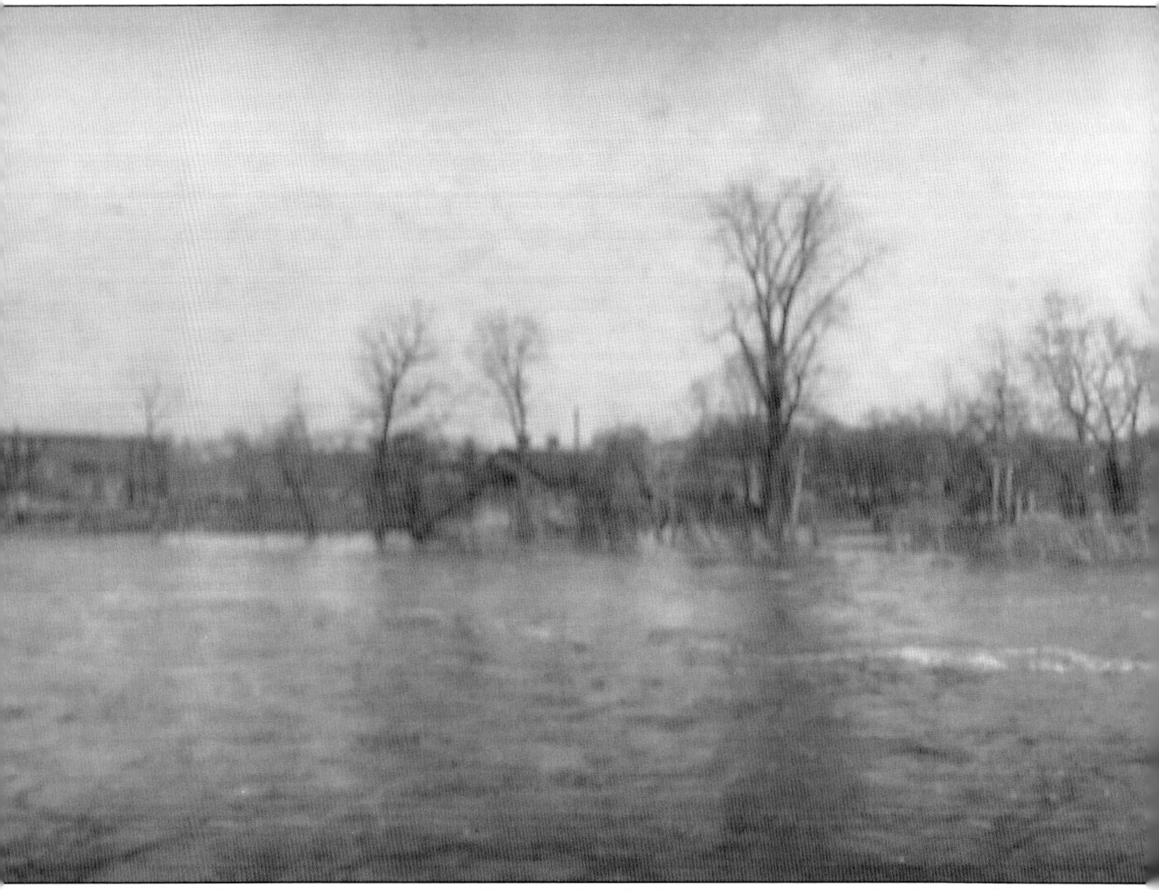

Looking East across the Grand River. This double-span Pratt truss bridge was located at the present day Grand River Avenue crossing of the Grand River. To the left of the bridge can be seen the confluence of the Grand and Looking Glass Rivers, while far in the distance, on

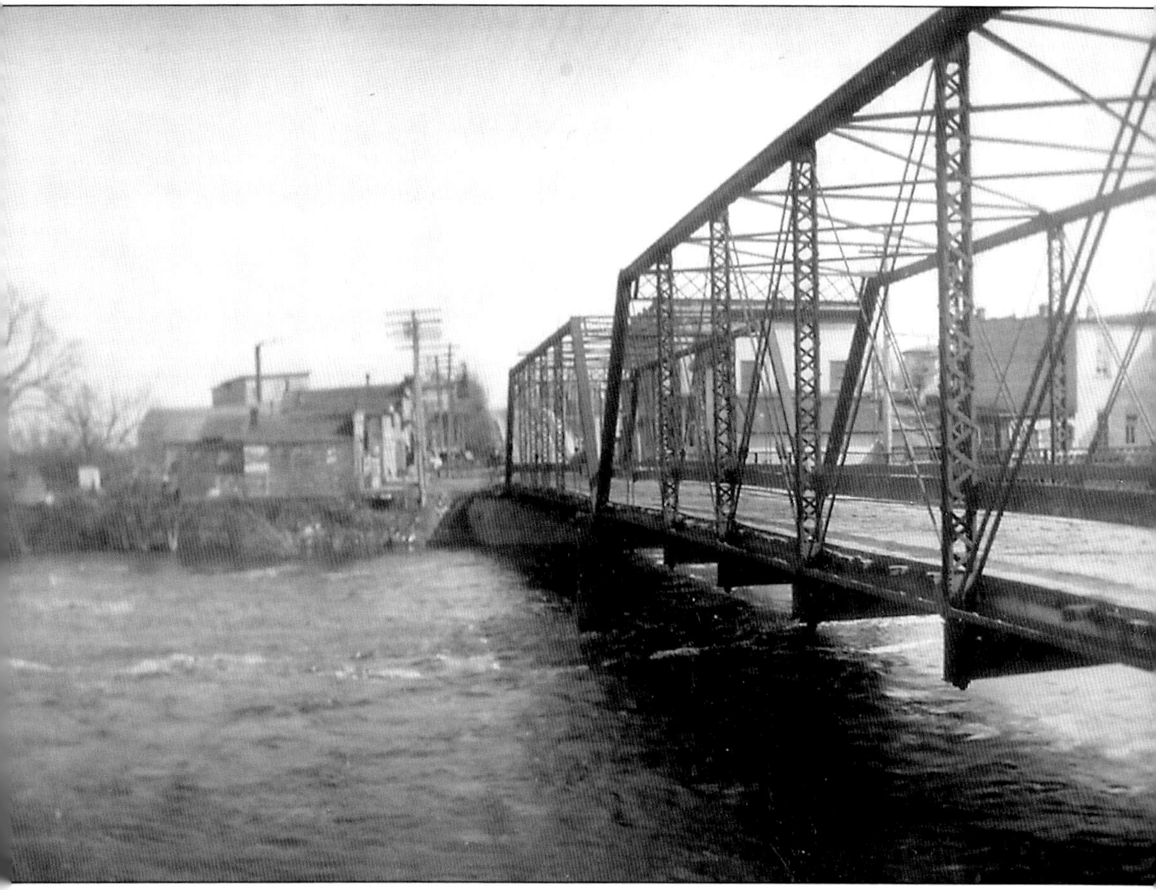

the left of the photograph, is the Ramsey-Alton Manufacturing Company. Visible through the bridge itself are the backs of the businesses along Kent Street. (Courtesy of Chuck Minkley.)

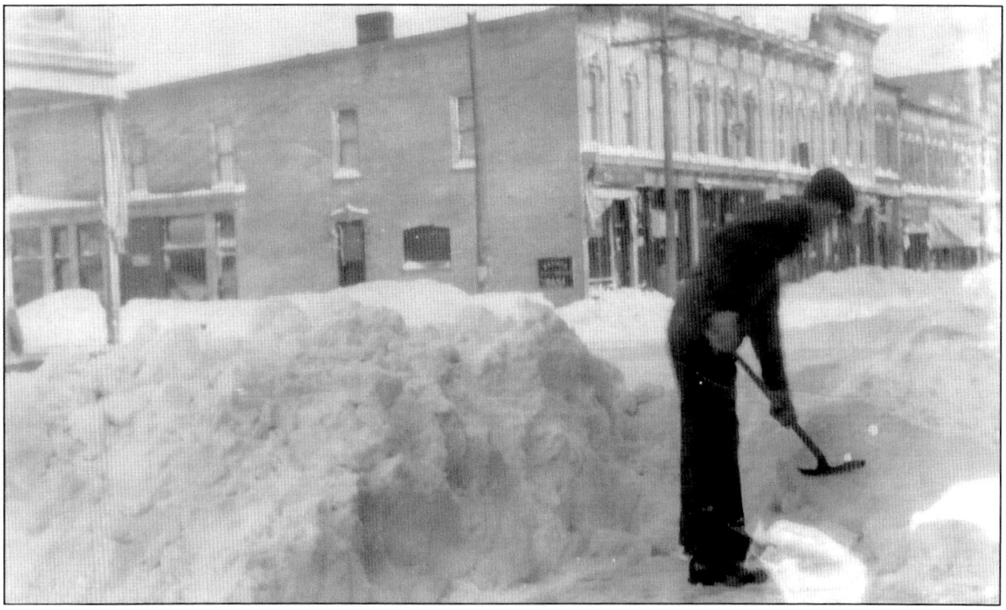

A Familiar Winter Scene. Some things in Michigan never change, regardless of the time period. Here, a man shovels snow outside of the McClelland store on the southeast corner of Kent and Bridge Streets. (Courtesy of the Portland Area Historical Society.)

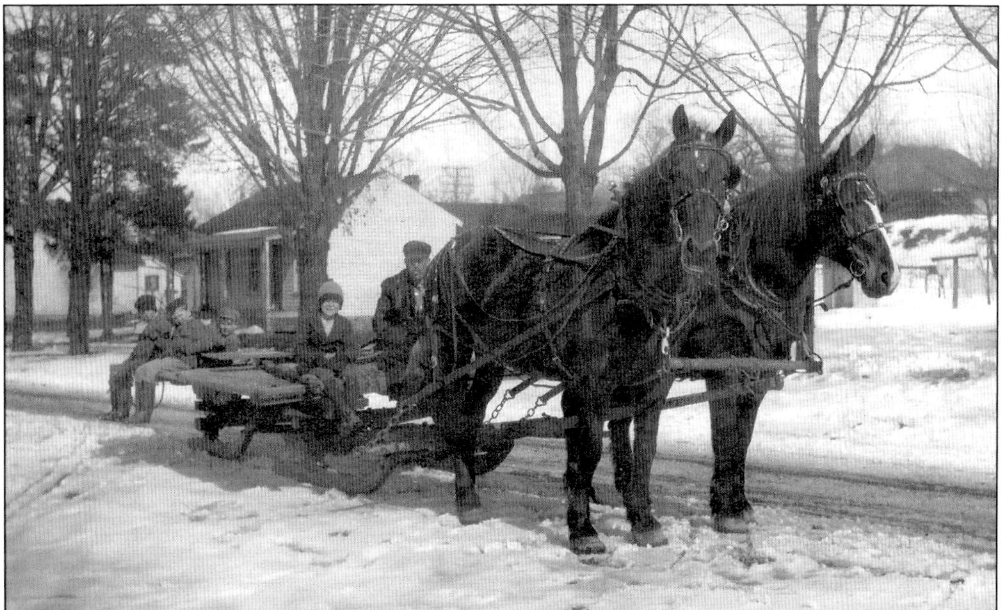

Winter on South Kent Street, c. 1910. A sled carrying a man and four excited boys passes by opposite the Portland library. (Courtesy of the Portland Area Historical Society.)

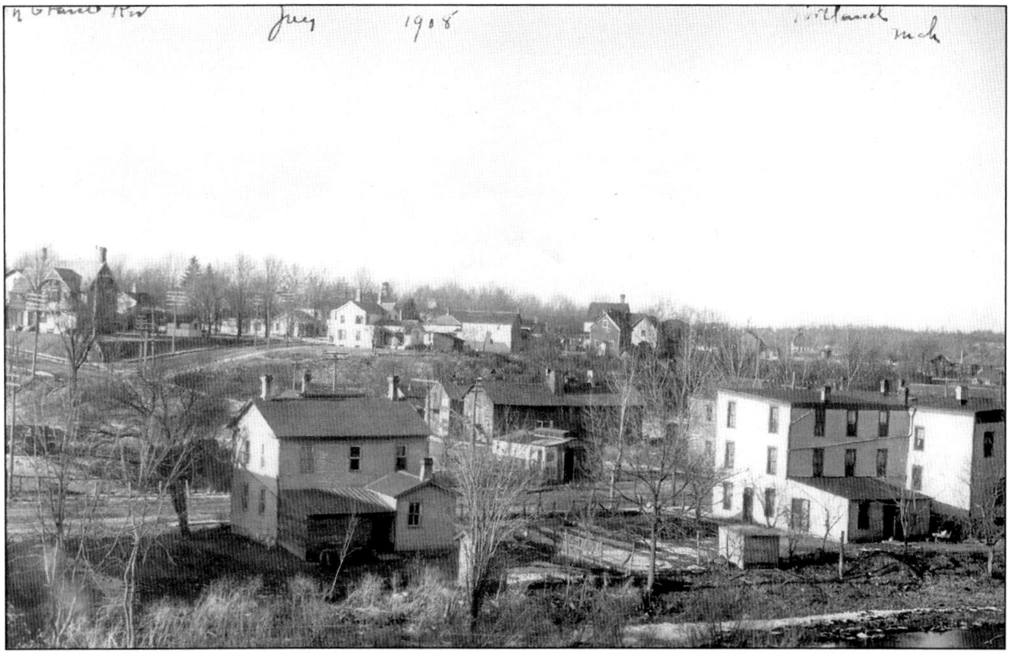

On the Grand River, Winter 1908. Both of these photographs were taken during the first two months of 1908. The picture on top is a view facing west across the Grand River. The building on the far right is the Rollins Hotel. The large Queen Anne Victorian house on the far left, with the gable brackets, was the home of Josiah Dilley. (Courtesy of Robert Torp-Smith.)

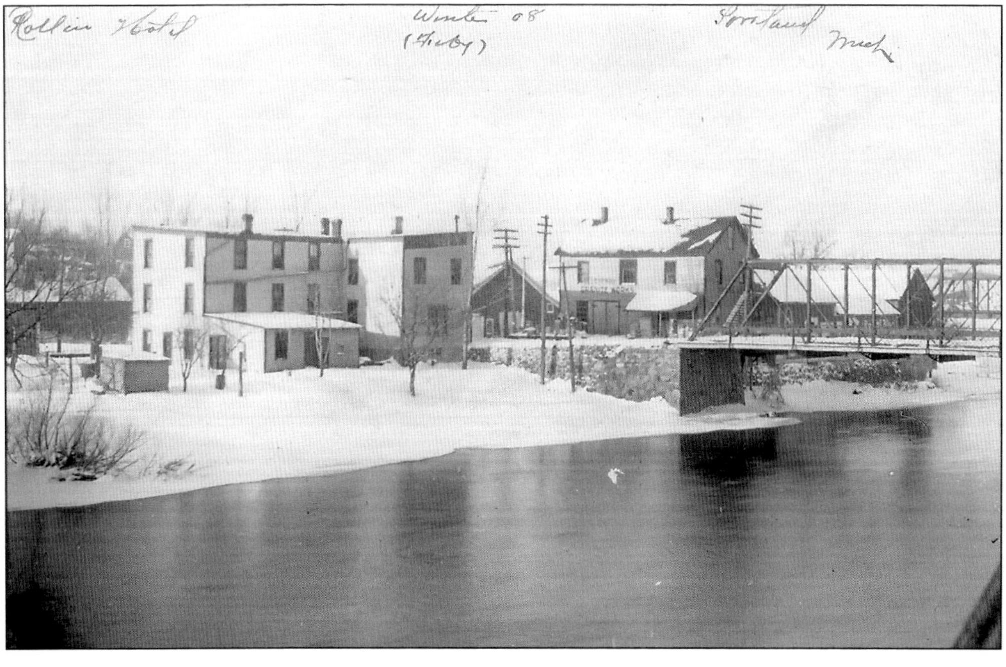

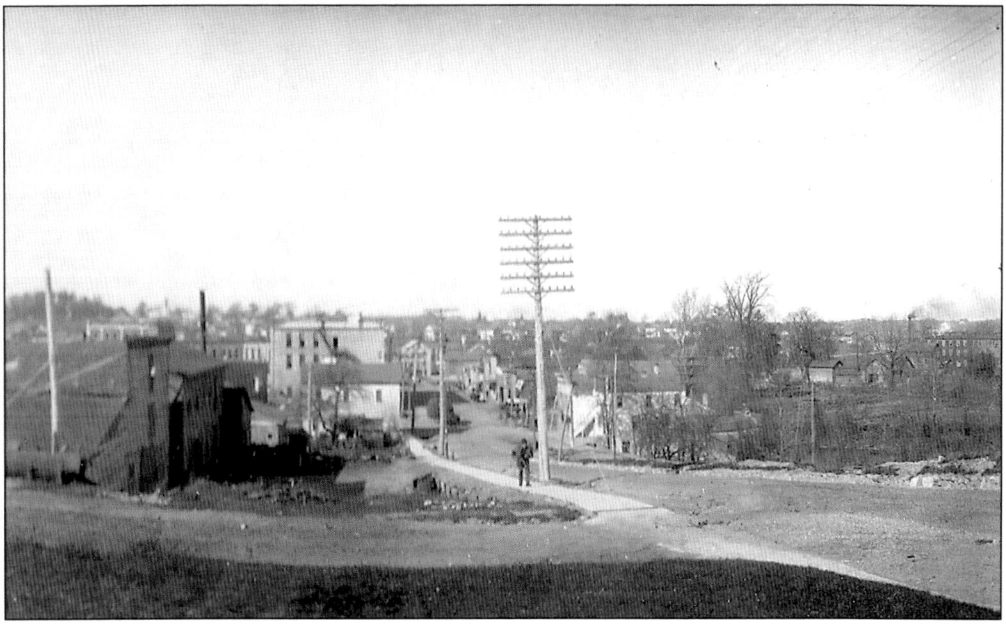

JAMES STREET. A lone figure makes his way up James Street. The large building in the middle distance is the Hotel Divine, seen from the back. The three-story building on the extreme right is the Ramsey-Alton Manufacturing Company. (Courtesy of Chuck Minkley.)

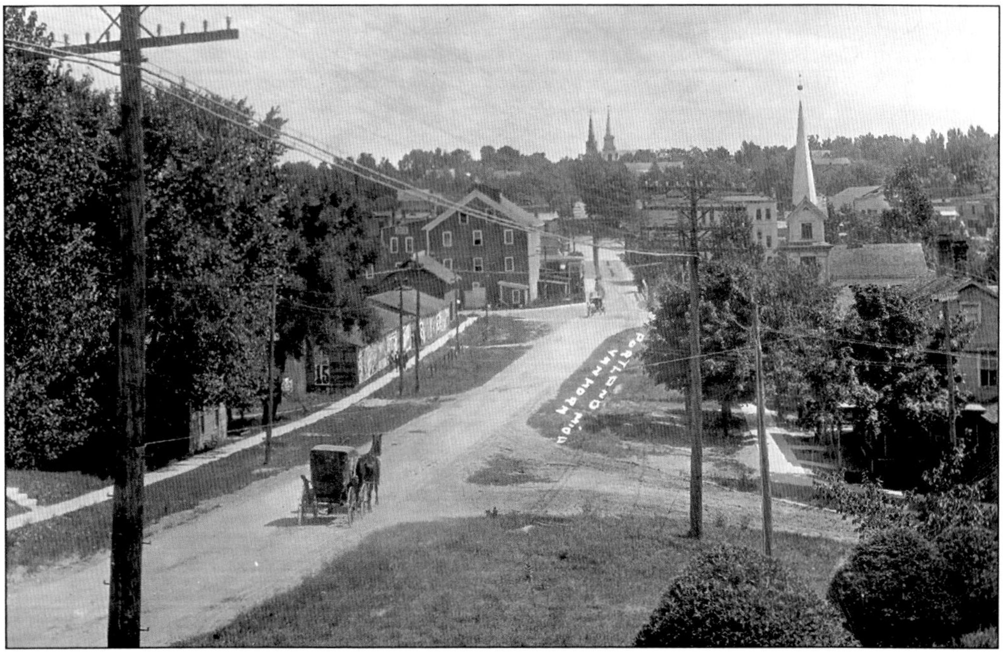

BROAD STREET. The stretch of Bridge Street west of the Grand River was once known as Broad Street. This is a view from the top of Dilley Hill. The large front-gabled building on the left-hand side of the road is the R.B. Smith Flour Mill. This photograph also provides an excellent view of the United Brethren Church (in the foreground) and the Methodist and Baptist Churches across the river.

Five

Churches and Schools

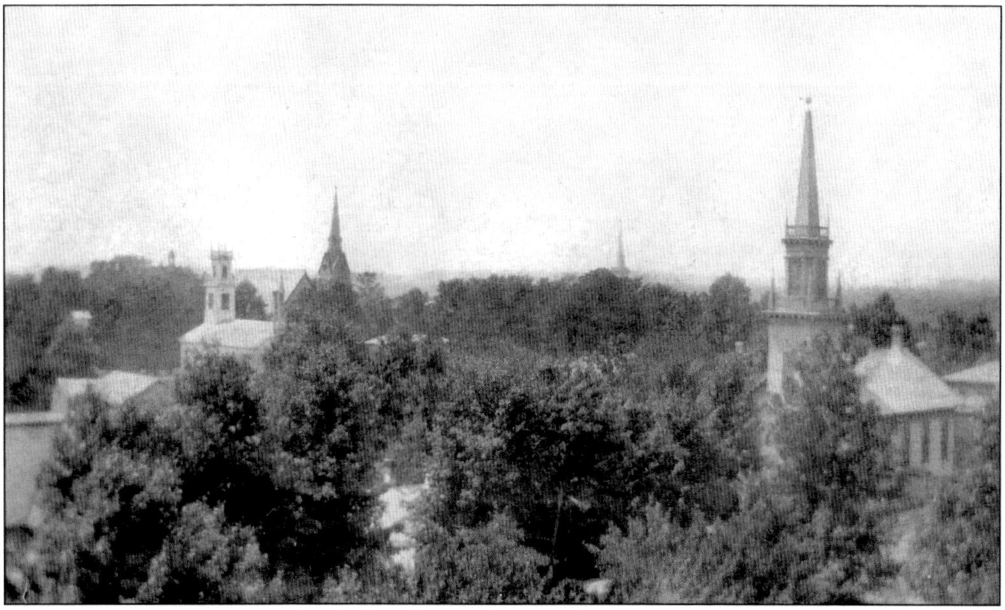

Panorama of Churches. Four church steeples can be seen in this photograph. The square tower on the left is the Congregational Church. The Baptist Church is just to the right of the Congregational Church. The steeple peaking over the trees in the distance belongs to the Methodist Church. The Universalist Church is clearly visible on the far right. The cupola of the old Portland High School is also visible to the right of the Congregational Church tower. Lorenzo Webber was most likely the photographer, and the picture was probably taken from the Webber house on James Street. (Courtesy of the Portland Area Historical Society.)

Methodist Episcopal Church. Portland's Methodist Episcopal Church was organized in 1838 and originally met at the home of early Portland settler Philo Bogue. The society occupied a few different locations until this church was built in 1866. It served the Methodist congregation until August 19, 1912, when a lightning bolt struck its steeple and the church burned to the ground. (Courtesy of Robert Torp-Smith.)

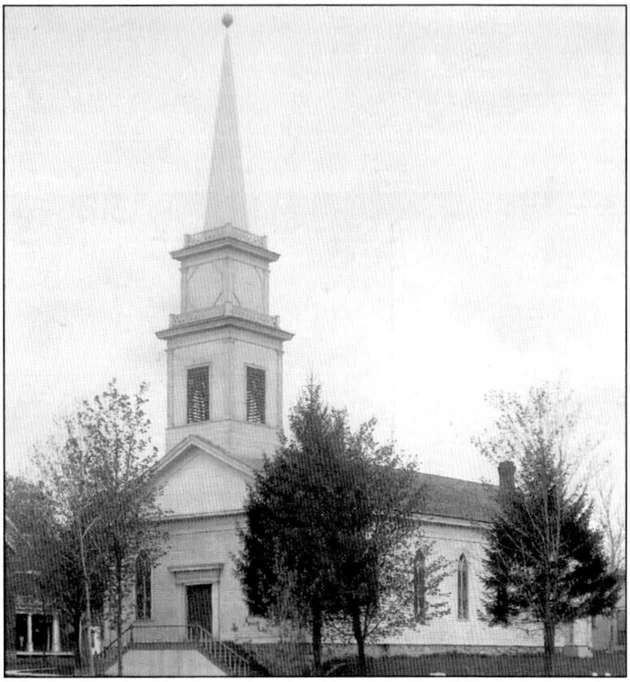

Ruins of the Methodist Episcopal Church. On the evening of August 18, 1912, at approximately 10:30 in the evening, lightning struck the steeple of the Methodist Episcopal Church. Nearby residents recalled hearing the sound of splintered timbers hitting the ground. Byron Smith and Thomas Turner, who were standing near the Webber State Savings Bank, were among the first to discover the steeple was on fire. They and other nearby citizens were able to sound the fire alarm. That night's electrical storm put the Bell and Citizens telephone lines out of commission, so operators were unable to reach some of the firefighters. By the time the hose wagon reached the church, the steeple was almost completely destroyed. The church organ and a few other items were all that was salvaged from the ruined building. (Courtesy of Robert Torp-Smith.)

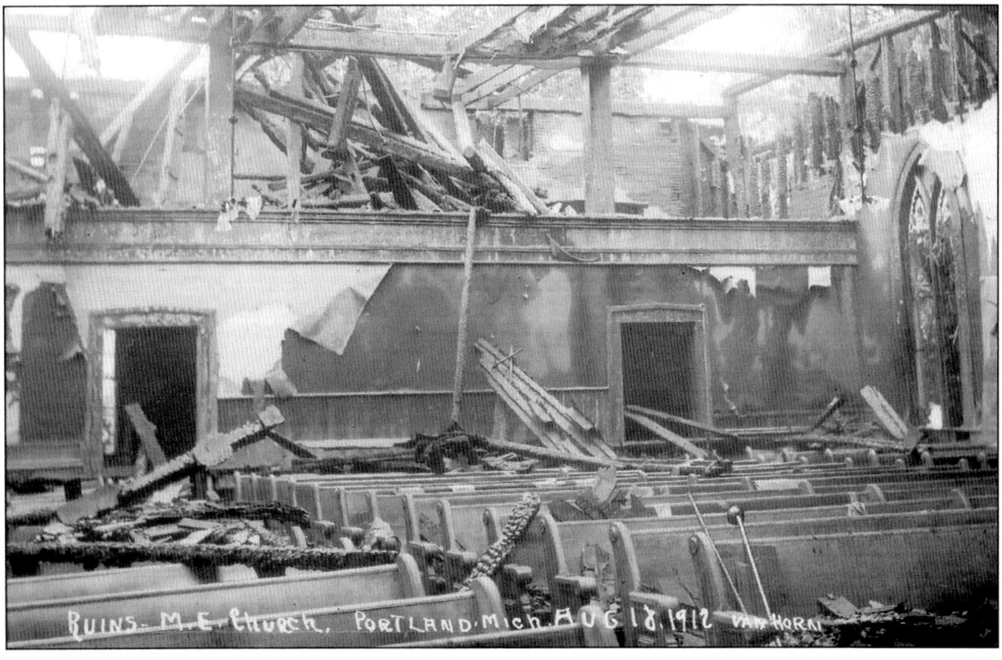

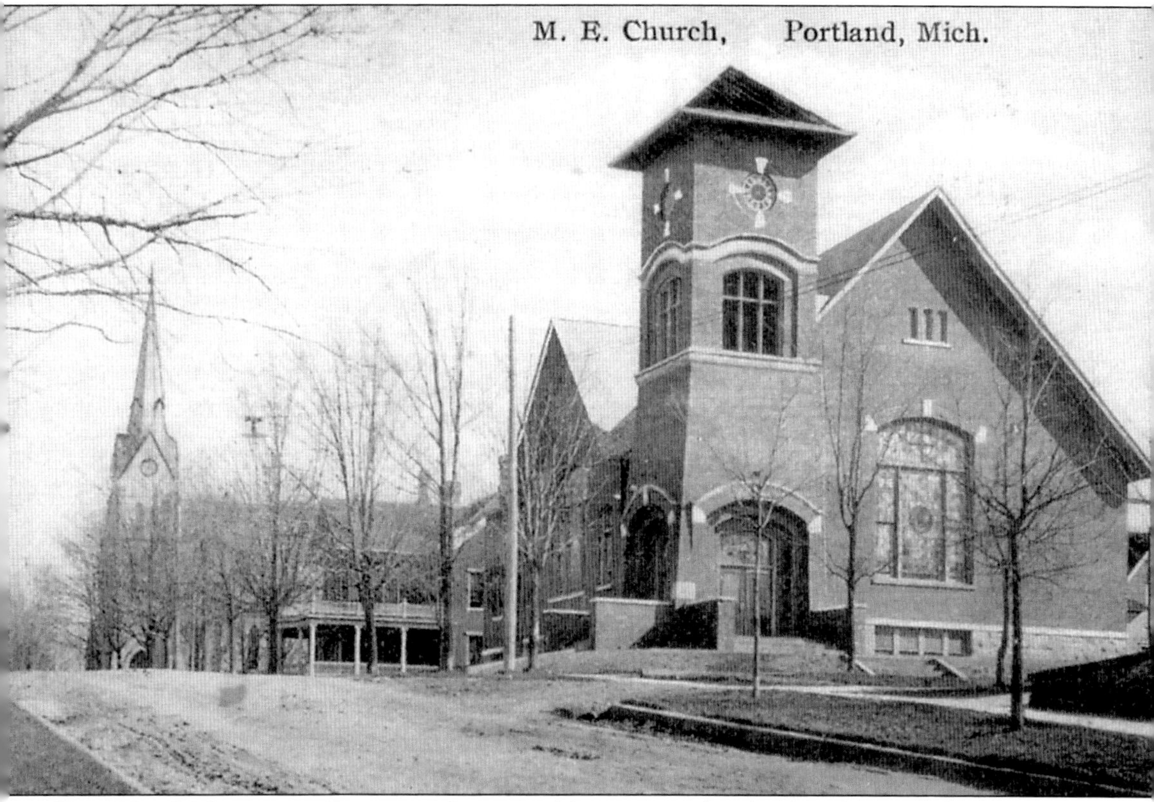

The "New" Methodist Episcopal Church. Almost immediately after the 1866 church was destroyed by fire, construction began on a new church. This church was built with dark red vitrified brick and trimmed with Ohio sandstone. The new church was dedicated in July 1913. (Courtesy of Robert Torp-Smith.)

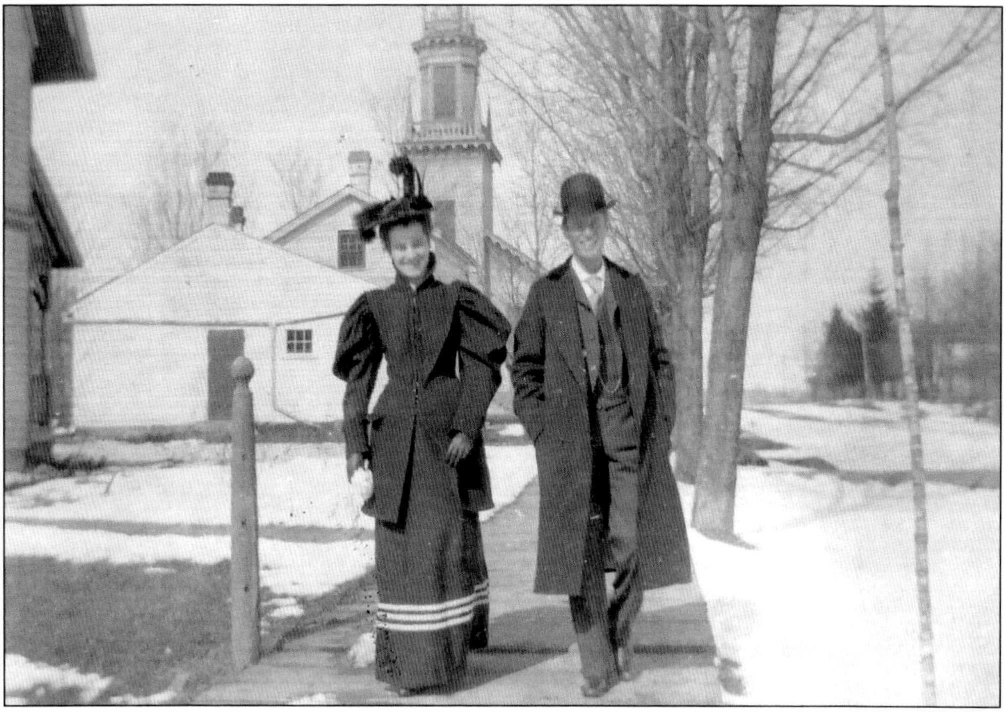

Coming Home from Church. A smiling and happy Meredith Smith and John Milne leave the Universalist Church on Sunday, March 17, 1895. Meredith sang soprano and John sang bass in the church quartet. (Courtesy of the Portland Area Historical Society.)

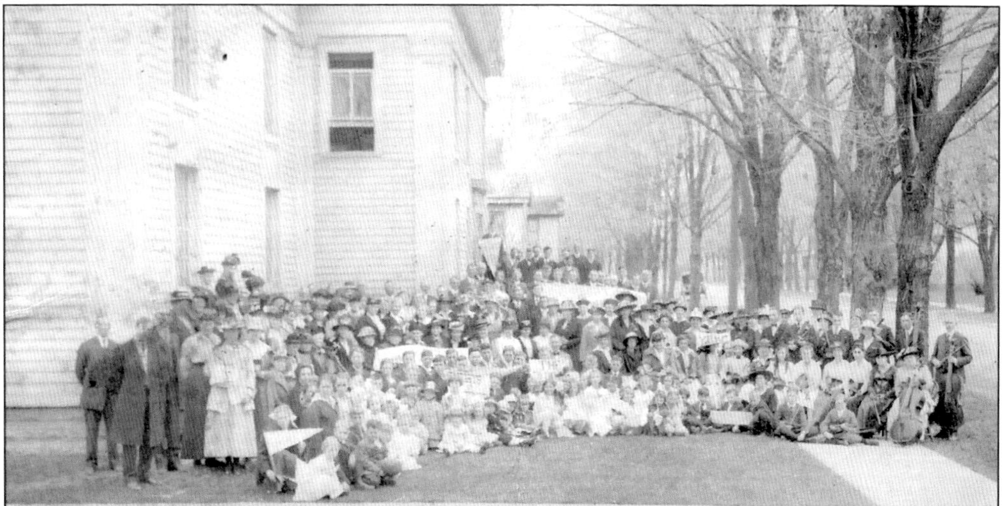

Congregational Church. On Sunday, May 13, 1917, George Van Horn's camera captured this image of the Congregational Church's Sunday school in front of the church. The Portland Congregationalists organized in 1843 and their Greek Revival-style church was built in 1853. Baruch G. Cooley of Greenwood, Massachusetts, supervised the church's construction. In 1877, the church was moved from its original Kent Street location to its present location at the corner of Warren and Bridge Streets. In 1984, the Portland Congregational Church was placed on the National Register of Historic Places. (Courtesy of Richard Teachout.)

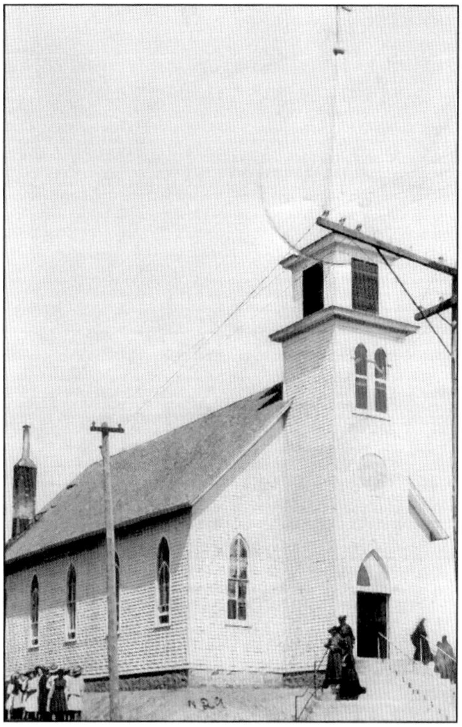

The First St. Patrick's Catholic Church. This church was built in 1870. By the early 1920s, the parish had outgrown the building. It was moved to the corner of West and Center Streets and converted to a parish hall. In 1931, it was destroyed by fire. (Courtesy of Robert Torp-Smith.)

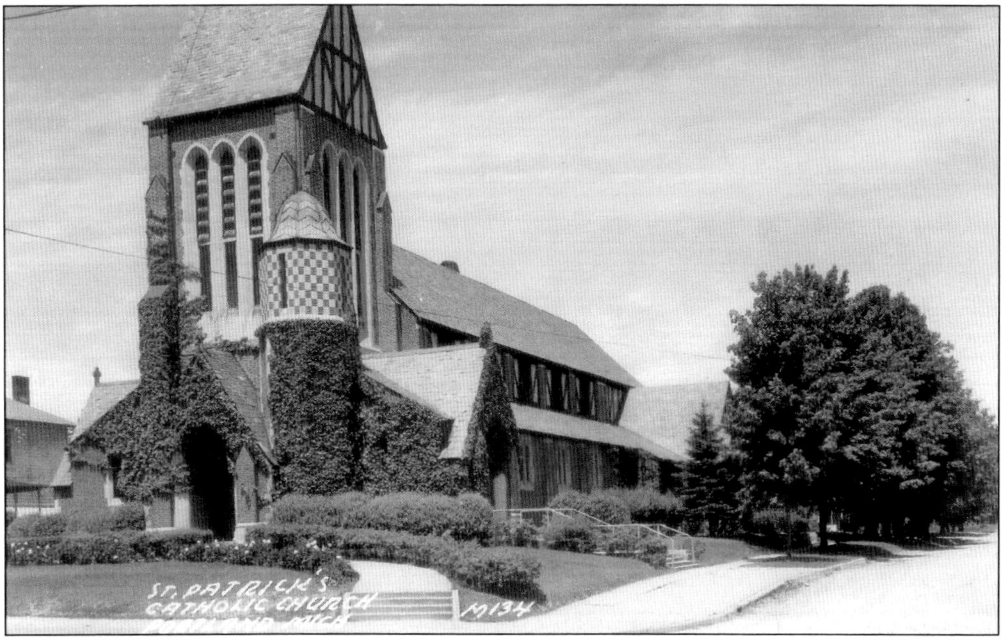

St. Patrick's Catholic Church. This church, which serves Portland's Catholic community to this day, was built in 1926. Father James O'Rourke obtained the plans of a Gothic-Tudor church in rural England; those plans were the basis for the design of the new St. Patrick's Church. The building was constructed at a cost of $80,000. (Courtesy of Richard Teachout.)

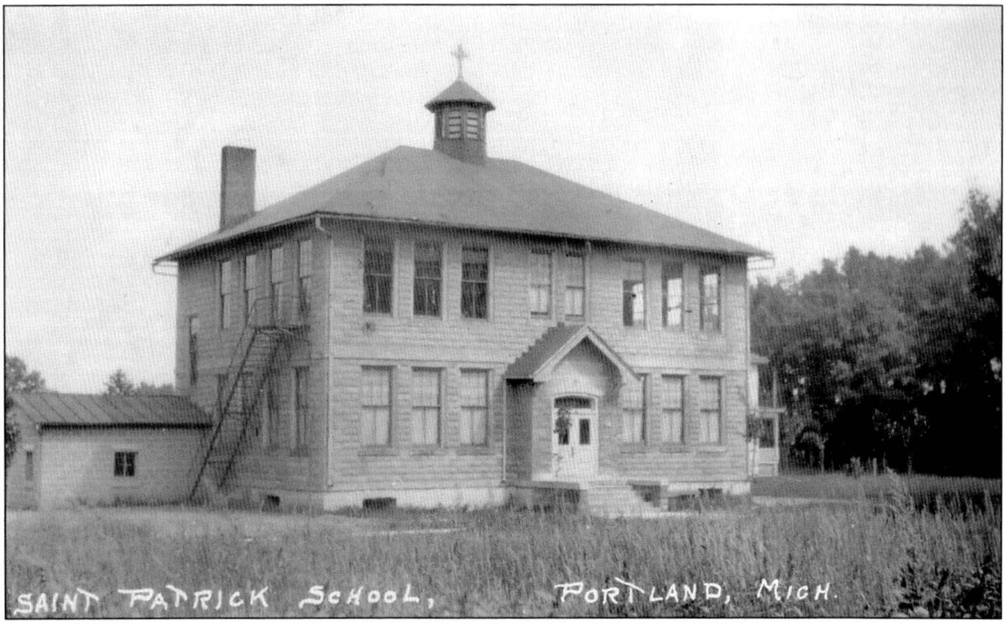

ST. PATRICK'S SCHOOL AND RECTORY. Above is the original Portland St. Patrick's School, built in 1906. Portland has a strong Catholic community that dates back to the 1870s. In 1878, Bishop Borges of Detroit authorized Charles G. Bolte of Ionia to build a church in Portland. The first Catholics to settle in the Portland area were of Irish descent, and they named the parish after the great Irish apostle. As the parish continued to grow, St. Patrick's pastor, Father Mathias Auer, directed the construction of this building. When it was finished, approximately 90 students were enrolled. The photograph below is the school and the rectory. The rectory was built by the parishioners for Father Auer in 1899. (Top photograph courtesy of Anne Rademacher. Bottom photograph courtesy of Robert Torp-Smith.)

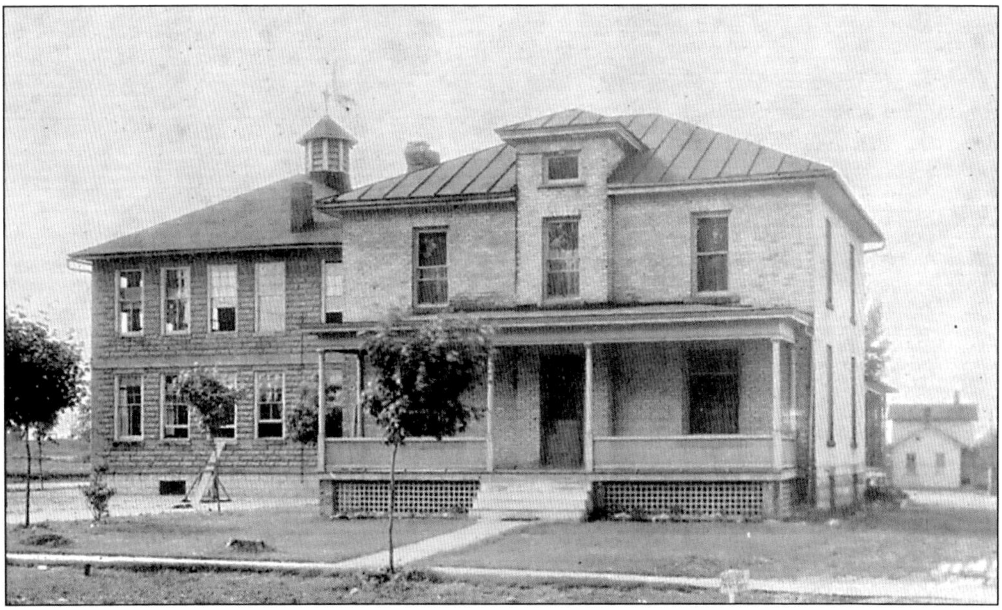

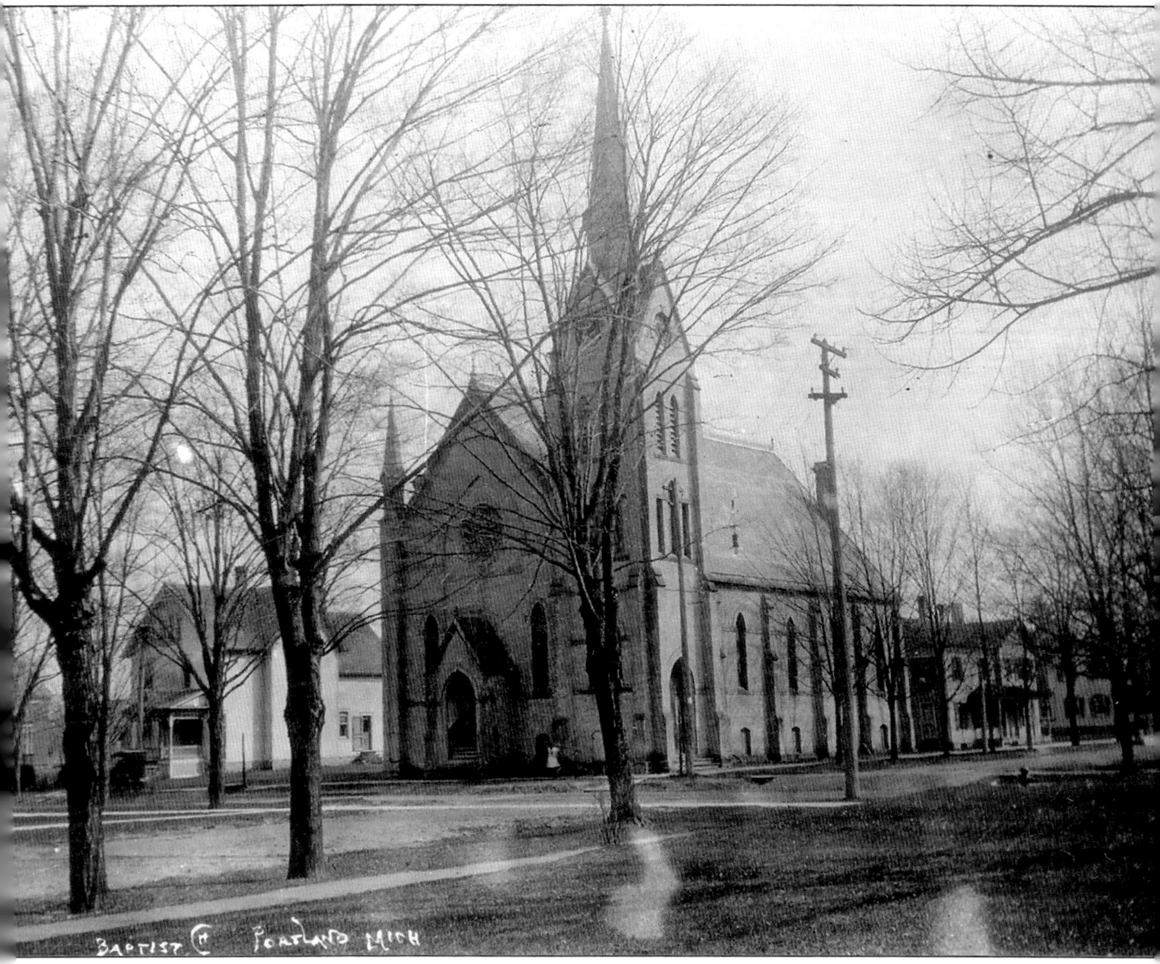

BAPTIST CHURCH. The church was built in 1877, at a cost of $17,500, on the southwest corner of Bridge and Smith Streets. The Portland Baptist Society was organized in 1840 and used the village schoolhouse as their meeting place until 1859, when their first wood frame church was built on Bridge Street. (Courtesy of Robert Torp-Smith.)

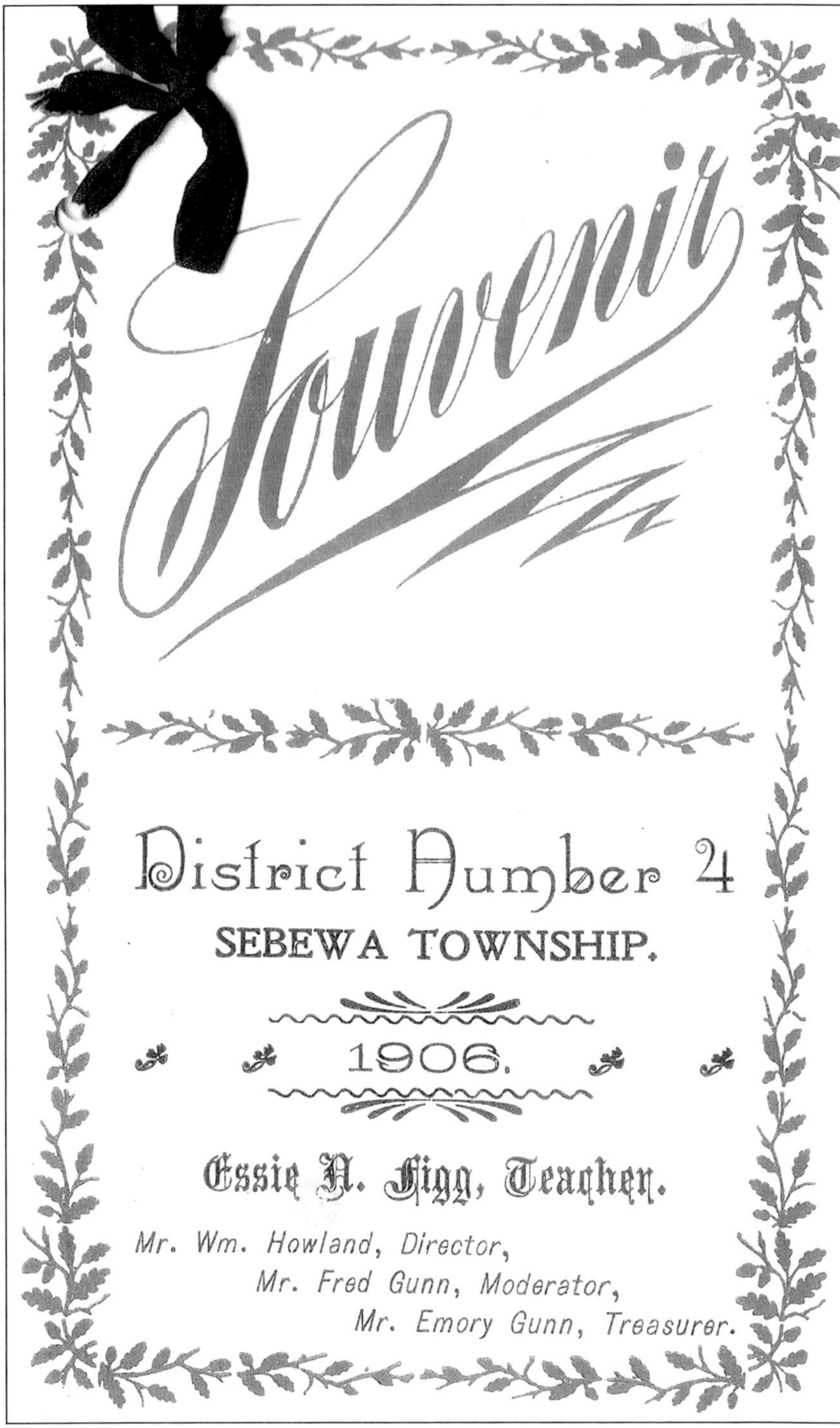

A SOUVENIR FROM THE SEBEWA TOWNSHIP SCHOOL. The first Sebewa Township District #4 School was built in 1856 at the corner of Sunfield and Bippley Road. The school was replaced with a brick structure in 1883. Essie Figg was hired as teacher in 1905 at a pay rate of $33 per month, and taught at the school until 1907. (Courtesy of the Portland Area Historical Society.)

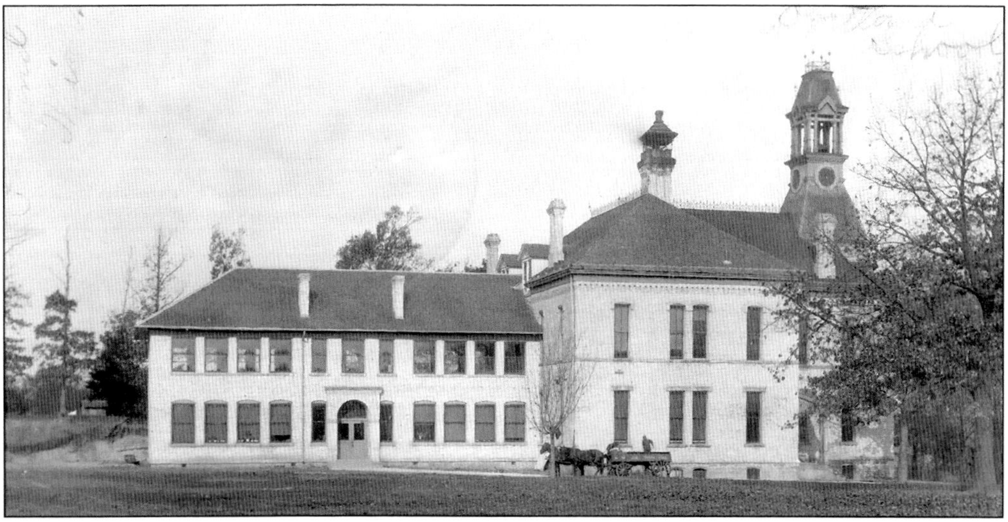

PORTLAND HIGH SCHOOL, C. 1907. In 1881, this impressive brick edifice, with its distinctive cupola, was built facing Brush Street between Elm and Maple Streets. When it was completed, it accommodated all grades except first and second. In the early 1900s, an addition was constructed on the south end and all grades went to the school. The school served the educational needs of Portland's young people until October 16, 1918, when it was destroyed by fire. (Courtesy of Richard Teachout.)

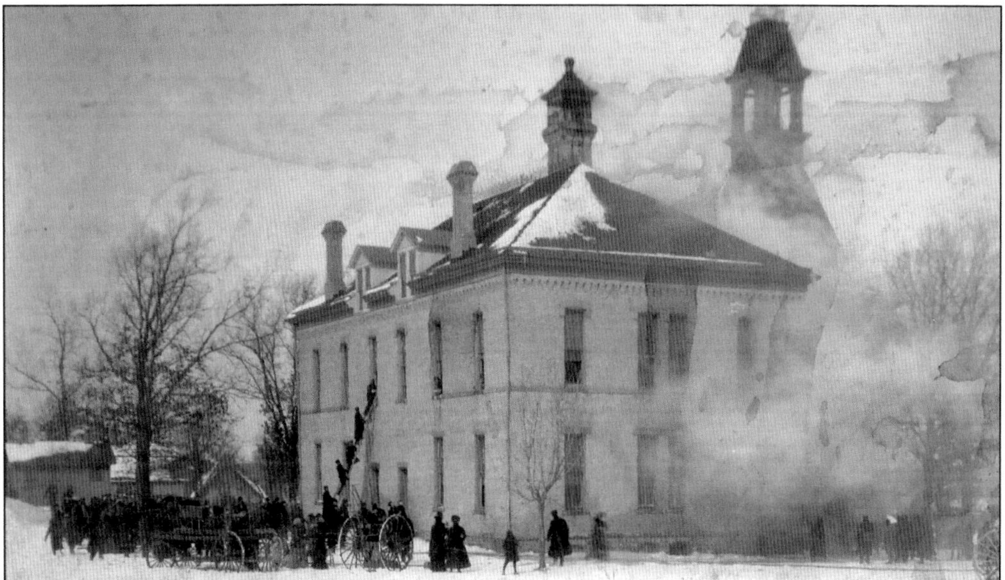

HIGH SCHOOL FIRE. On the morning of Thursday, February 16, 1905, a fire broke out in the basement of the Portland High School building. The recently installed telephone was used to summon the fire department. Firefighters had a difficult time containing the fire and it eventually reached the second story. Fortunately, the wind was blowing in the opposite direction and this allowed the firefighters to finally extinguish the flames. The fire was blamed on overheated furnace pipes with the cost of damage totaled at about $4,000. Luckily, no one was hurt by the fire. Although the school was spared in this particular blaze, the building was eventually destroyed by a fire in 1918. (Courtesy of the Portland Area Historical Society.)

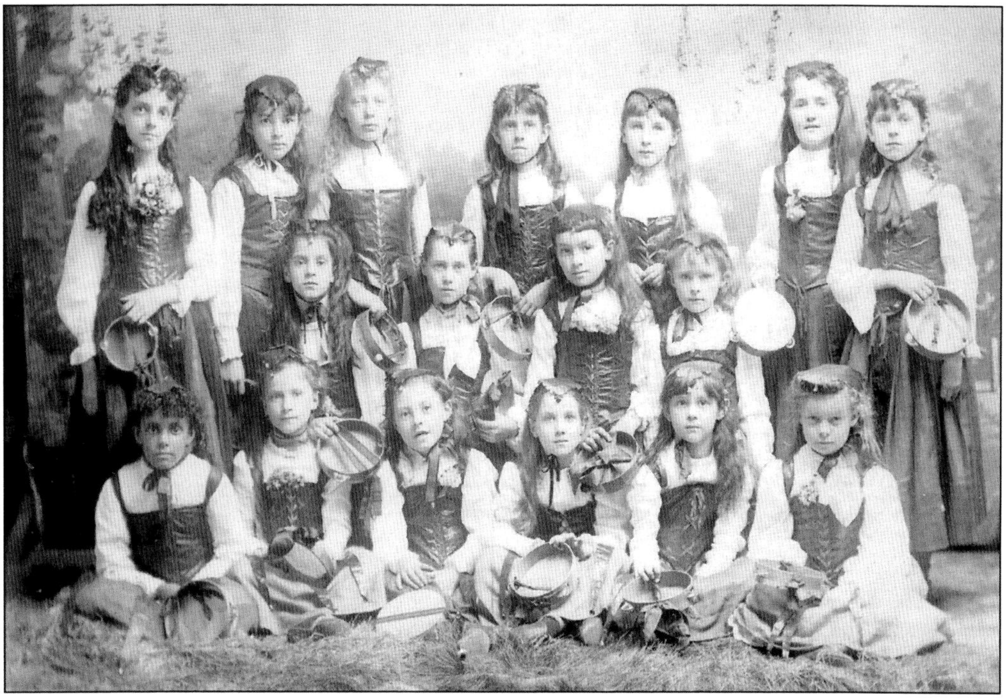

Grade School Class Picture, c. 1890s. The girls in this photograph appear to be dressed for some sort of pageant. Pictured here are, from left to right: (seated) Maud Pratt, Reva Earl, Ethel Alton, Minnie Newman, Emma Pilkington, and Bessie Adams; (middle row) Alice Allen, Minnie Adams, Mary Newman, and Gertie McClelland; (top row) Reva Crane, Lula Anderson, Jessie Moe, Nettie Smith, Harold Benedict, Rubie Brady, and Nellie Smith. (Courtesy of the Portland Area Historical Society.)

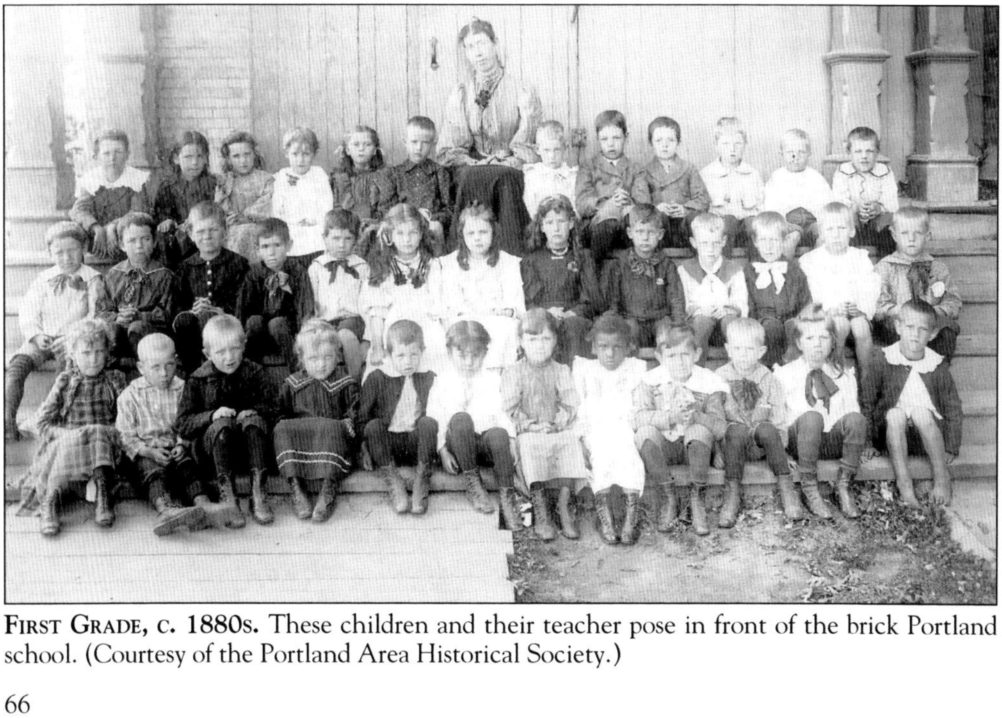

First Grade, c. 1880s. These children and their teacher pose in front of the brick Portland school. (Courtesy of the Portland Area Historical Society.)

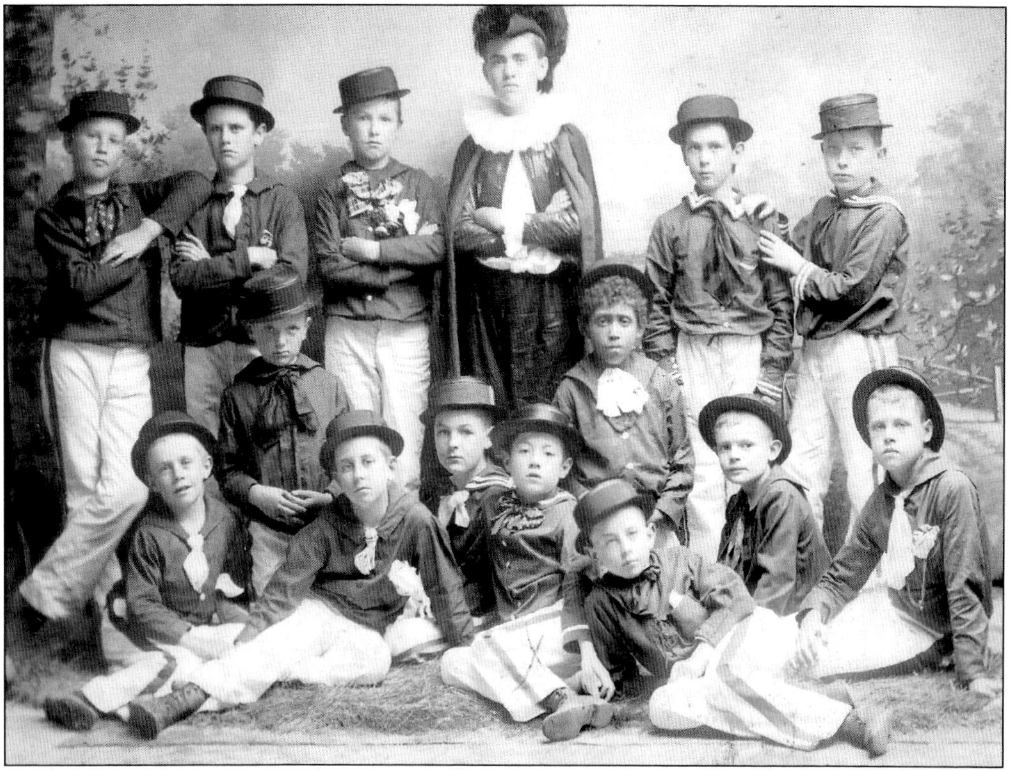

CLASS PICTURE, C. 1890S. Some of the boys pictured in this photograph include Eston Smith, Arthur Pilkington, Howard Stevens, Jay Clark, Fred England, Richard Bates, and Harold Bandfield. Two other students are particularly noteworthy. Clarence Budington Kelland, seated second from the right, became a prolific writer with 60 novels and over 200 short stories, one of which, "Opera Hat," was the basis for the film "Mr. Deeds." "Pedro" Pratt, the curly-haired youngster seated third from right, became a renowned local baseball star. He once registered 38 consecutive scoreless innings as a pitcher. (Courtesy of the Portland Area Historical Society.)

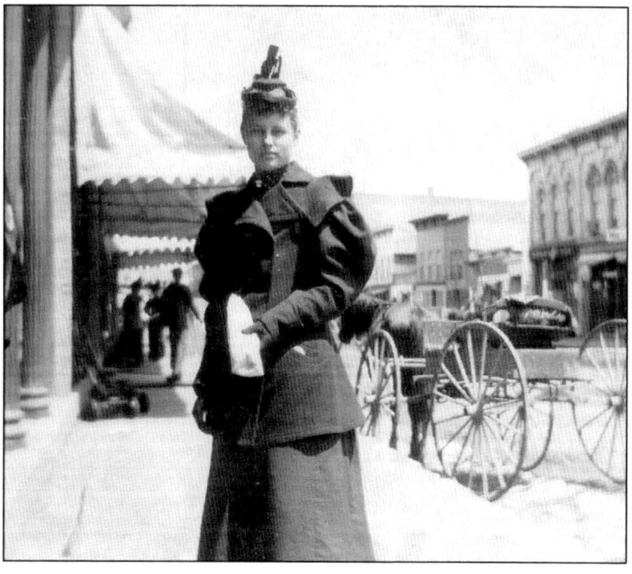

SCHOOLTEACHER HOPE THOMAS. Hope Thomas taught music and drawing in the Portland Public Schools in the late 1890s and early 1900s. She was about 19 years old when this photograph was taken. Hope's two younger sisters, Anna and Ruth, were also schoolteachers. By the early 20th century, what was once a male-dominated profession became a largely female domain. Victorian-era school boards viewed women as more morally virtuous than men, and preferred them as teachers. (Courtesy of the Portland Area Historical Society.)

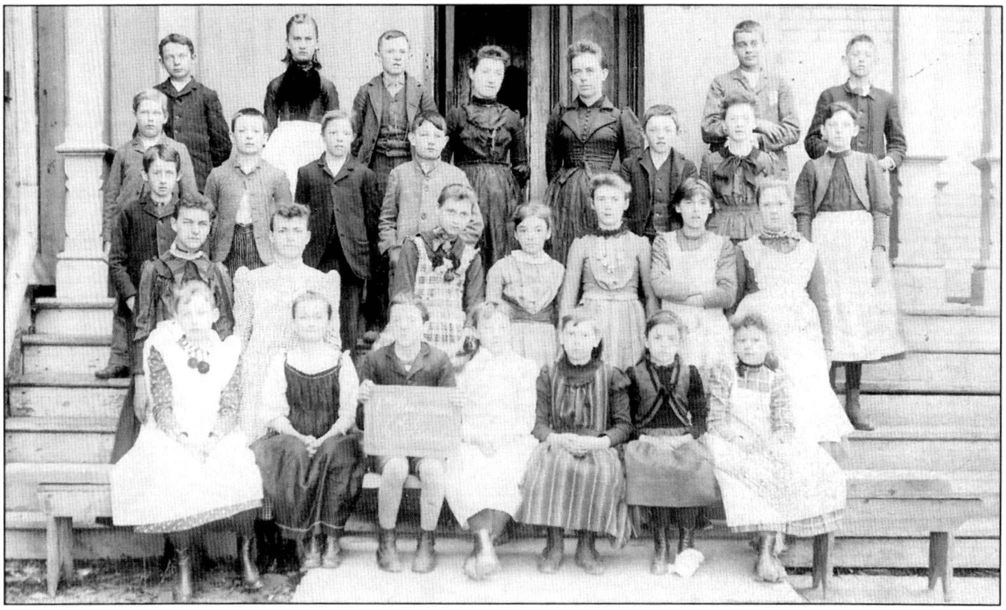

(*above*) **SIXTH GRADE, 1892.** Identified on the back of the photograph, from left to right, are as follows: (front row) Billie Day, Francelia Fuller, Willie Halladay, Maud Fishbeck, Carrie Ward, Clara Albro, and Mary Ryerson; (second row) Willis Brooks (boy with dark hair and dark jacket), Maud Soules (girl with striped dress), Susie Russell, Nellie Gilden, Lula Anderson, Daisy Smith, Edith Moore, and Iva Scofield; (third row) Willie Browning, Willie Dilley, Chester Norwood, Bret Dickson, Glenn Bradley, Eva Sanger, and Grace Wood; (top row) Seth Wright, Millie Derby, George Whitney, Mary Newman, teacher; Genevra Walker, teacher; Dee Pierce, and Fred Leland. (Courtesy of the Portland Area Historical Society.)

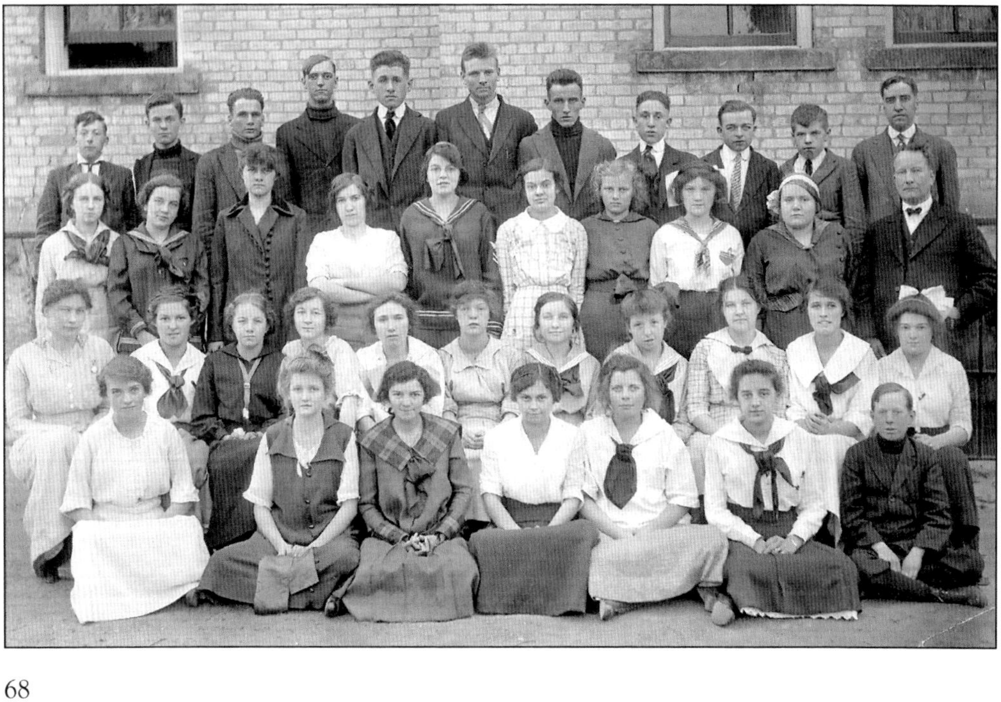

Motto of Class—Second to None.

CLASS OF 1882.

English Course.

GRADUATING CLASS.

RY WHITE,
KITTIE SCRIBNER.

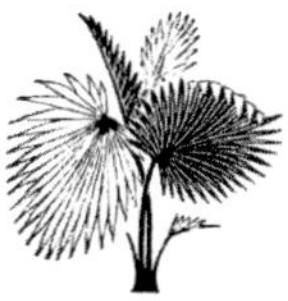

JUNIOR CLASS.

A ADAMS,
DELLA BROWN,
MARY STALEY,
MINNIE HINMAN,
GLENN SMITH,
EDWARD WAY,
CLARA HORNER,
HARVEY BENSCHOTER.

PROGRAMME.

MUSIC—Make a Joyful noise unto God—HAROLD B ADAMS

PRAYER

MUSIC—This is my Commandment—W. F. WORSCHKUL.

ORATION............................Modern Literature
IRA ADAMS.

ESSAY...................................Perseverance
DELLA BROWN.

ESSAY..............................Old Times and New
MARY STALEY.

MUSIC—Come Down in the Meadow—S. W. STRAUB.

ESSAY......................................Self Reliance
MINNIE HINMAN.

ORATION...Music
EDWARD WAY.

ESSAY......................................Class History
CLARA HORNER.

MUSIC—A Home by the Sea...........R. D. RUFERT

ORATION......................Advantages of Education
GLENN SMITH.

BIOGRAPHY................................Victor Hugo
MARY WHITE.

MUSIC—Roll on Mississippi................S. W. STRAUB

EULOGY............................On Dr. Bolland
KITTIE SCRIBNER.

PROPHESY..Class
HARVEY BENSCHOTER.

MUSIC—O Say not Life is Dark..........FRANK M. DAVIS

PRESENTATION OF DIPLOMAS—BY CAPT. E. M. ALLEN

BENEDICTION.

FIRST PORTLAND HIGH SCHOOL GRADUATING CLASS. This is the program from the first-ever commencement ceremony for Portland High School. The 1882 senior class was the first to attend the brick high school building. (Courtesy of the Portland Area Historical Society.)

(*opposite, bottom*) **SOPHOMORE CLASS, 1916.** Identified on the back of the photograph, from left to right, are as follows: (front row) Katrine Keusch, Dorothy Blanchard, Dorothy Kenyon, Hermine Hamlin, Nettie Shotwell, Marie Hath, and Dean Tyler; (second row) Mary Brown, Elise Crane, Lena Dawdy, Gertrude Whitman, Zorva Ward, Mae Sherman, Lula Avery, Marion Pryer, Mildred Hoover, Margery Scadin, and Mildred Schultz; (third row) Margery Kenyon, Viola Howe, Helen Bissinger, Esther Kenyon, Mary ?, Bertha Selleck, Lucille Keefer, Edna Schults, Martina Baugh, and Superintendent J.D. Gourlay; (top row) Lawrence Friend, Fred Maurn, Dewey Clark, Howard Gilford, Dan Moriarty, Harvey Peabody, Elmer Van Sickle, Bill Sulpizio, Leo Phillips, Frederick Knox, and John Kanter. (Courtesy of the Portland Area Historical Society.)

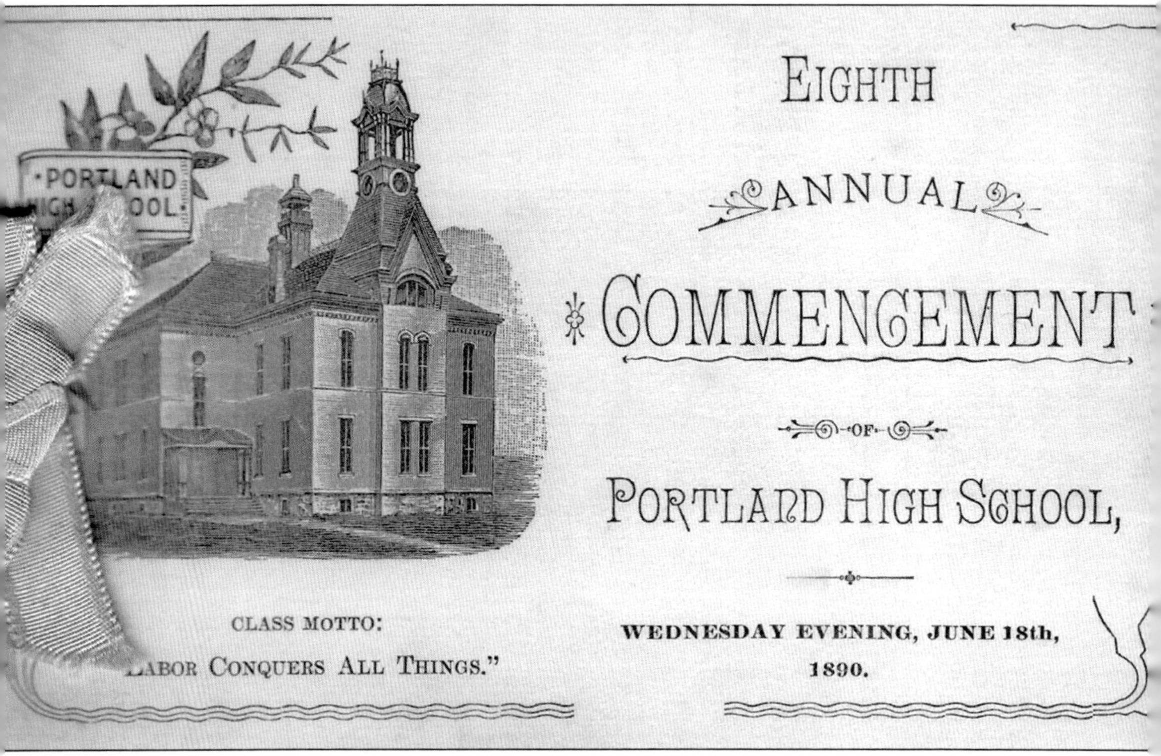

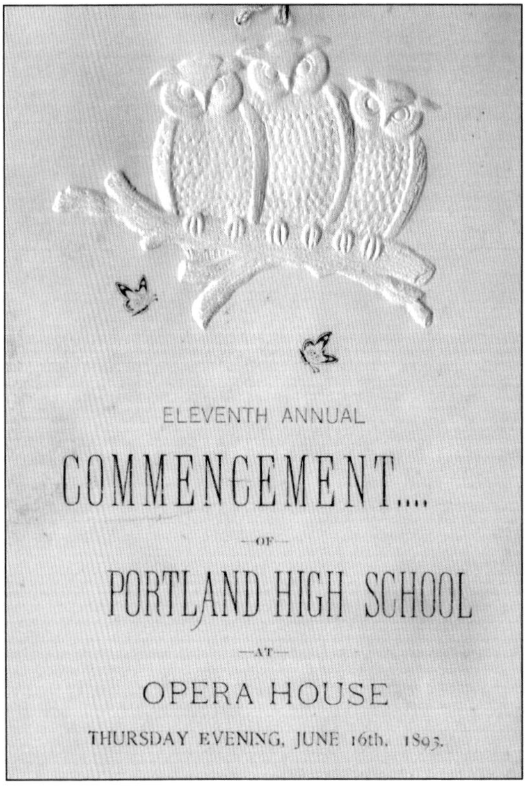

PORTLAND HIGH SCHOOL COMMENCEMENT PROGRAMS. The 1890 program boasts an attractive drawing of the high school, and the 1893 program is decorated with three embossed owls perched on a tree limb. For many years in the late 1800s and early 1900s, high school commencement ceremonies were held in the opera house. (Courtesy of the Portland Area Historical Society.)

Six

Agriculture and Rural Life

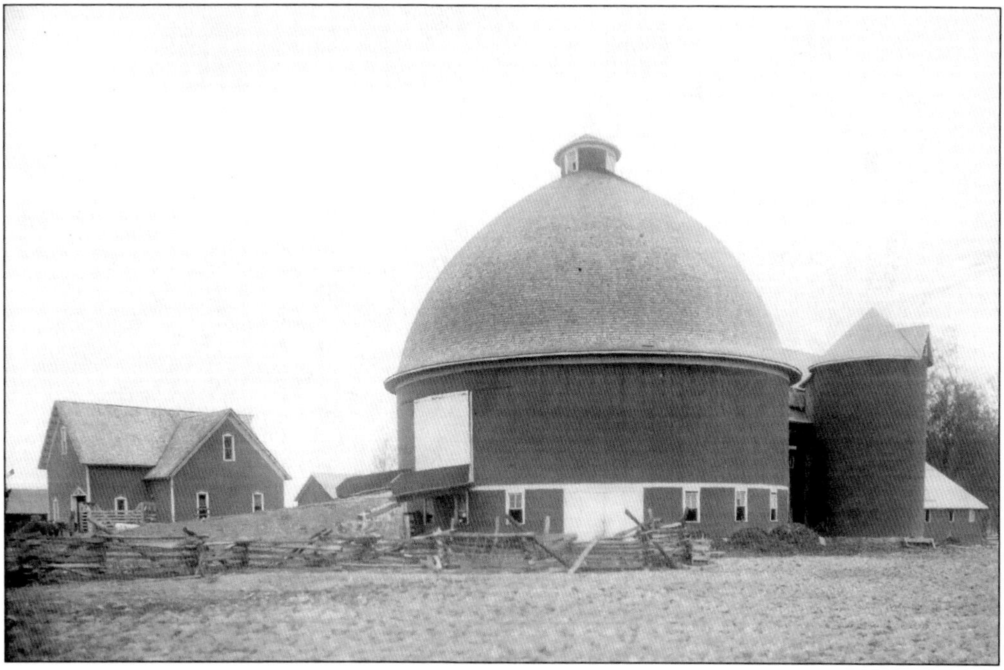

Round Barn. This round barn was located west of Portland along the north side of Grand River Avenue. The barn, along with the other out-buildings pictured, was built by a farmer named Love. This farmer also owned a lumber yard in Portland, which enabled him to build these grand structures. Unfortunately, the round barn was struck by lightning and burned down in 1925. (Courtesy of the Portland Area Historical Society.)

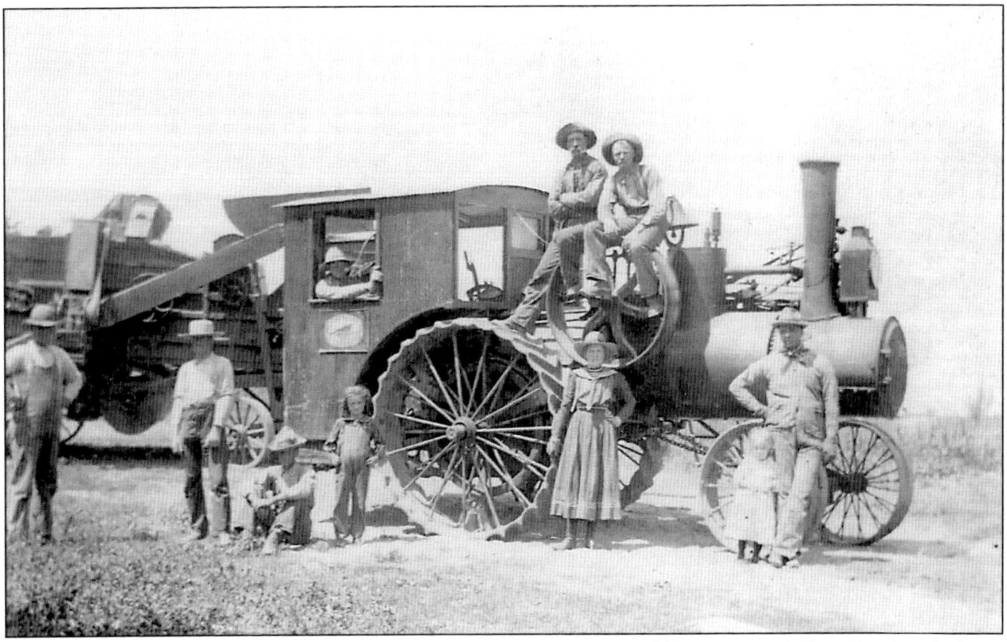

Posing on and around a Steam Tractor, c. 1910s. (Courtesy of the Portland Area Historical Society.)

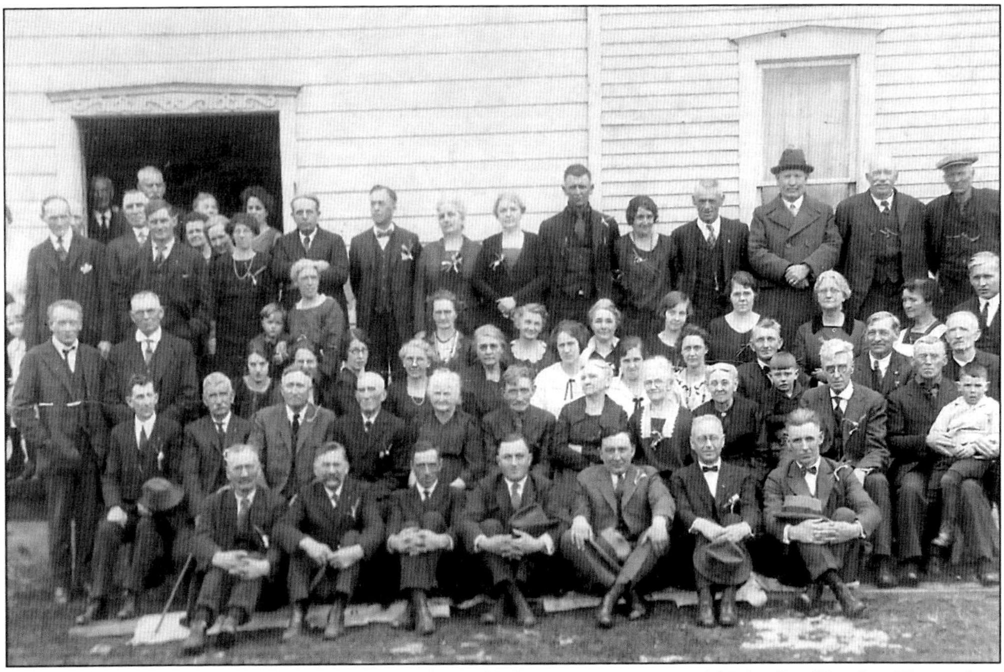

Danby Grange. Upon the occasion of its 50th anniversary in 1934, the Danby Township Grange assembled for this group photograph. The National Grange, officially known as the Order of Patrons of Husbandry, was formed in 1867. The organization's mission was, and still is, to protect the interests of farmers. Through its lobbying efforts, the Grange was able to establish better educational opportunities for rural residents, rural free delivery, and the Farm Credit System. (Courtesy of the Portland Area Historical Society.)

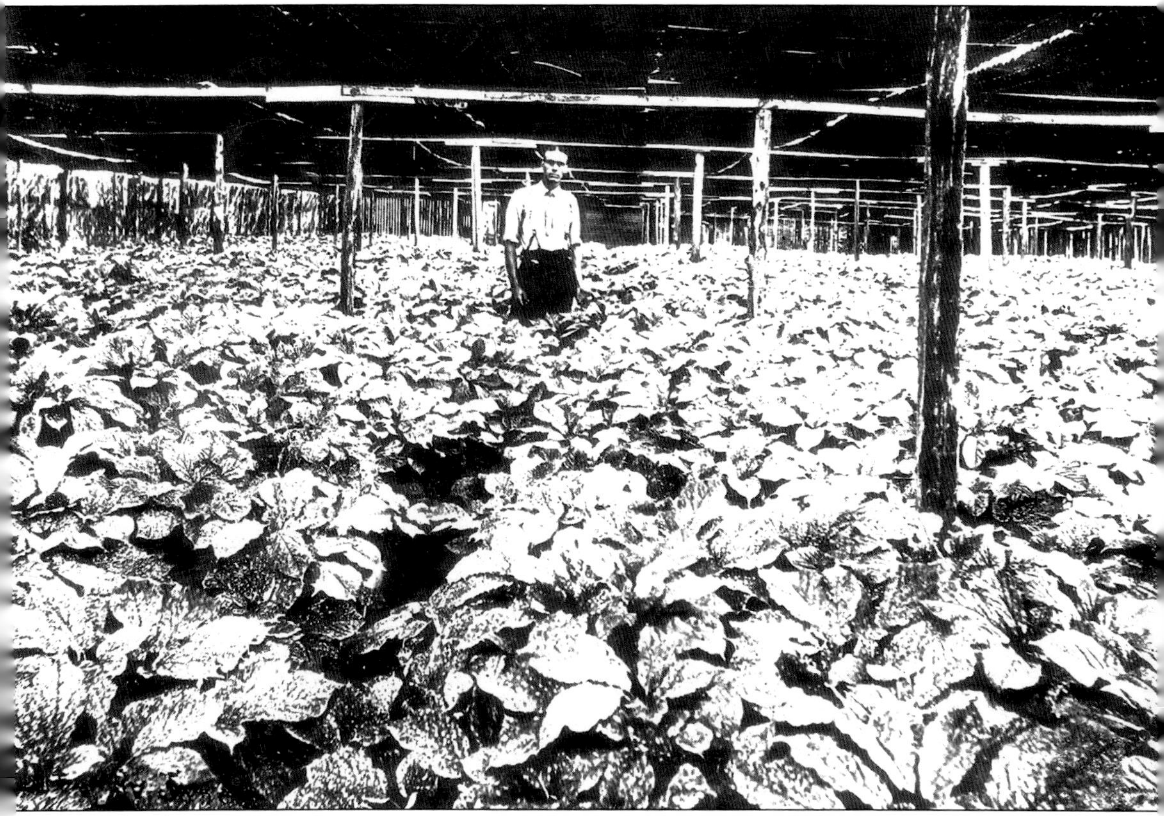

Dale Pierce, 1922 President of the Michigan Ginseng Society, on his Ginseng Farm. Between 1905 and 1933, Dale Pierce ran a ginseng farm on East Grand River Avenue (near the Charlotte Highway intersection). He began the operation with his father. They visited various farms in Michigan searching for ginseng roots and brought what they found back to Portland in order to get the farm started. The Pierces sold their ginseng to New York and Chicago agents, who in turn sold them to China. (Courtesy of Robert Torp-Smith.)

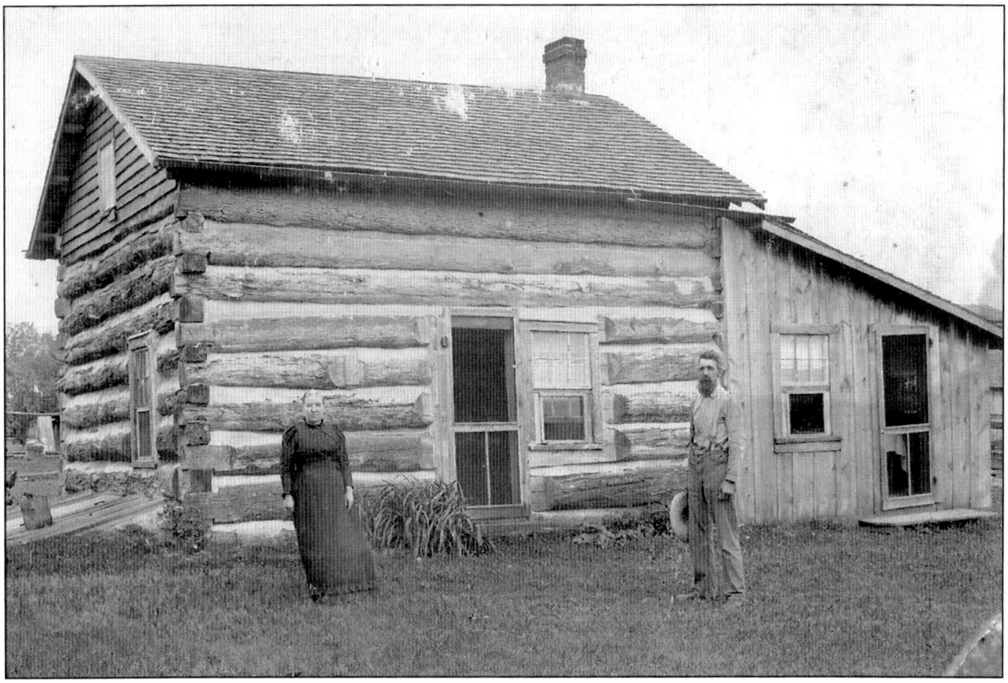

LOG HOUSE. These rural people stand in front of their hand-hewn log home with its board-and-batten lean-to addition. (Courtesy of the Portland Area Historical Society.)

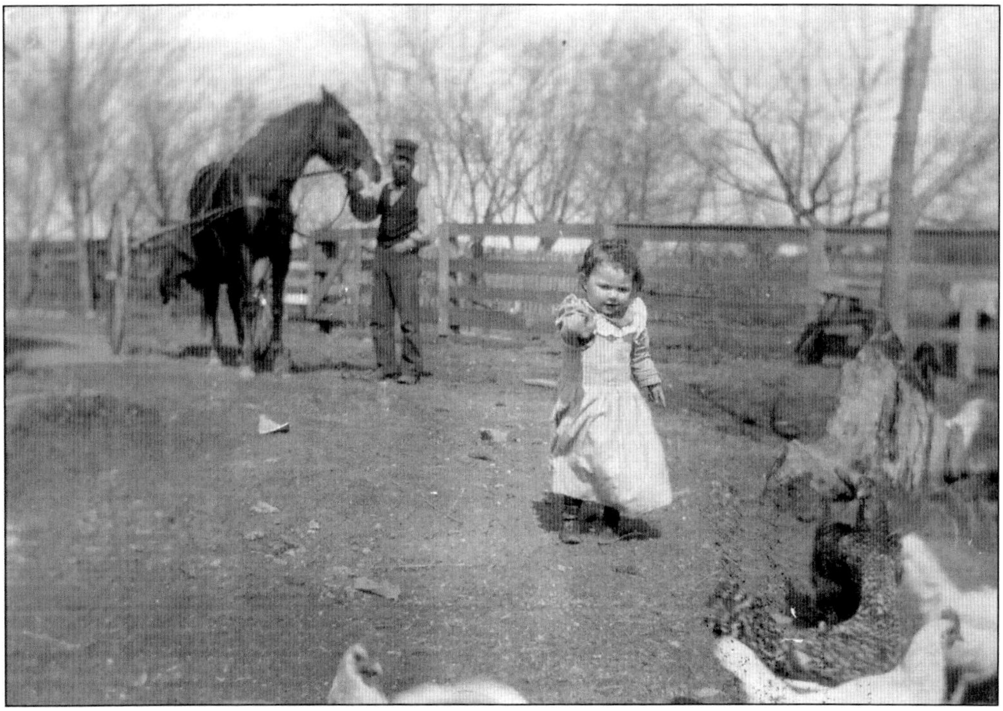

LITTLE GIRL FEEDING CHICKENS, C. 1895. This photograph was taken at the John Webber residence. During this time period, even people who lived inside the village kept poultry and/or livestock. (Courtesy of the Portland Area Historical Society.)

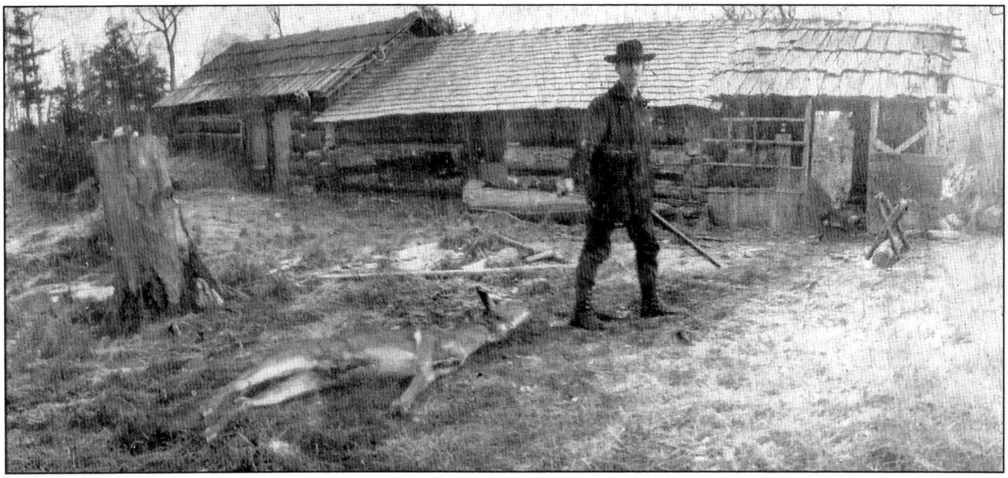

Successful Deer Hunt. This is Portland-area resident Clyde Moore after what appears to have been a successful hunting expedition. Based on the number of tree stumps on the property, the land was probably recently cleared. Clyde Moore became assistant postmaster and also served as a trustee of the Portland School Board. (Courtesy of the Portland Area Historical Society.)

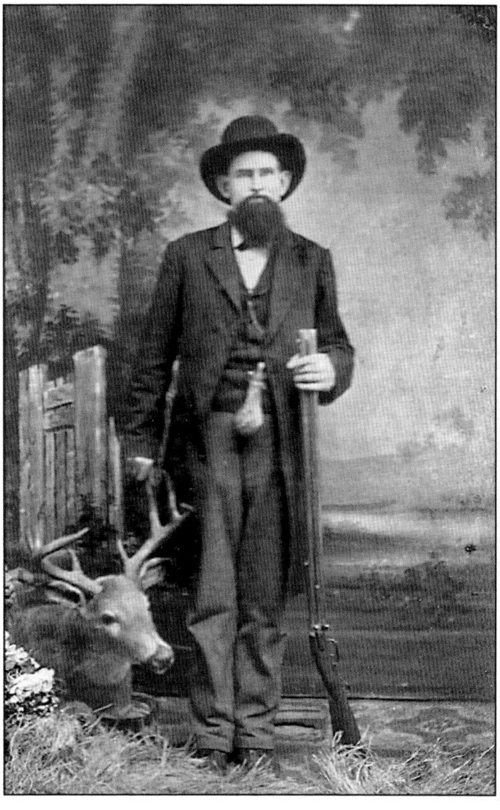

Hunting. Luther (Lute) Van Horn was born in New York in 1820. He was a farmer and also the father of renowned Portland photographer George Van Horn. Lute Van Horn also had the reputation of being a great hunter, as this photograph attests. By the mid-19th century, hunting portraits such as these became very popular among sportsmen. (Courtesy of the Portland Area Historical Society.)

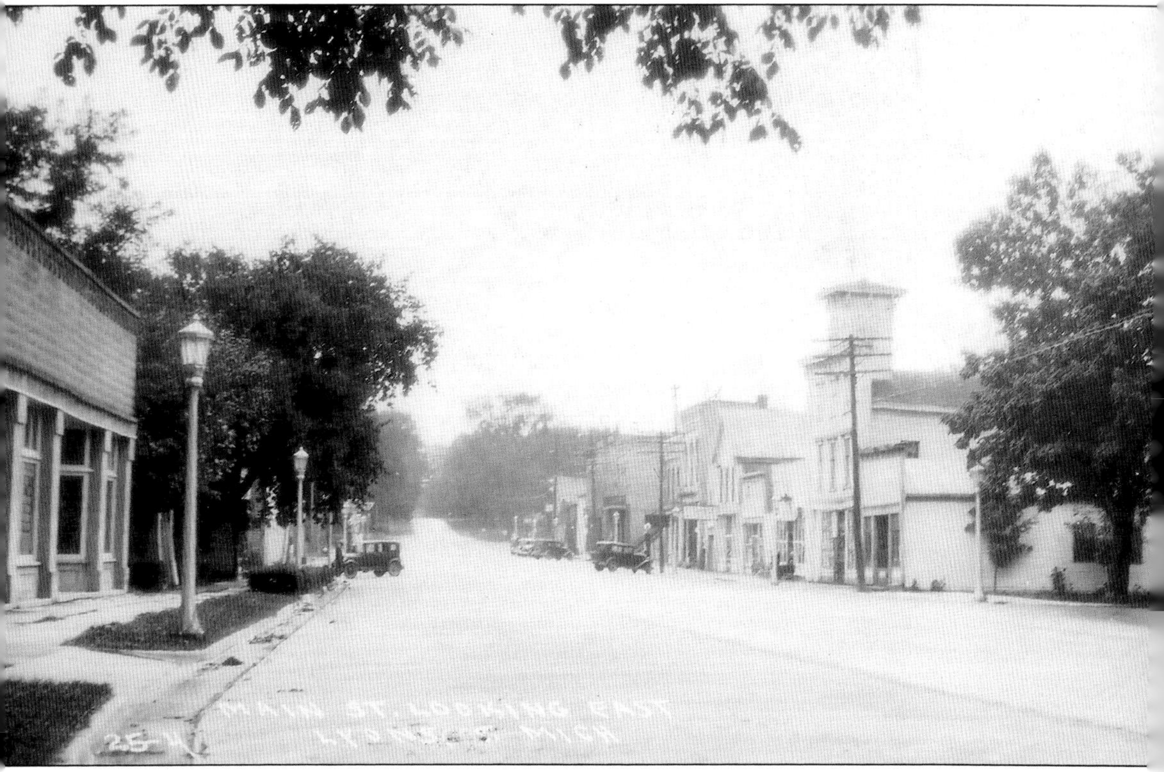

DOWNTOWN LYONS. Lyons is a small community about 10 miles north of Portland. Like Portland, the area now known as Lyons was first inhabited by Native Americans. The H.V. Libart family settled there in 1833 and named the area Arthursburg. Three years later, Lucius Lyons arrived, platted the village, and renamed it Lyons, the name it has had ever since. Lyons was incorporated as a village in 1859 and flourished during the boom lumber years of the late 1800s. (Courtesy of Robert Torp-Smith.)

Seven

FLOODS AND OTHER DISASTERS

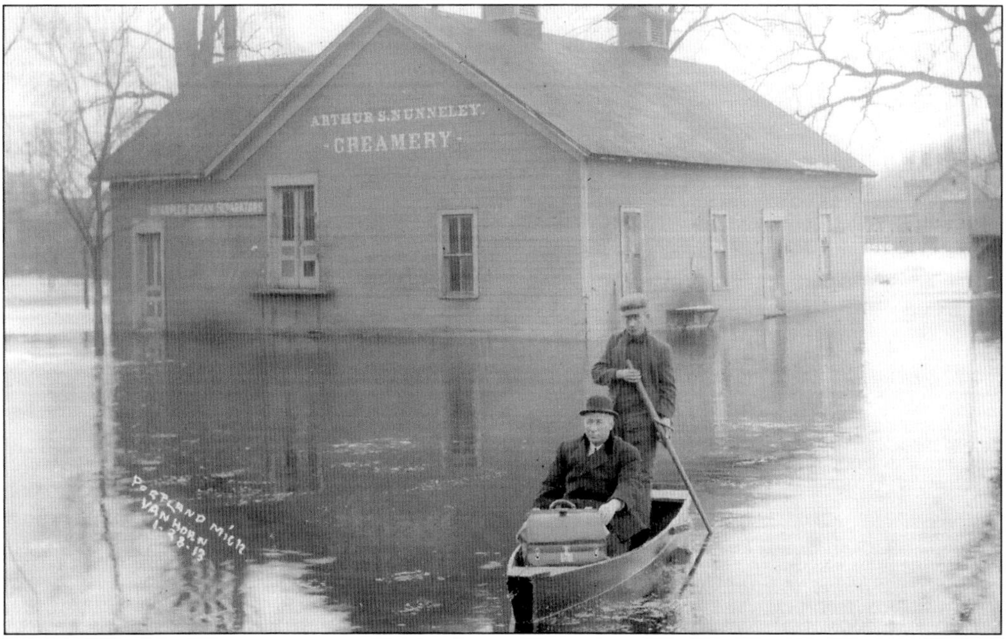

JANUARY 1913 FLOOD. Because of its location at the confluence of two rivers, and the volatility of Michigan's winters and springs, Portland has always been susceptible to flooding. Here, a man who appears to be a doctor on a house call is ferried through the flood past Arthur Nunnely's creamery. The creamery was located on the east bank of the Grand River, just south of the Ramsey-Alton Manufacturing Company near the confluence of the Grand and the Looking Glass Rivers. (Courtesy of Robert Torp-Smith.)

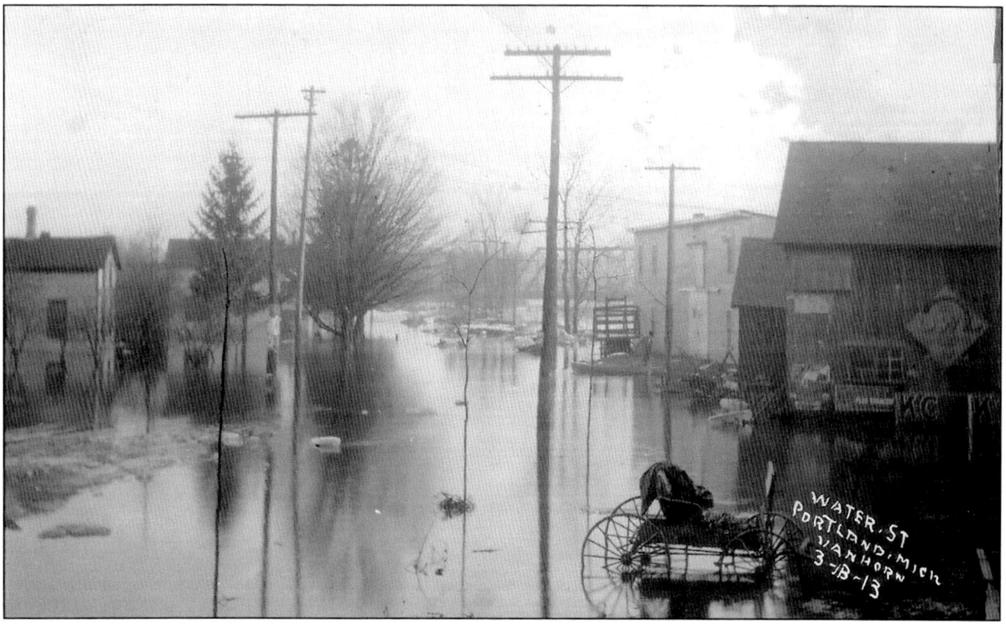

MARCH 1913 FLOOD ON WATER STREET. This flood took place on March 13, 1913, and was the second of two major floods that took place during that year's winter. Water Street, on the west bank of the Grand River, was hit especially hard. Many residents were removed from their homes in boats. Husbands were seen carrying their wives upon their shoulders. Fortunately, by the next day the water had receded considerably and life returned to normal for the residents of Water Street. (Courtesy of Robert Torp-Smith.)

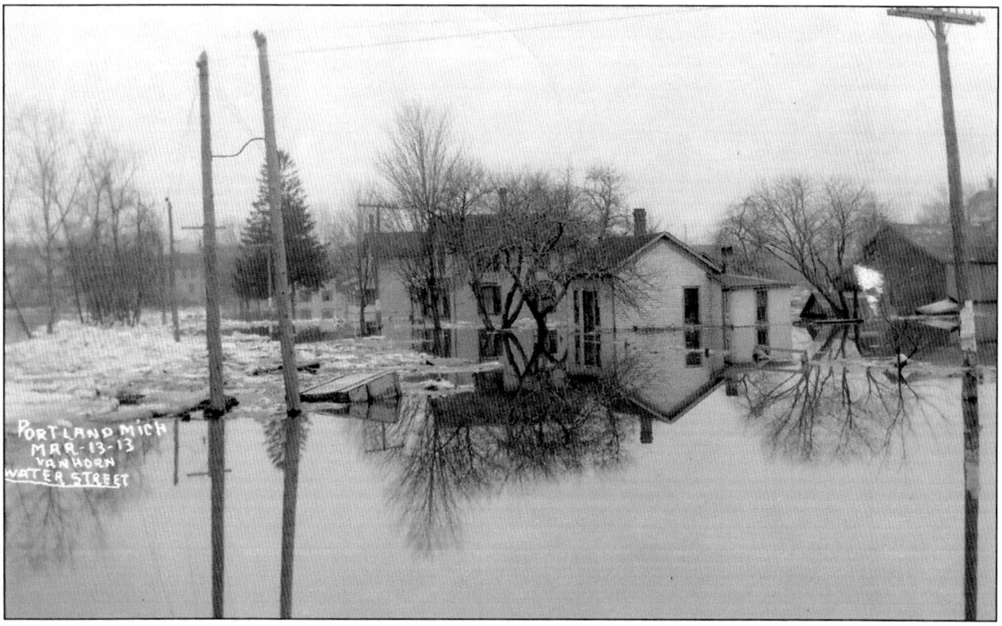

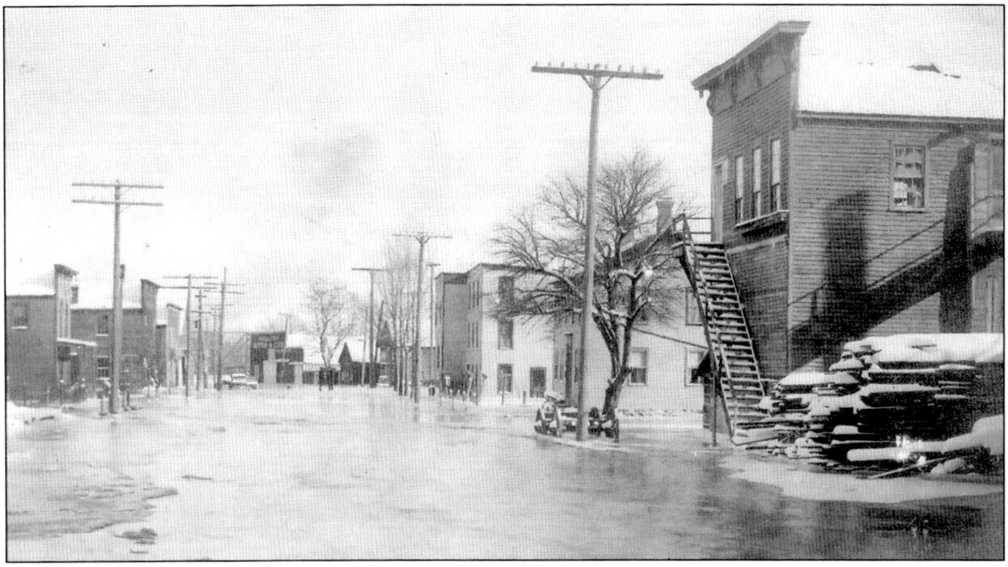

January 1907 Flood. On January 18, balmy weather, combined with a rain storm, created high waters. Cellars of businesses on Kent Street were reported to have been filled with between four to six feet of water. To make matters worse, the next day brought a cold front and blizzard which froze the water. Ice was piled high against the railroad bridge across the Looking Glass River and dynamite was used to dislodge it. (Courtesy of Robert Torp-Smith.)

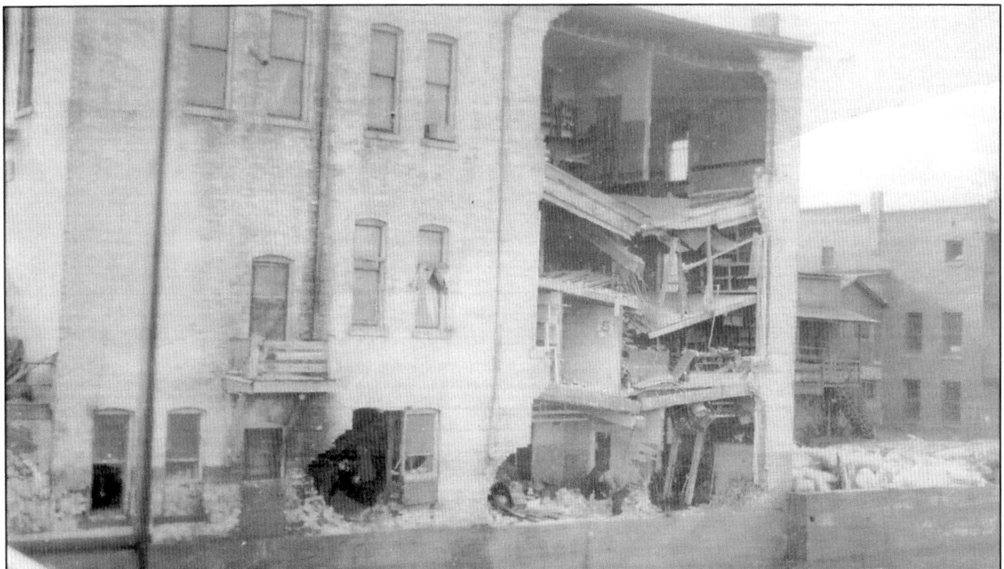

Disastrous Flood of 1920. The flood of March 15, 1920, was the worst flood in Portland history. The heaviest accumulation of winter ice that had ever moved down the Grand River raised the water level to an unprecedented 17.5 feet. A portion of the back of the Blanchard-Knox Block (currently known as the Kramer Building) collapsed into the Grand River. The *Portland Observer* wrote, "The floors collapsed and the falling brick and mortar filled the air with a great cloud of dust that resembled the effect of an explosion. The crash was almost deafening, causing many by-standers to involuntarily shriek with terror." (Courtesy of Robert Torp-Smith.)

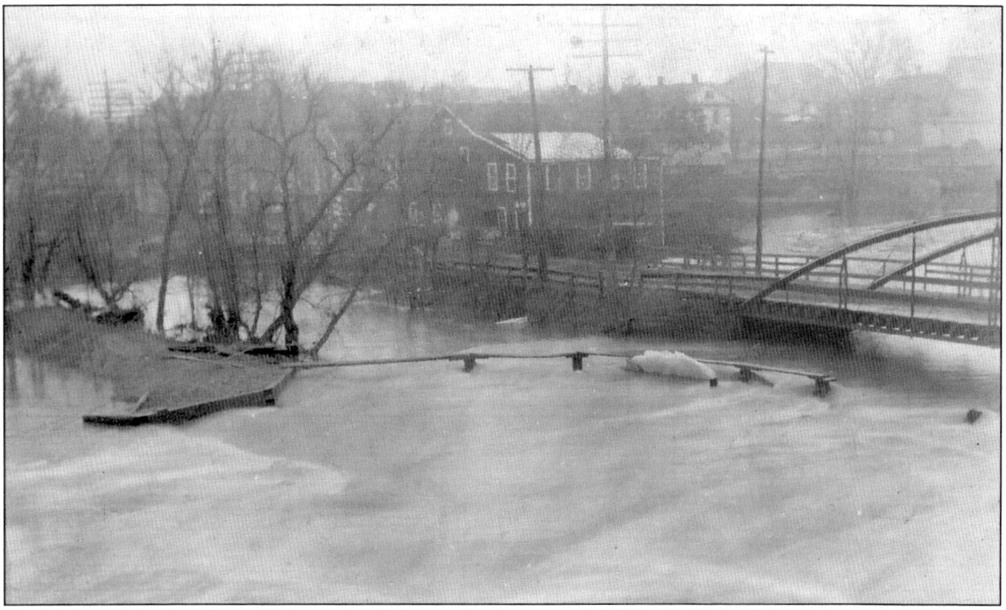

HIGH WATER ON THE LOOKING GLASS RIVER. This view looks northeast toward Divine Highway. The building in the foreground was the Wolverine Soap Company. (Courtesy of Robert Torp-Smith.)

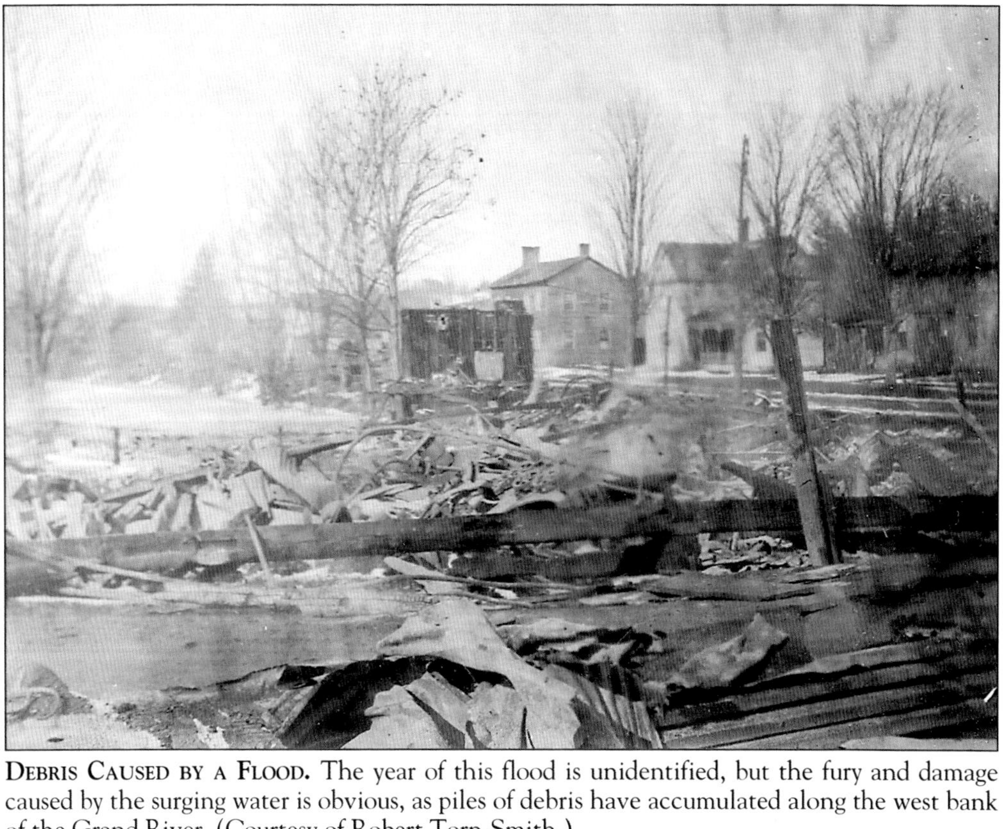

DEBRIS CAUSED BY A FLOOD. The year of this flood is unidentified, but the fury and damage caused by the surging water is obvious, as piles of debris have accumulated along the west bank of the Grand River. (Courtesy of Robert Torp-Smith.)

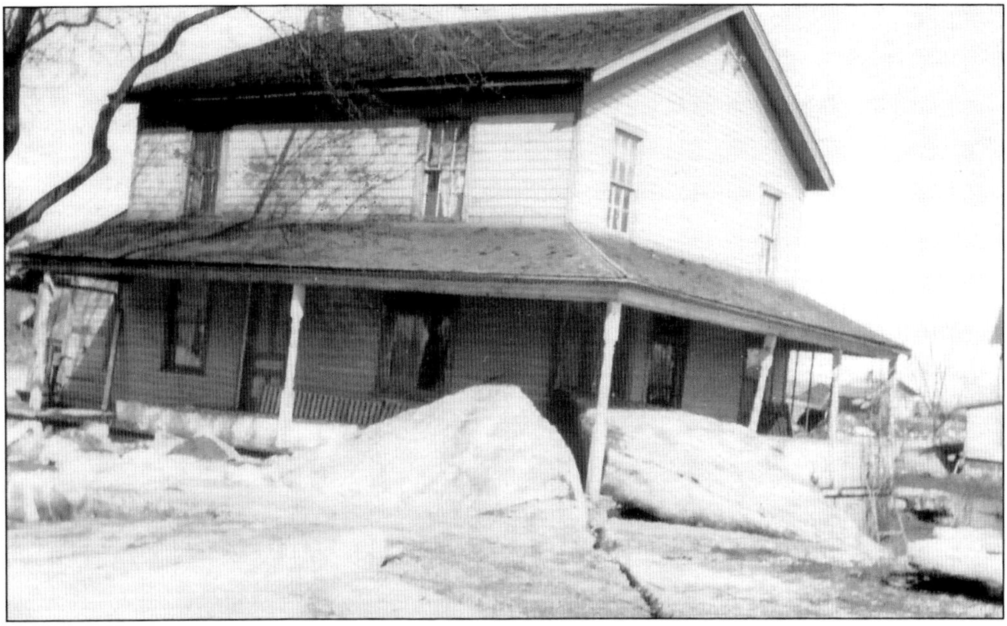

Two More Views of the 1920 Flood. In the picture above, a house is completely surrounded by enormous blocks of ice. Below, both banks of the Grand River are piled high with ice chunks and other debris. These lethal ice chunks were swept down the river and destroyed almost everything in their wake. (Courtesy of Robert Torp-Smith.)

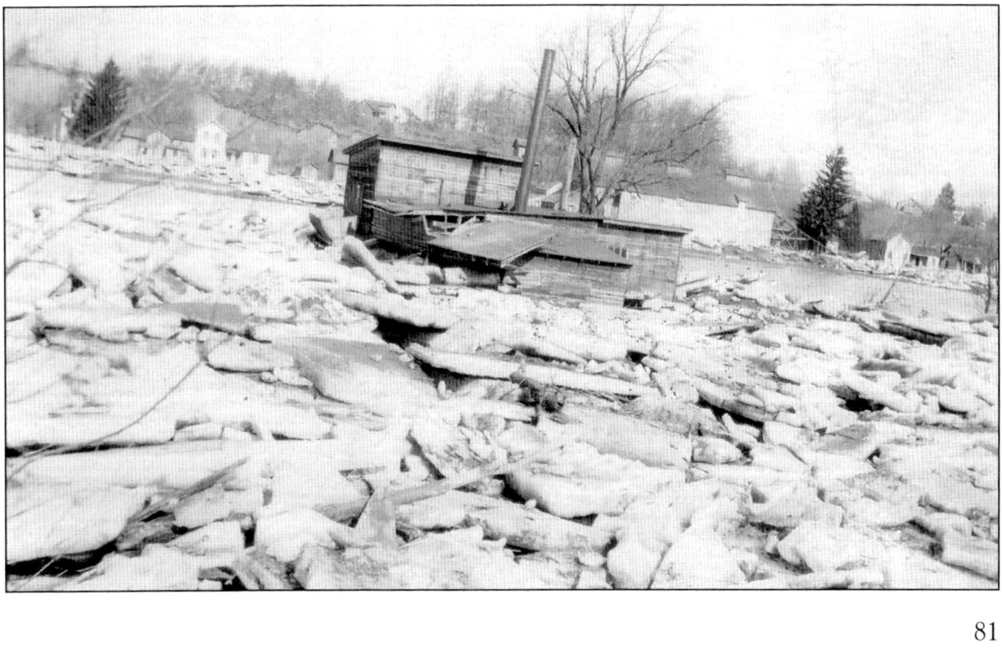

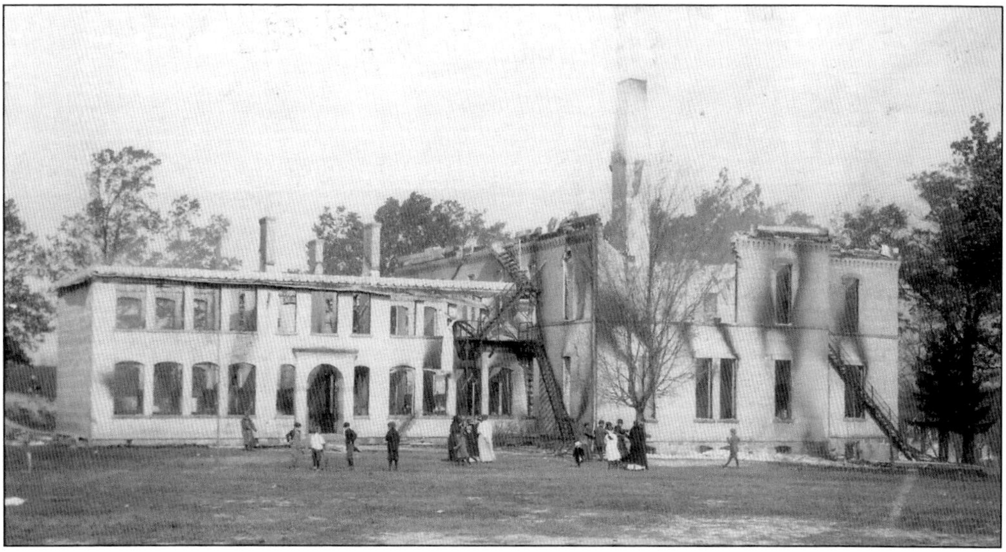

PORTLAND HIGH SCHOOL FIRE OF 1918. In the early evening of October 16, 1918, Portland's high school was destroyed by fire. The cause was believed to be from an incendiary device. High school students were forced to continue the rest of the school year at the Congregational Church while the grade school children were dispersed to the old West Side school, St. Patrick's auditorium, the Nazarene Church, and the basement of the Carnegie Library. Taxpayers quickly voted for a $100,000 bond to build a new school on the same site. The school opened in September 1920. (Courtesy of Robert Torp-Smith.)

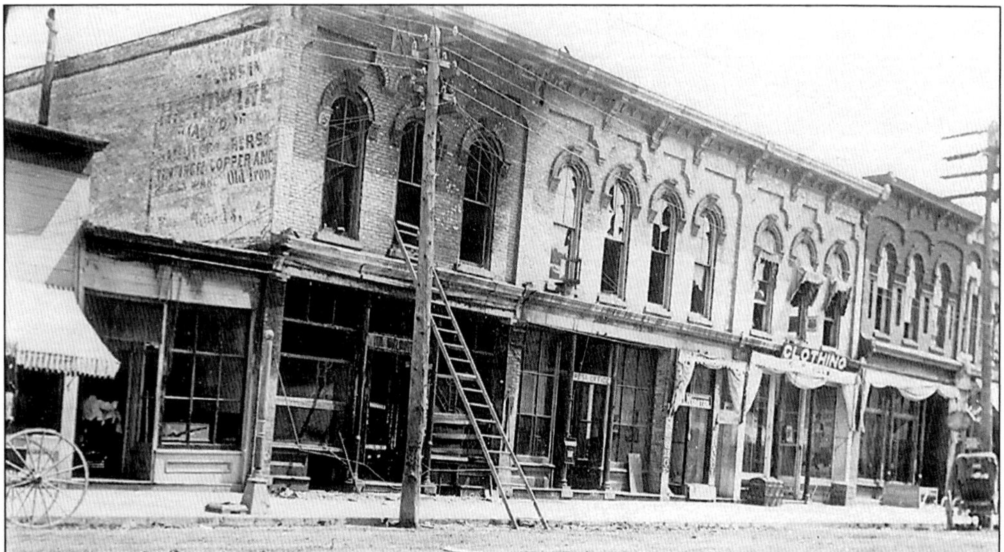

KENNEDY & DERBY HARDWARE STORE FIRE, 1907. In July 1907, Duncan Kennedy watched helplessly as his business of 25 years was destroyed by fire. People were alerted to the fire when smoke filled the office of the adjacent Citizens Telephone and Postal Telegraph. Firefighters quickly responded to the alarm, but were hindered in their ability to fight the fire because several hose nozzles had been misplaced or stolen. Fortunately, Kennedy's business was insured and he was able to rebuild the hardware store. He continued as owner and proprietor of the store until his retirement in 1916. (Courtesy of Robert Torp-Smith.)

Eight

Residences

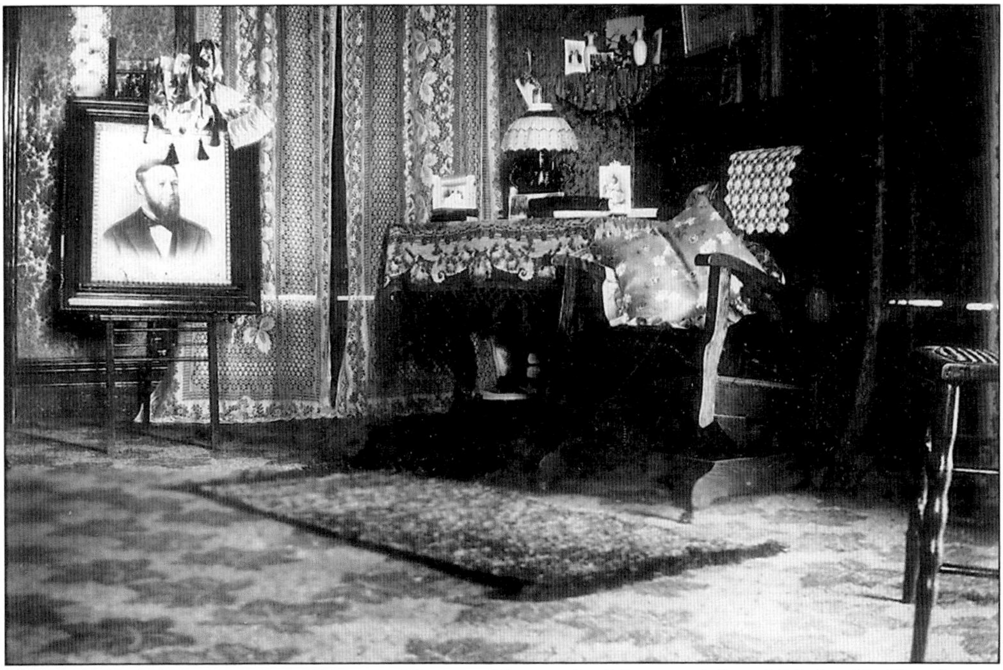

Interior View of the Old Webber House. This is the library of the old John Webber house that stood at James Street until the early 1890s, when it was moved to the corner of Lincoln and Academy Streets to make way for the second John Webber house. John Webber, along with his father Lorenzo (the grandfather of Lorenzo Webber, the photographer) established the Webber Bank. (Courtesy of the Portland Area Historical Society.)

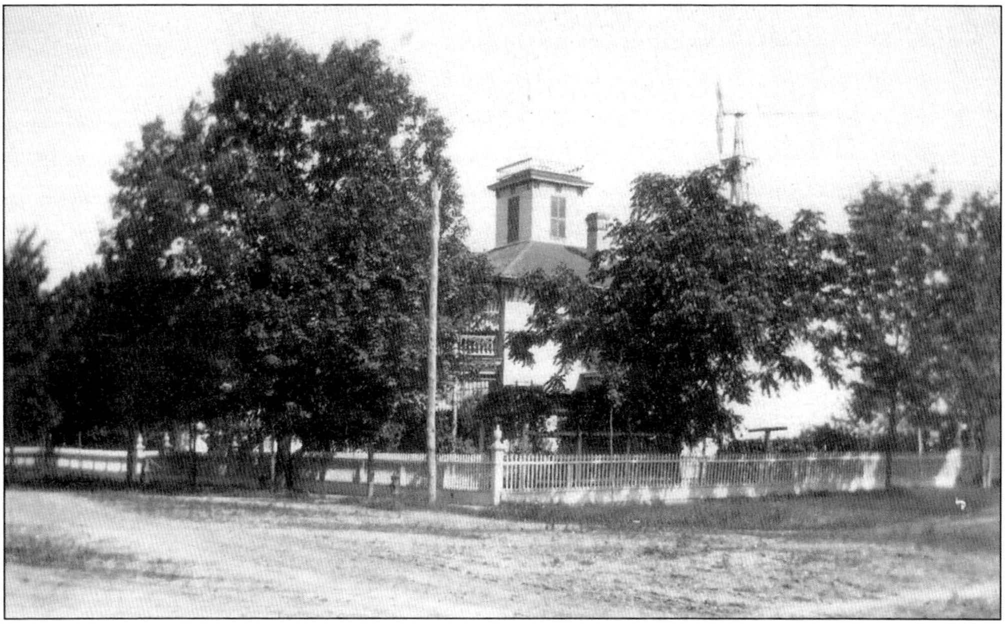

Old and New John Webber Houses. The house pictured above, which stood on James Street near Lincoln Street, was the original Webber residence. The new John Webber house is shown below under construction on August 18, 1893. At about the time this picture was taken, work was progressing on the second story and the stone tower on the east side. This large house, with its distinctive half-timbering, still stands on James Street to this day. It remains one of Portland's landmark residences. (Courtesy of the Portland Area Historical Society.)

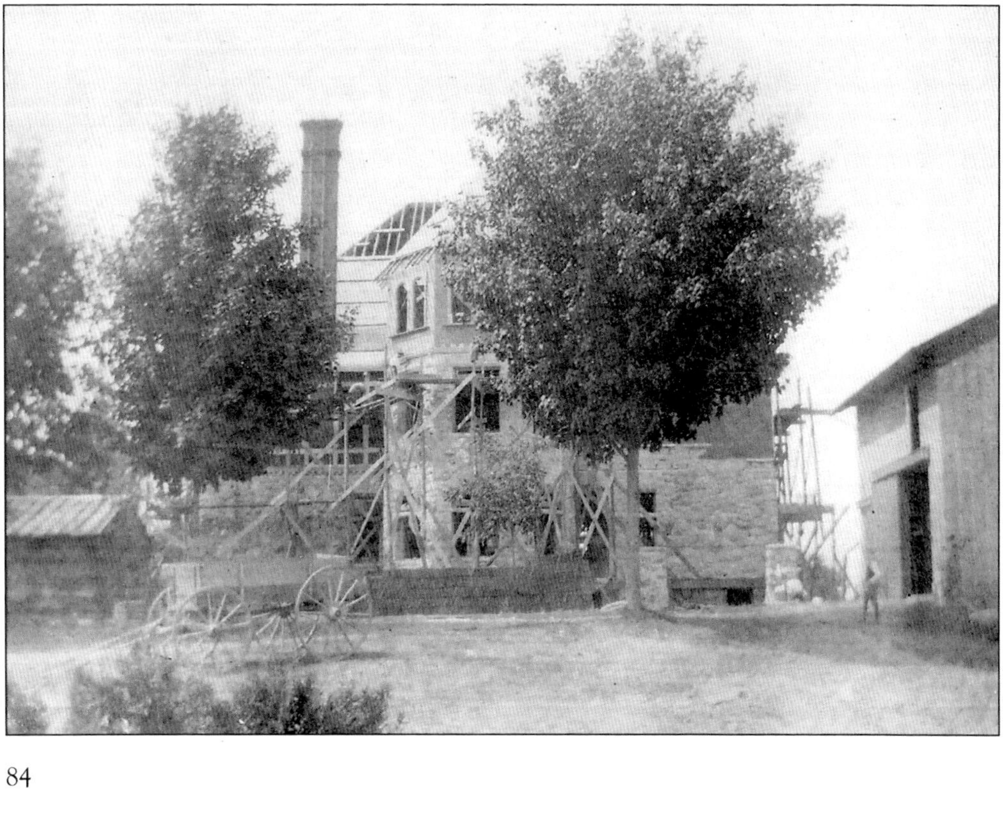

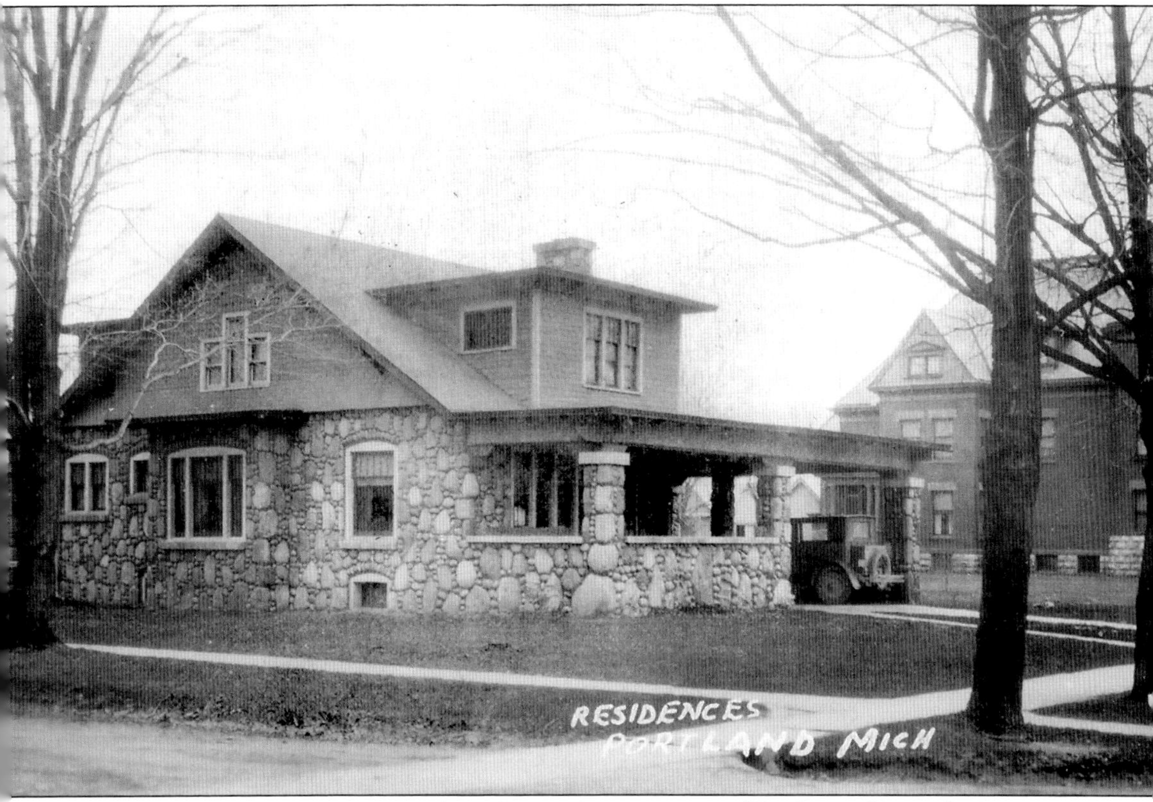

EDWARD GOODWIN HOUSE. Located on the southwest corner of Bridge and Lincoln Streets, this house is one of Portland's finest examples of the Craftsman bungalow style. The house was built in 1920 by Edward (Ed) Goodwin, who owned a monument works business in Portland. The stones used for the construction were quarried locally. The property was purchased by Goodwin for $1,000. The house that originally stood on the property was moved next-door along Lincoln Street. Ed Goodwin lived in this attractive stone bungalow until 1952. (Courtesy of Richard Teachout.)

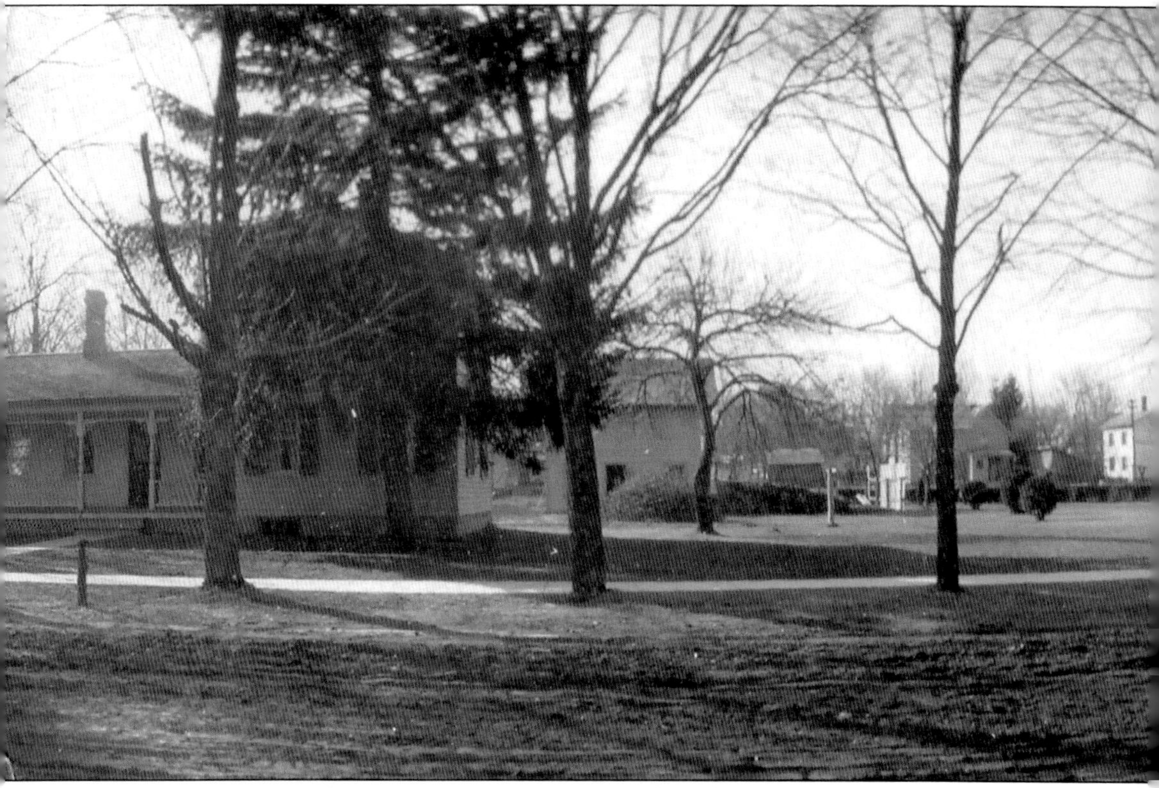

PANORAMIC VIEW OF BRIDGE STREET RESIDENCES. Along the tree-lined lane of Bridge Street is the Charles Maynard house. This red pressed-brick Queen Anne house, with its Portage stone trim, prominent tower and distinctive *porte cochere* (not visible in the photograph), was built in 1896. Charles Maynard was half of the Maynard-Allen State Bank, a Portland financial

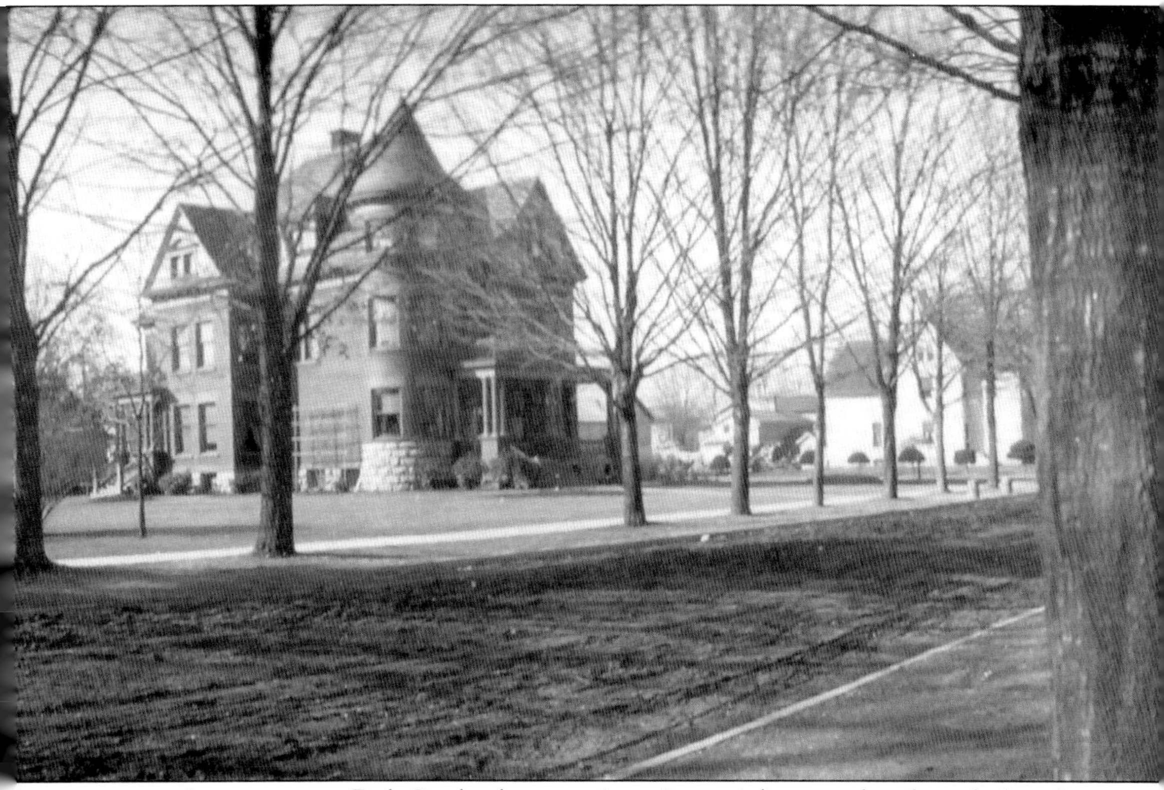

institution for many years. Early Portland pioneer Isaac Perrigo's house is the white clapboard front-gabled house somewhat obscured by the trees. This house was the one moved to make way for Edward Goodwin's stone bungalow. (Courtesy of the Portland Area Historical Society.)

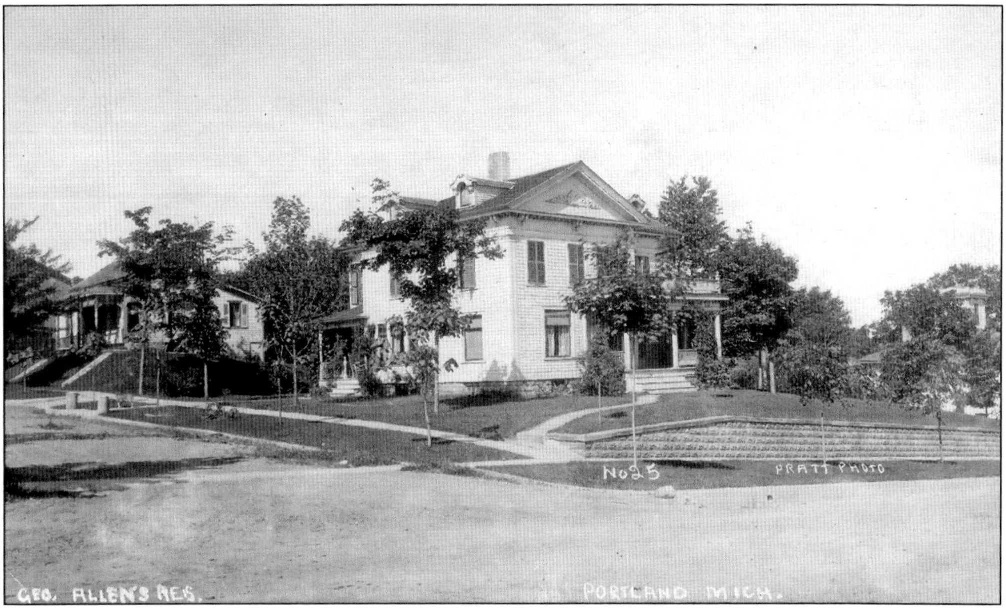

George Allen House. This house, which stands on the southwest corner of Bridge and Elm Streets, was originally built by James Webster Jr. in the late 1840s. Over the years, it underwent a number of additions and changes until it reached its present appearance. The house is perhaps best known as the former residence of Portland physician George Allen. After Allen died, the house was purchased by Arthur Bandfield in 1937, who converted half of the building into a funeral home. The house is currently a single-family residence. (Courtesy of the Portland Area Historical Society.)

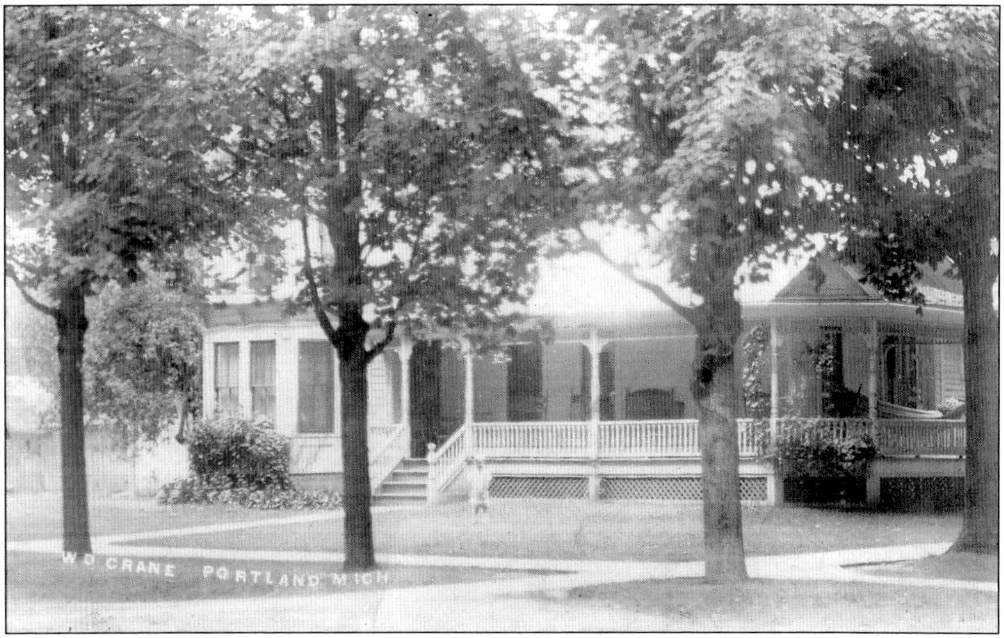

Wallace D. Crane House. This upright-and-wing house, with its wraparound porch, is located on the southeast corner of Bridge and Lincoln Streets. Wallace D. Crane was a prominent Portland druggist. (Courtesy of the Portland Area Historical Society.)

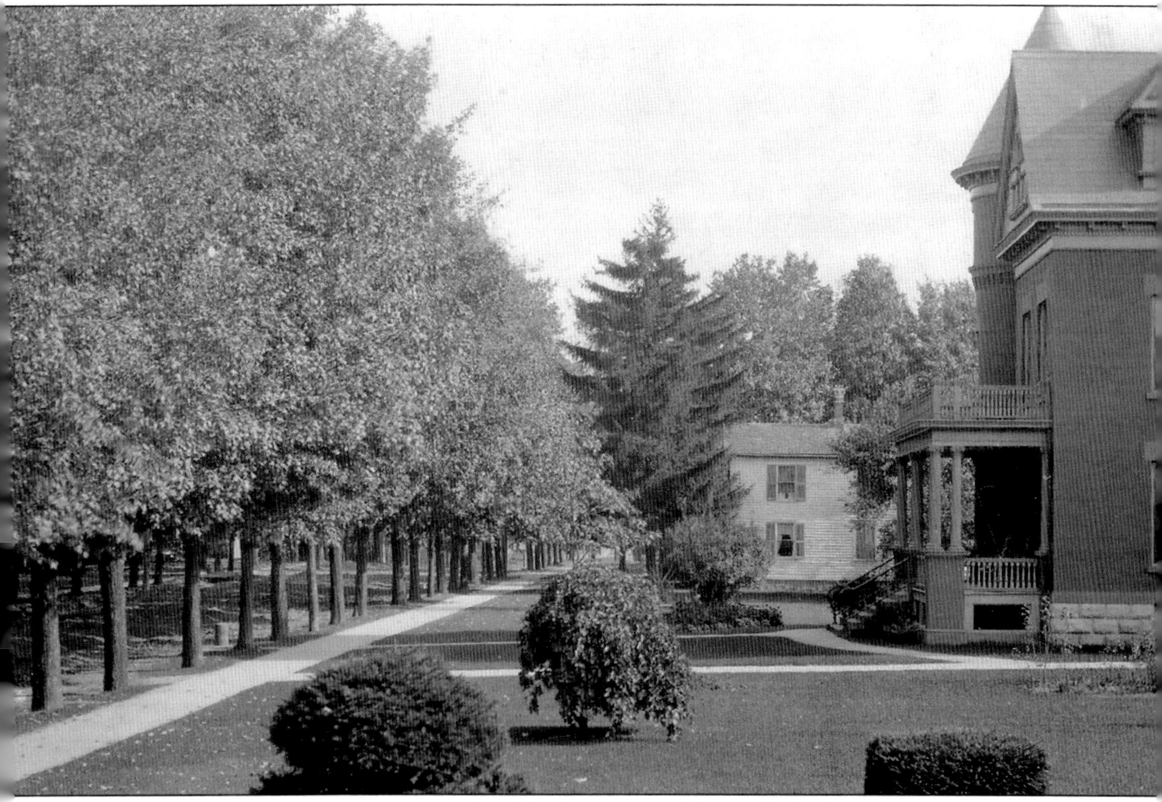

FACING EAST ALONG BRIDGE STREET. The Charles Maynard house is in the foreground, and the white clapboard house next door is the Isaac Perrigo house. The two houses offer an interesting contrast: one is a large, imposing and ornate mansion displaying the wealth of Portland near the turn of the century, the other is a handsome, yet utilitarian structure emblematic of Portland's early pioneer spirit. When construction of the Charles Maynard house was completed and the family was about to move in, the *Portland Observer* wrote a long description of the home in its January 13, 1897 issue. The *Observer* noted, "The structure has an imposing appearance and gives one an idea of solidity from the foundation up. It is symmetrical in proportion and all together is one of the handsomest residences in Ionia County." (Courtesy of the Portland Area Historical Society.)

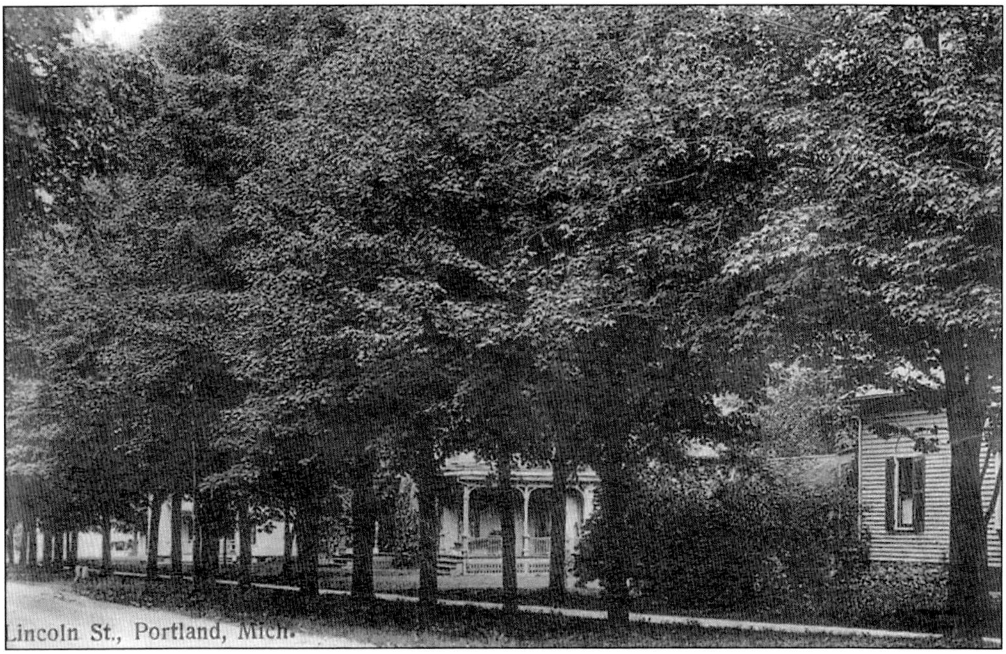

THICK CANOPY OF TREES ALONG LINCOLN STREET. This is the east side of Lincoln Street, looking north from Bridge Street. The homes are barely visible through the thick foliage of trees. The house in the center was the E.M. Allen house. E.M. Allen was a Civil War veteran and, along with Charles Maynard and J.B. Roe, one of the founders of the Maynard-Allen Bank. (Courtesy of Robert Torp-Smith.)

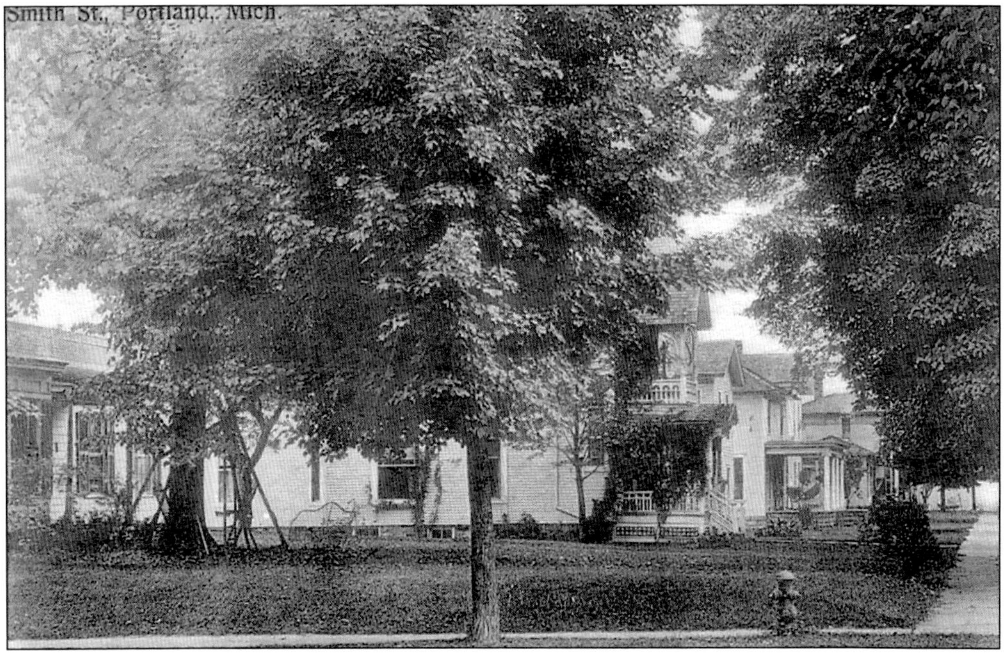

RESIDENCES ON SMITH STREET. This is a view, from the Bridge Street intersection, facing north along Smith Street. (Courtesy of Robert Torp-Smith.)

Nine

Townspeople

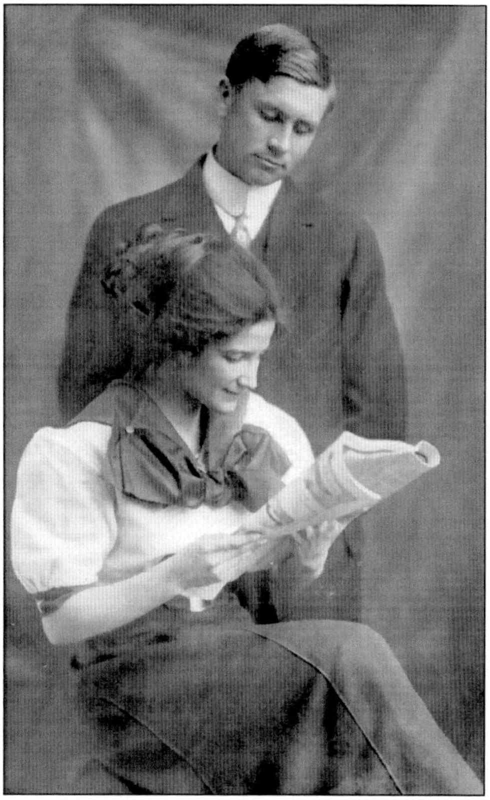

Reading the Newspaper. The man and woman pictured in this George Van Horn postcard are identified as Leon Lockwood and Maude Samain. If it appears that there is warmth between the two, it was genuine and not merely fabricated for the camera. Leon and Maude eventually married. (Courtesy of the Portland Area Historical Society.)

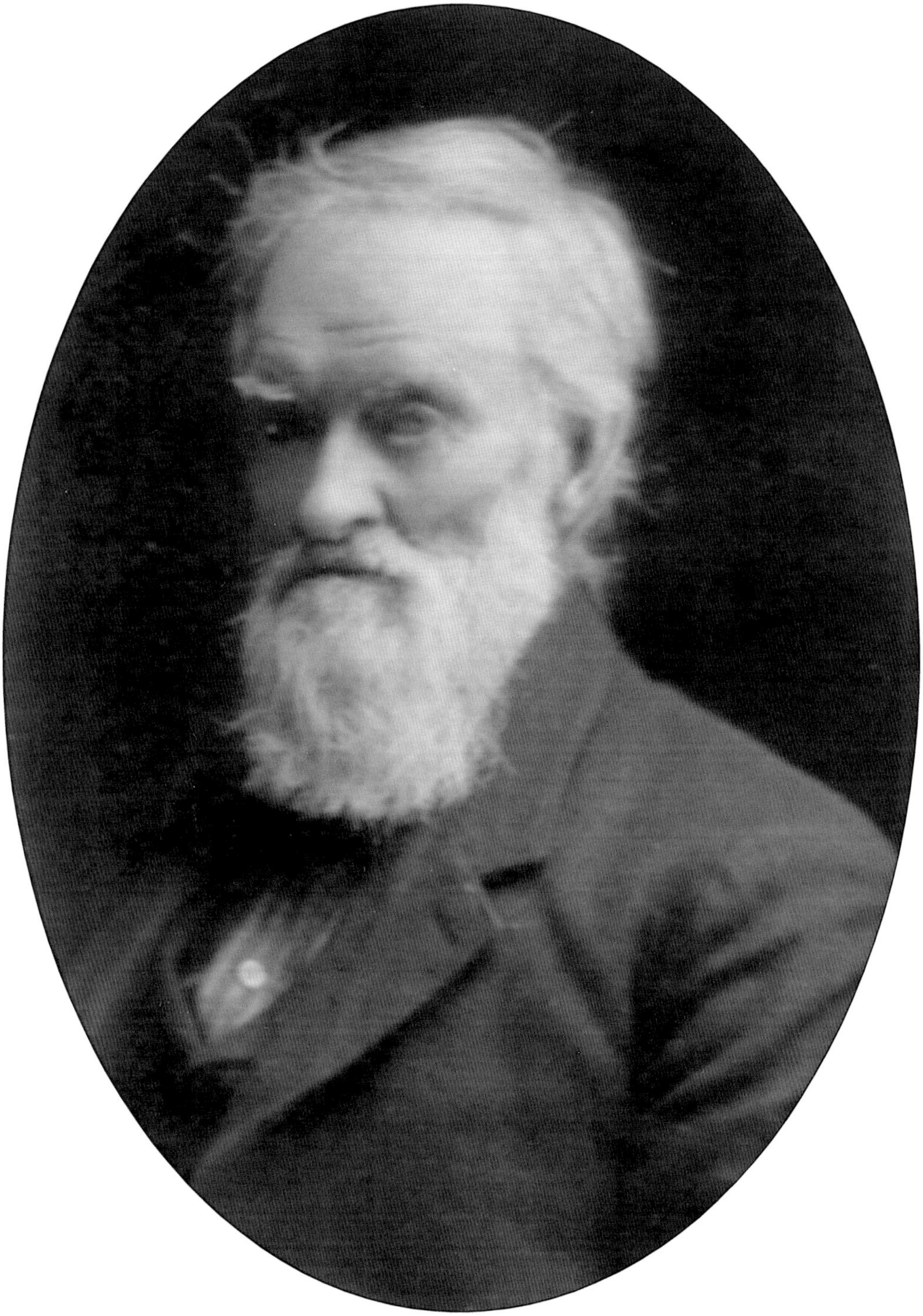

"J.K. Swipes." Portland may have never produced an Edgar Allen Poe or Ernest Hemingway, but it is not without its own literary characters. Charles E. Goodwin wrote under the pen name "J.K. Swipes." He was well-known to Portland newspaper readers in the early 1900s, writing verse on whatever subject struck his fancy. (Courtesy of Richard Teachout.)

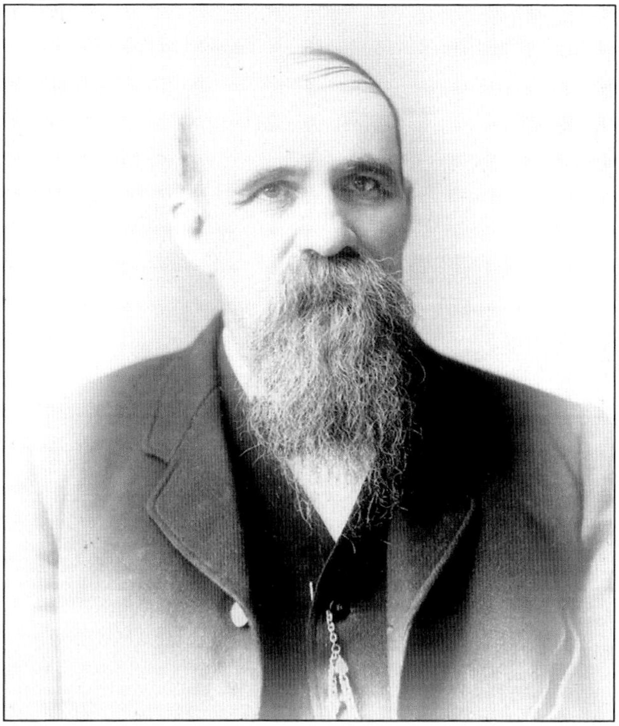

Isaac Perrigo. One of Portland's early pioneers, Isaac Stephen Perrigo was born in New Jersey on January 24, 1832, and arrived in Portland with his mother and two sisters in 1857. He opened a blacksmith shop upon his arrival in Portland and continued in that line of work until 1872. That year, he and a partner, S.S. Hinman, went into business together as carriage makers. Their shop was located on Maple Street, south of Bridge Street. Isaac Perrigo outlived his partner and remained a carriage maker until about 1904. Perrigo died in 1914, and was survived by his wife of 48 years, Stella.

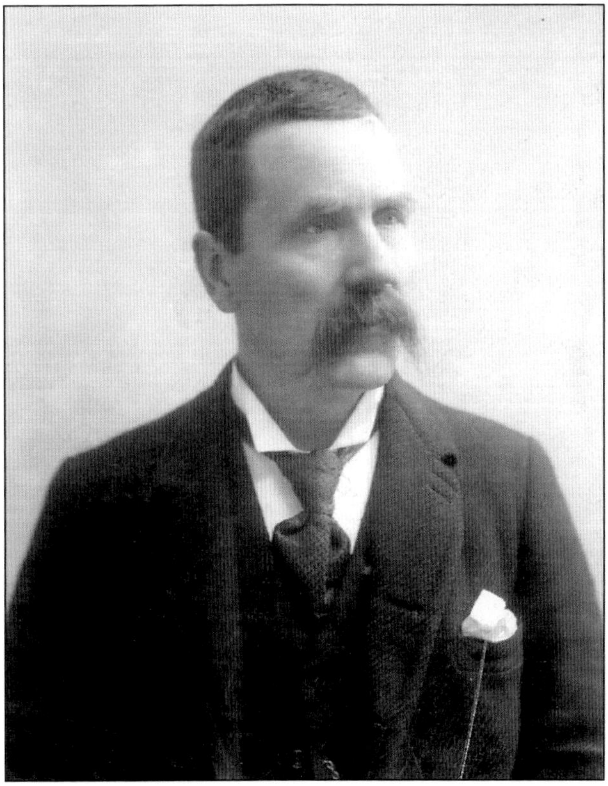

Duncan Kennedy. A native of Ireland, Duncan Kennedy was mayor of Portland several different times. He owned and operated two hardware stores in the village and his wife sang contralto in a singing quartet at the Universalist Church. (Courtesy of the Portland Area Historical Society.)

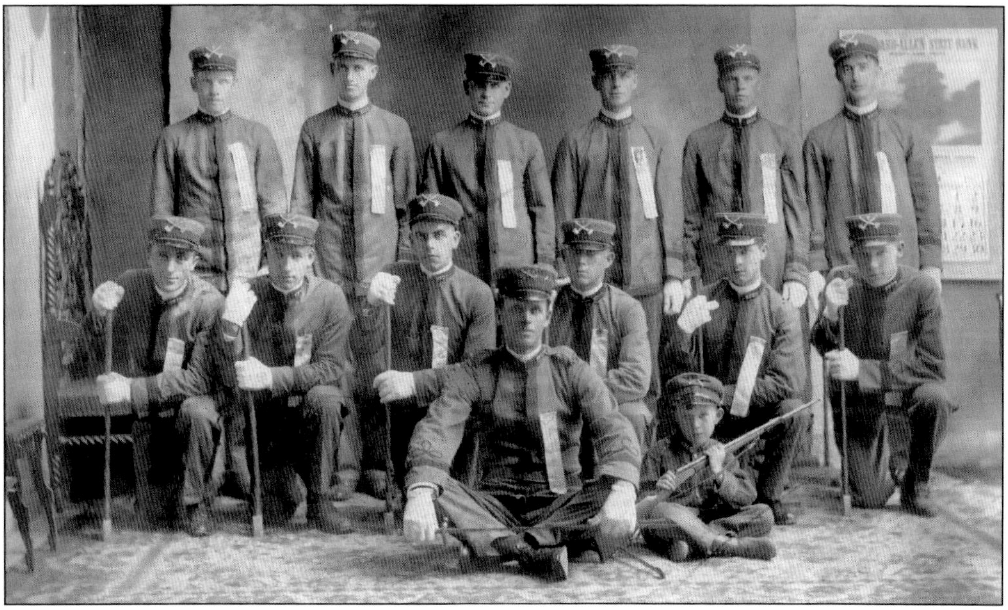

PORTLAND FIREFIGHTERS, 1917. The first organized firefighters in Portland formed on June 12, 1876. The unit was known as the Wabanah Engine Company No. 1. (Wabanah is a Native American name for "Looking Glass.") These independent volunteer firefighters served the community until February 7, 1896, when the village forced them to disband because they had not adopted formal by-laws. Two days later, the Wabanah Company re-formed under the direction of the village. In 1912, its name was changed to the Portland Fire Department. From left to right, these 1917 firefighters are identified as: (seated) Bert Weed and Willard North; (kneeling) ? Shepard, Laurence Miller, Kelly Penfield, Frank Potter, Clifton Lyttle, and Carl Williams; (standing) Ernest Stiffler, Ray ?, Charles Goodwin, Orville Stiffler, and Dan Watson. (Courtesy of the Portland Area Historical Society.)

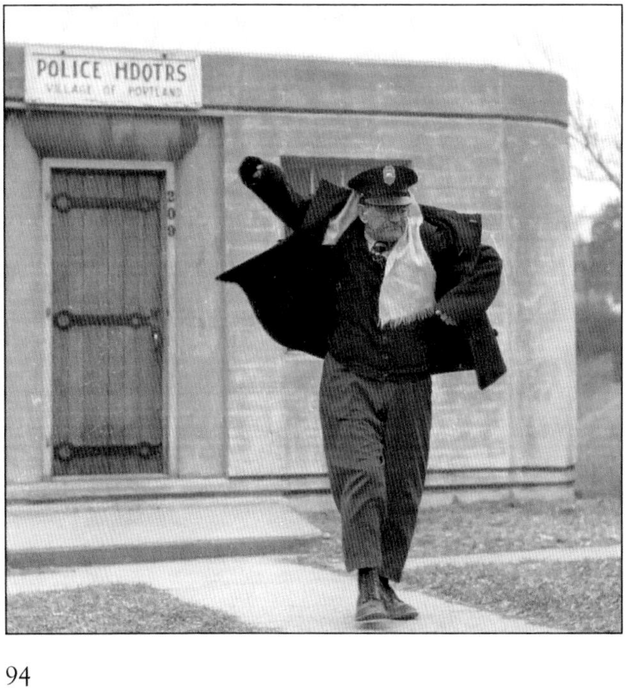

FIREMAN IN A HURRY. Fireman Howard Lowry is leaving Portland Police Headquarters with great purpose and determination. This old police headquarters, with its interesting Art Deco-inspired architecture, was located on Water Street and is currently used as the Portland Parks and Recreation office. (Courtesy of the Portland Area Historical Society.)

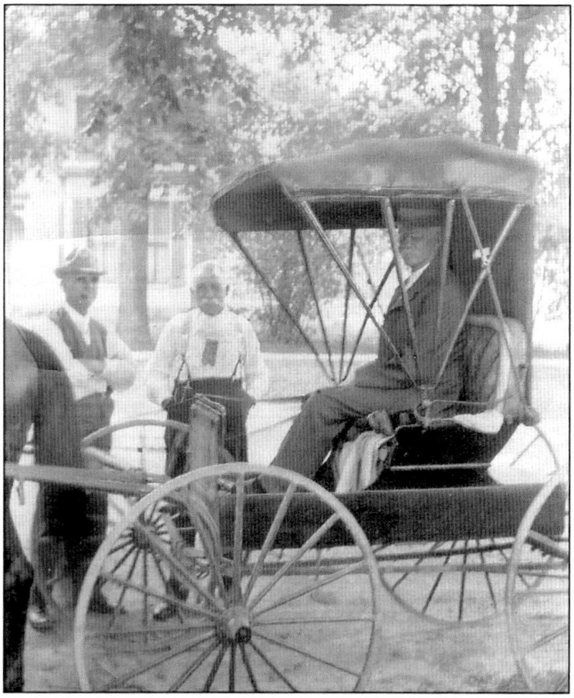

George Allen. The dapper gentleman in the buggy is Dr. George Allen. He was born July 11, 1839 in Orleans, New York, and attended medical college in Cleveland, Ohio. Arriving in Portland in 1867, he established his medical practice. Over the next 56 years, he delivered over 2,000 babies and gained the nickname, "baby doctor." Illness forced Dr. Allen to retire in 1923 and he died three years later. (Courtesy of the Portland Area Historical Society.)

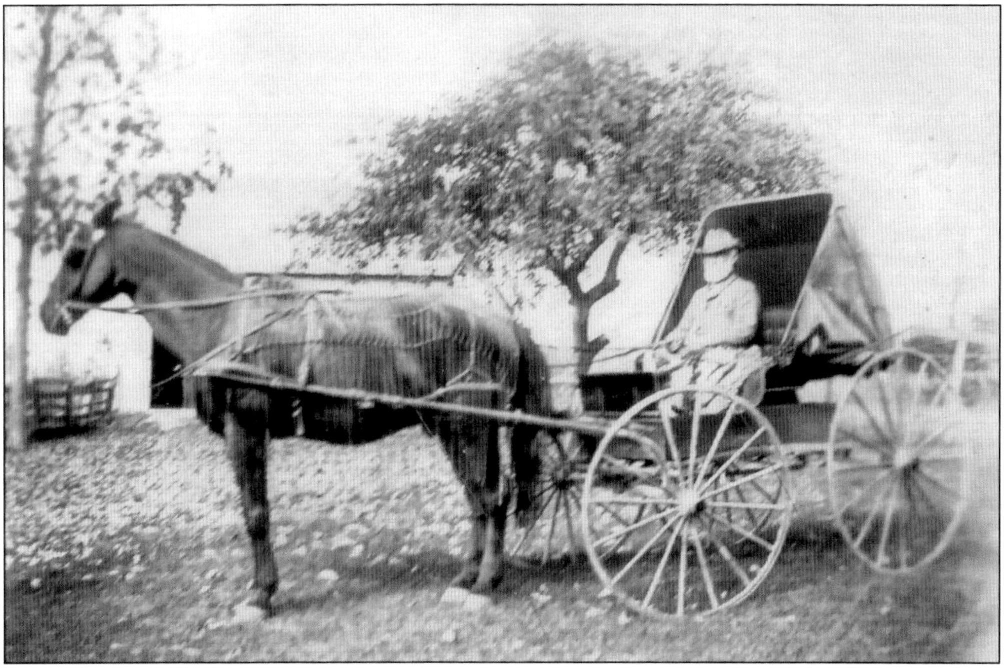

N.B. Rice. N.B. Rice is pictured behind the reins of his horse, "Old Fred," c. 1900. Napoleon Bonaparte (N.B.) Rice married Mary Newman, the granddaughter of Elisha Newman, who was the first person to enter a land claim in what would eventually become Portland. Mary was the first non-Native American born in Portland. Upon his marriage, N.B. went to work in father-in-law James Newman's flour mill. N.B. and Mary Rice were highly respected members of the community. N.B. died in 1912 and Mary in 1927. (Courtesy of the Portland Area Historical Society.)

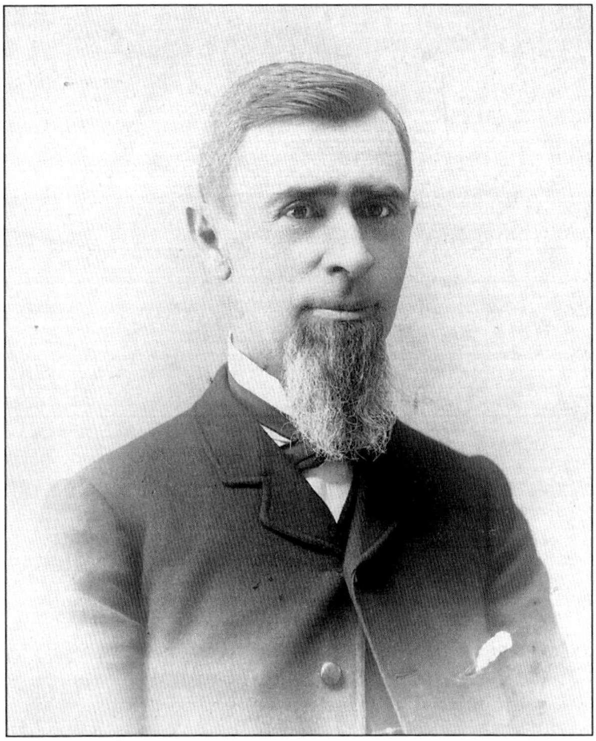

Charles C. Dellenbaugh. These are two photographs of Dr. C.C. Dellenbaugh; one is a candid shot by Lorenzo Webber and the other is a portrait from the Casey & Whitney Photographers studio in Lansing. Dellenbaugh was one of three doctors in Portland in the late 19th century. Former Portland resident Queen Robinson Stone recalled, "Whenever he saw me he would begin to talk German as fast as he could—then ask me what he said. Of course I didn't know. Then he would slap his knee and laugh. Then he would pinch my cheek and go laughing down the street—still talking German." (Courtesy of the Portland Area Historical Society.)

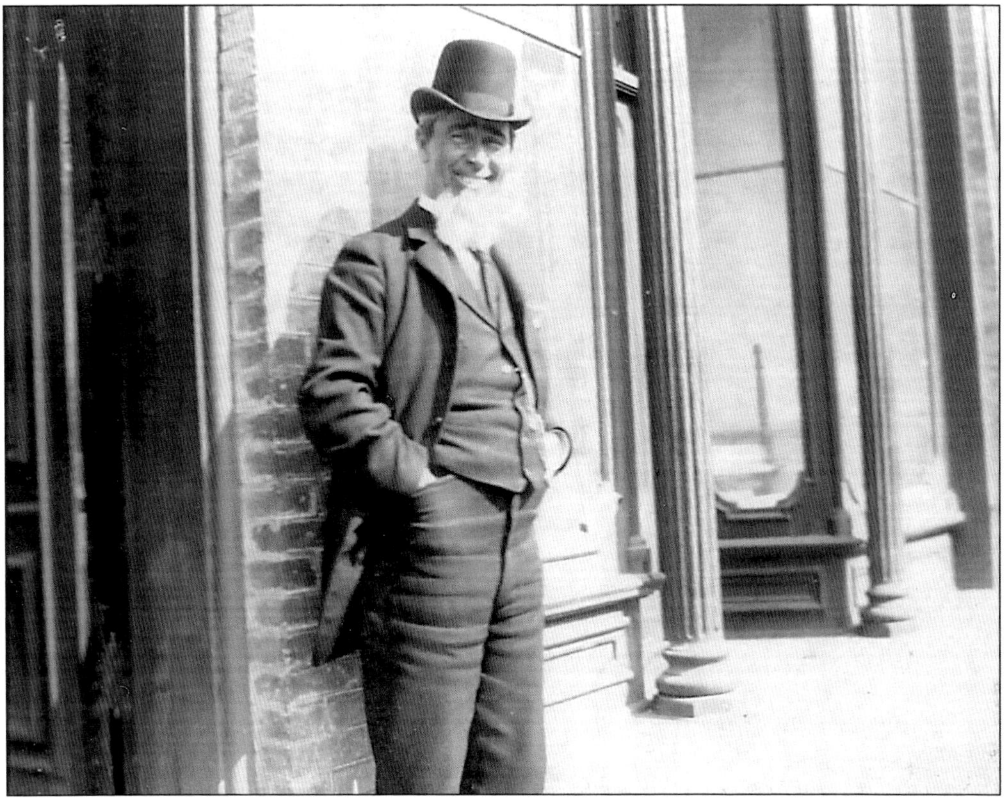

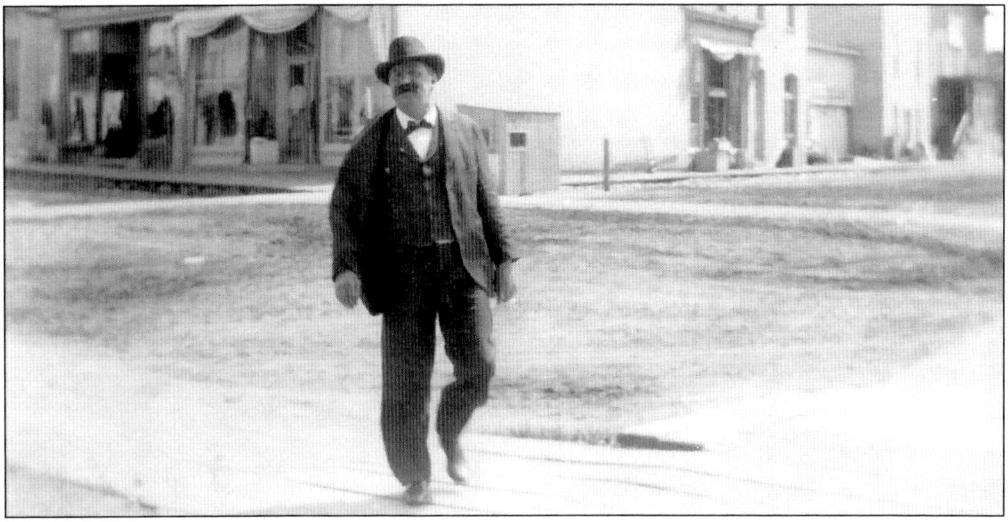

STRIDING TO THE WEBBER BANK. James "Jimmie" Churchill owned and operated the Churchill & Woodbury store. James H. Churchill was born August 27, 1844, in a building that stood on the northeast corner of Bridge and Kent Streets. He was the son of one of Portland's early pioneer families. By the age of sixteen, he was a clerk for Charles H. Maynard, who in 1860 operated a general store. When Churchill was 35 years old, he joined Erastus D. Woodbury and F.R. Savage and the three men formed Churchill, Savage & Woodbury. Savage severed his connection two years later and the general store became known as Churchill & Woodbury. James Churchill remained in the business until his death in 1916. (Courtesy of the Portland Area Historical Society.)

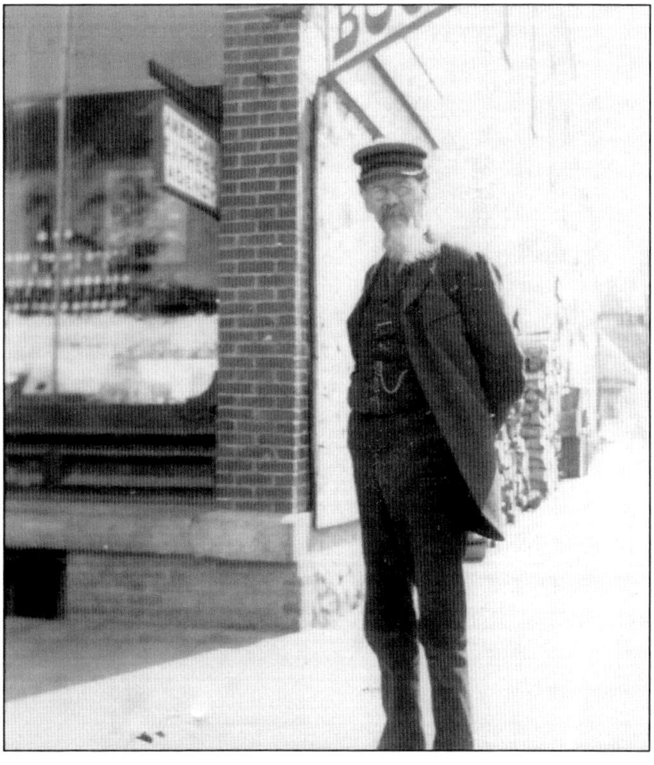

W.H. STONE STANDING NEXT TO HIS DRUG STORE. This photograph was taken by Lorenzo Webber in April 1895. W.H. Stone was a well-known druggist in Portland for many years and was also Lorenzo Webber's father-in-law. His drug store was located on the northeast corner of Bridge and Kent Streets. As is evident from the sign above his head, W.H. Stone also sold books. (Courtesy of the Portland Area Historical Society.)

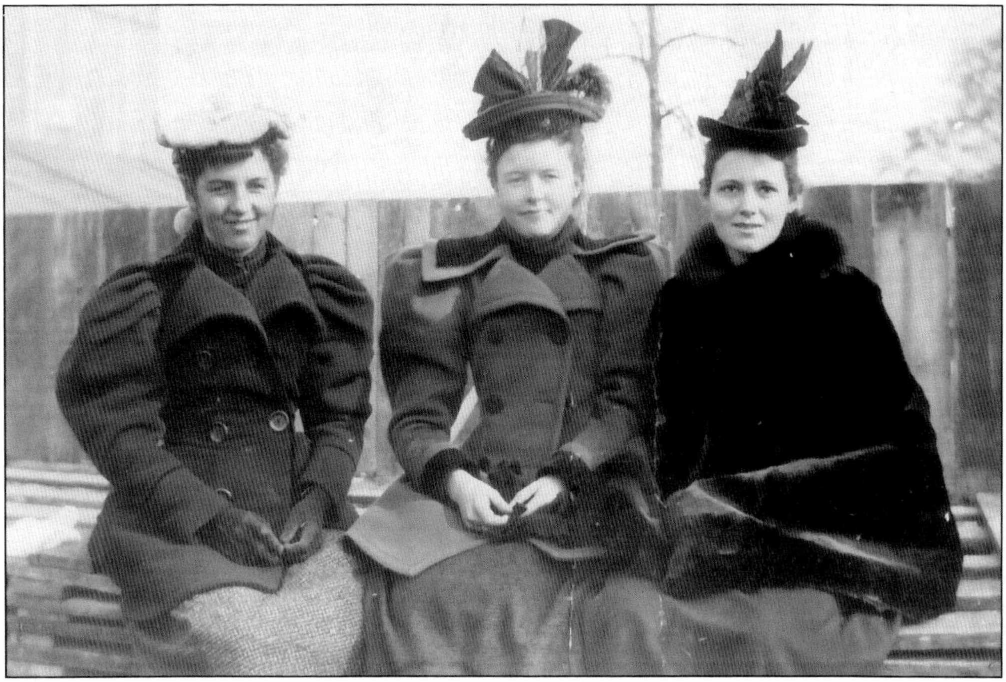

THREE YOUNG WOMEN, OCTOBER 1895. From left to right are Dora Stone Webber, Lulu McClelland Richards, and Christine Webber Latta. Dora was the wife of Lorenzo Webber, Lulu's father was John McClelland (owner of the McClelland & Son general store), and Christine was Lorenzo Webber's sister. (Courtesy of the Portland Area Historical Society.)

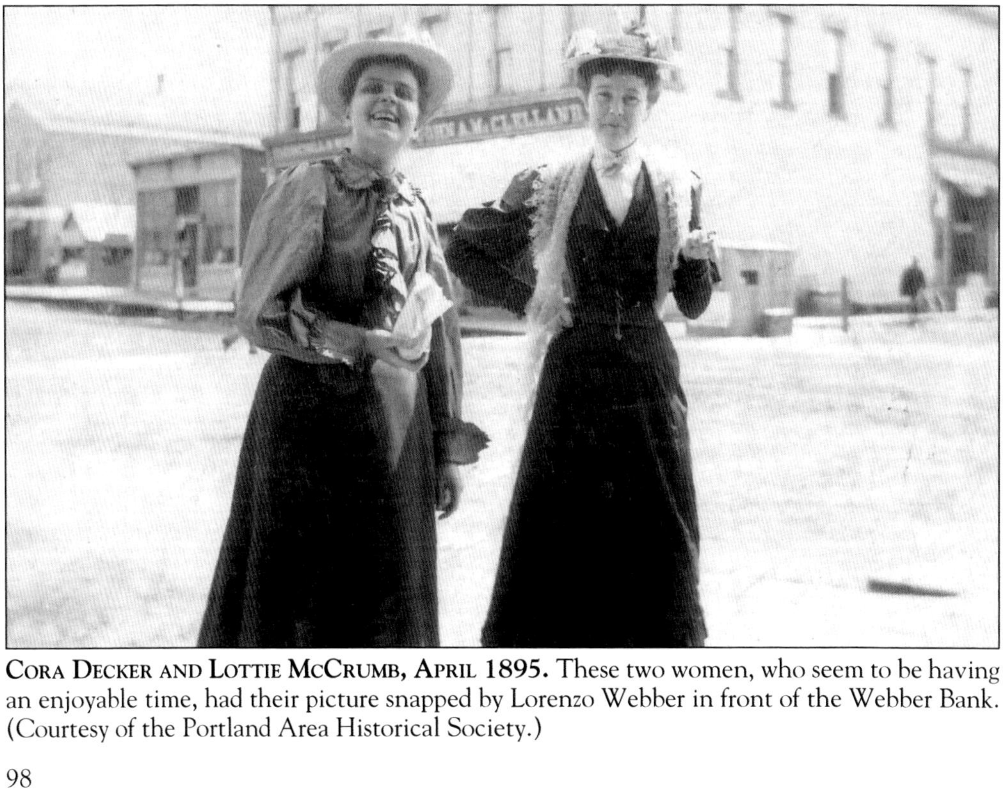

CORA DECKER AND LOTTIE MCCRUMB, APRIL 1895. These two women, who seem to be having an enjoyable time, had their picture snapped by Lorenzo Webber in front of the Webber Bank. (Courtesy of the Portland Area Historical Society.)

Jacob Revels. Jacob Revels was one of few African Americans to live in Portland in the village's formative years in the late 19th and early 20th centuries. A native of Canada, Revels was born in 1863. His father was born in Georgia and his mother in Virginia. Both were probably former slaves. Revels arrived in the United States from Canada in 1878 and eventually made his way to Portland, where he established his own barbershop. He remained a barber well into the 1930s. Revels died in January 1944. (Courtesy of the Portland Area Historical Society.)

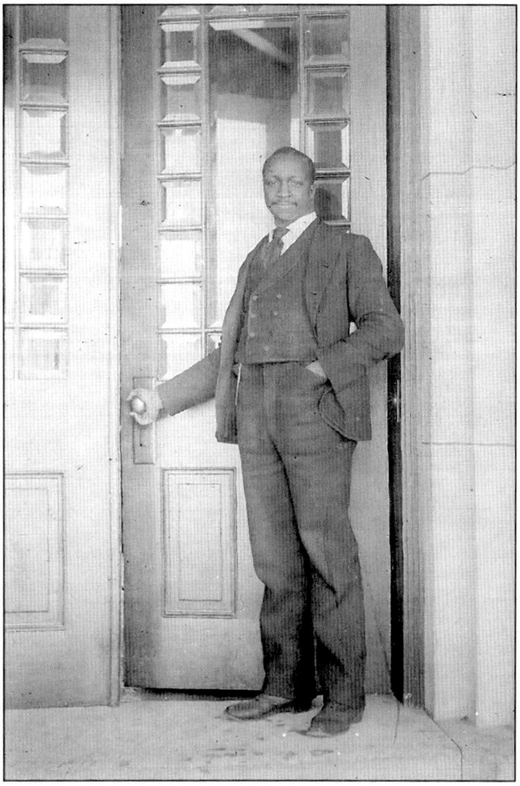

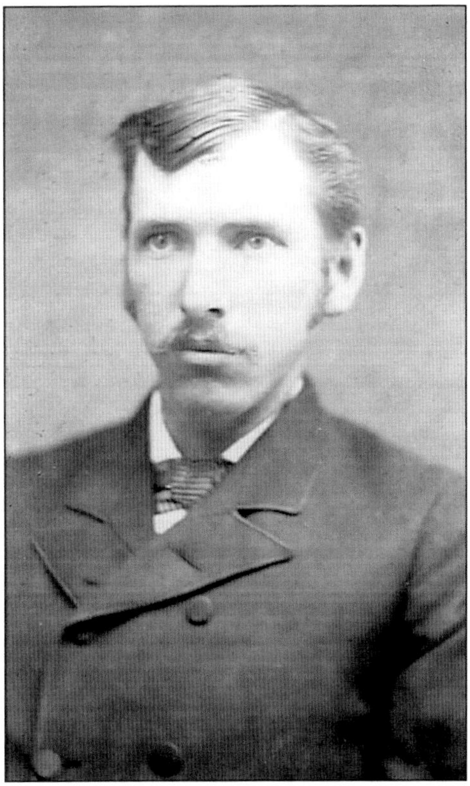

Fowler Martin. Fowler Martin was a Portland-area farmer. This small portrait was taken c. 1880s. Fowler was born in 1860 and was the only son of William and Elizabeth Martin. By the time he was 20 years old, Fowler had taken over the farm from his retired father. He married and had a son, but died prematurely, in 1905, at the age of 44. (Courtesy of the Portland Area Historical Society.)

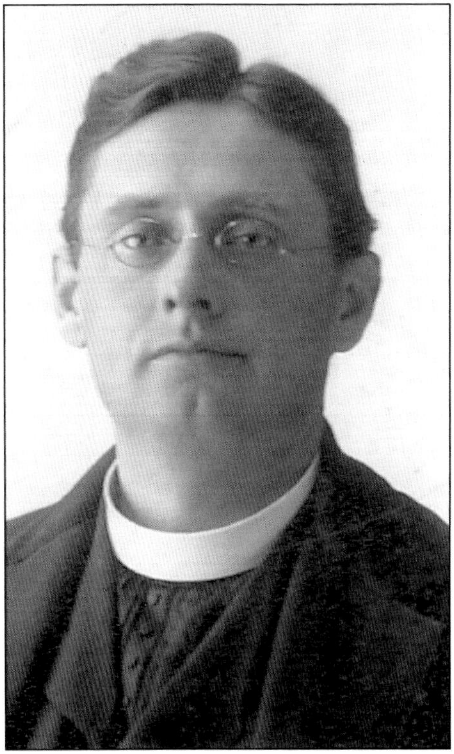

FATHER MATHIAS AUER. Mathias Auer was born in Germany and in 1890 came to the United States. In 1899, he became the first pastor of St. Patrick's Catholic Church. St. Patrick's parishioners built a rectory for him shortly after his arrival. In 1906, Father Auer directed the construction of St. Patrick's School. Unfortunately, he was not able to enjoy the fruits of his labor for long. Father Auer died in 1908 at age 42. (Courtesy of the Portland Area Historical Society.)

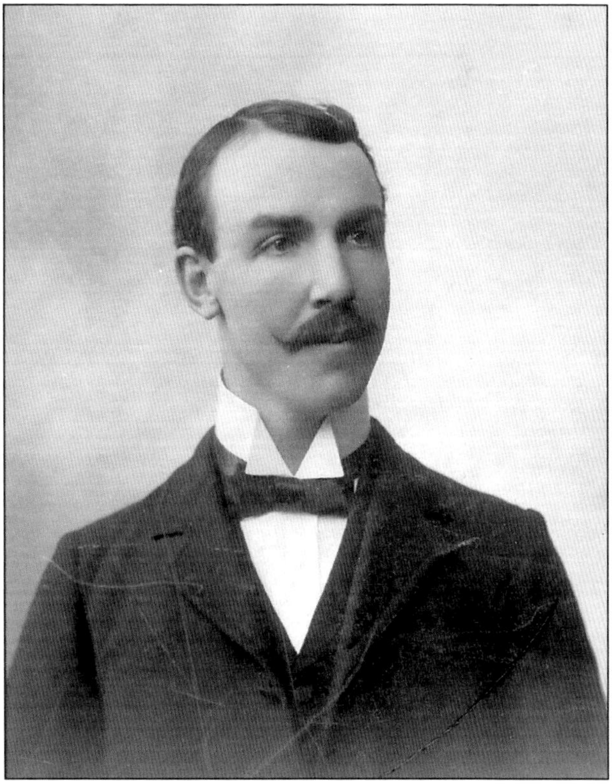

H.E. AGNEW. Hugh E. Agnew was superintendent of Portland Public Schools in the late 1890s and early 1900s. Agnew was a graduate of the University of Michigan and was only in his early twenties when he assumed the superintendent position. After working in Portland, he later moved to Oakland, California, where he worked in advertising for a trade journal. (Courtesy of the Portland Area Historical Society.)

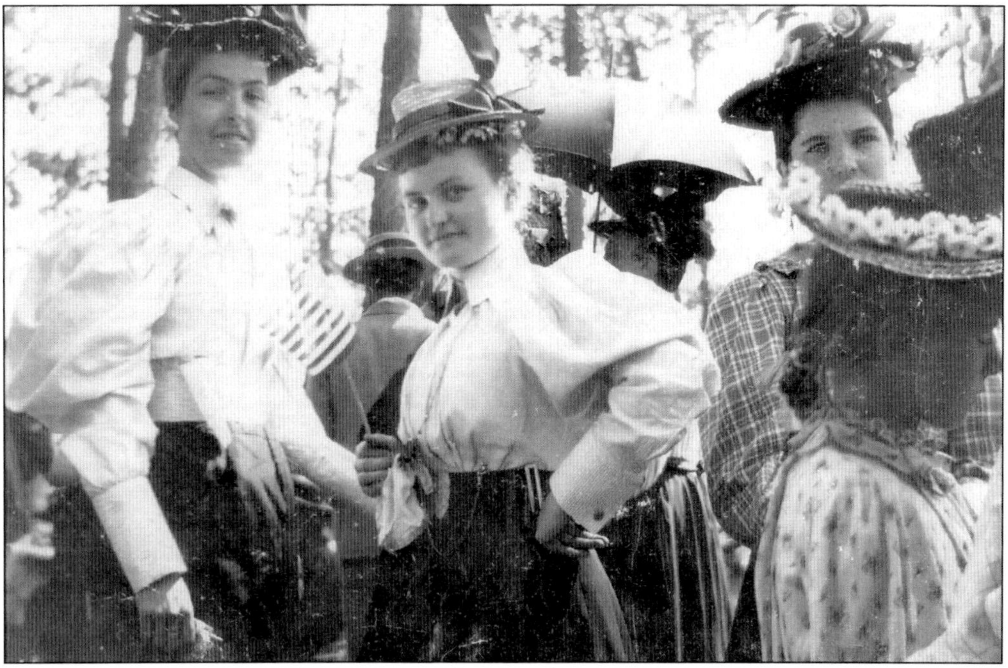

Italy Dey. The woman in the center is Italy Dey. She married Tom Horner, a man who played coronet in a circus band. She joined the circus with him and was a bareback rider. She and her husband spent their winters with his parents in Portland. (Courtesy of the Portland Area Historical Society.)

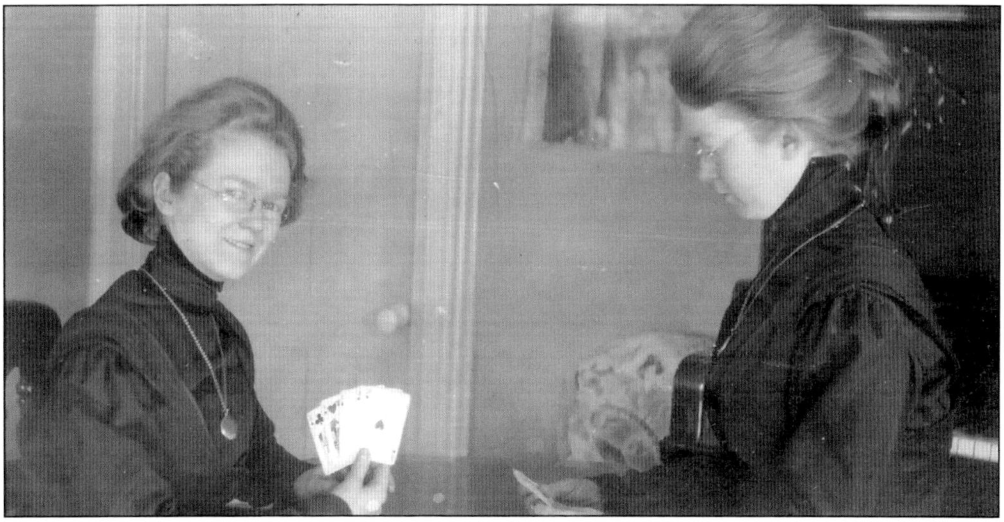

Sara Rice. With the assistance of some trick photography, Sara Rice plays cards with herself in this George Van Horn novelty postcard. Sara McCormick Rice was born in 1885 and briefly attended Ferris Institute (present-day Ferris State University). Upon leaving Ferris, she took a job as stenographer at the Portland Manufacturing Company. On September 30, 1907, Sara married Oscar Rice in a quiet ceremony at Detroit's Forest Lawn Presbyterian Church. (Oscar Rice was the grandson of N.B. and Mary Newman Rice.) In April 1920, Sara Rice became the first woman ever elected to public office in Portland Township when she defeated her female competitor, Nora Bates Young. (Courtesy of the Portland Area Historical Society.)

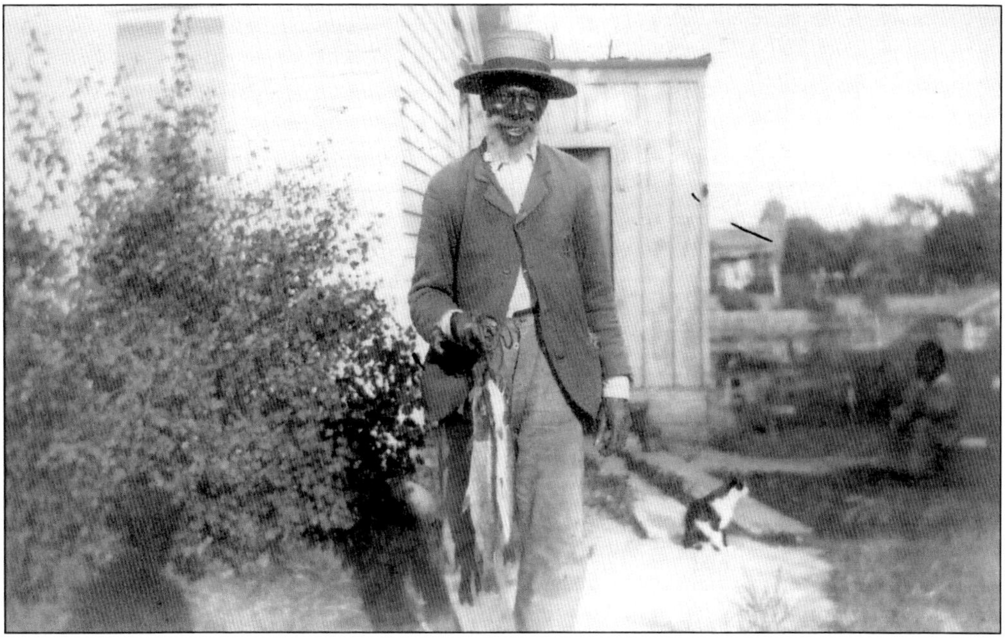

John Peterson. Peterson was purported to be the first African American to settle in Portland. Born in 1837, he was a native of New York State. Peterson made his living as a handyman for the residents of Portland's east side. (Courtesy of the Portland Area Historical Society.)

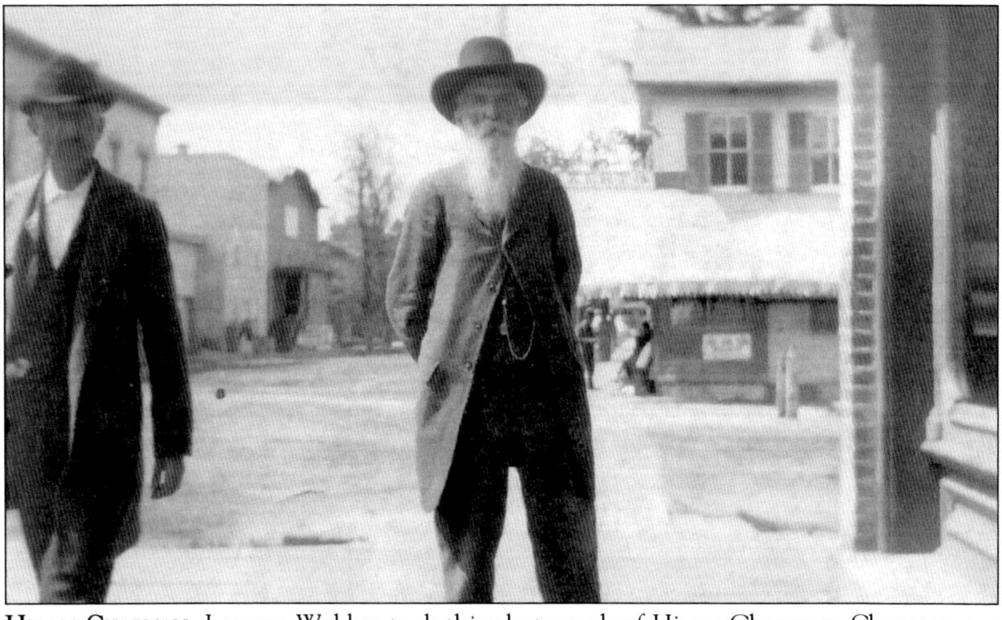

Hiram Chapman. Lorenzo Webber took this photograph of Hiram Chapman. Chapman was born in Vermont in 1825 and made his living primarily as a musician. He lived in Ionia for most of his life until relocating to Portland in the 1870s, where he lived with and worked for the T.J. Bandfield family. (T.J. Bandfield owned and operated the Bandfield Furniture Company.) According to former Portland resident Queen Robinson Stone, Chapman once made a violin out of a cigar box for Bandfield's son Harold and taught him how to play it. (Courtesy of the Portland Area Historical Society.)

Dr. Robert W. Alton. Dr. Alton practiced medicine in Portland for many years and was also deeply involved in the village's industry; he was the "Alton" in the Ramsey-Alton Manufacturing Company. Dr. Alton was born in Lansing and educated at the University of Michigan's medical school. In 1878, Dr. Alton arrived in Portland at the age of 25. Soon after, he married Florence Wolcott; together they had a daughter. Unfortunately, Mrs. Alton died in 1890 and Dr. Alton remained a widower for the rest of his life. He died in 1930 an extremely well-respected member of the community. Michigan Governor Fred W. Green attended his funeral. Shortly after his death, the *Portland Observer* wrote of Dr. Alton, "He was endowed with all those qualities which secured confidence, integrity and fidelity." (Courtesy of the Portland Area Historical Society.)

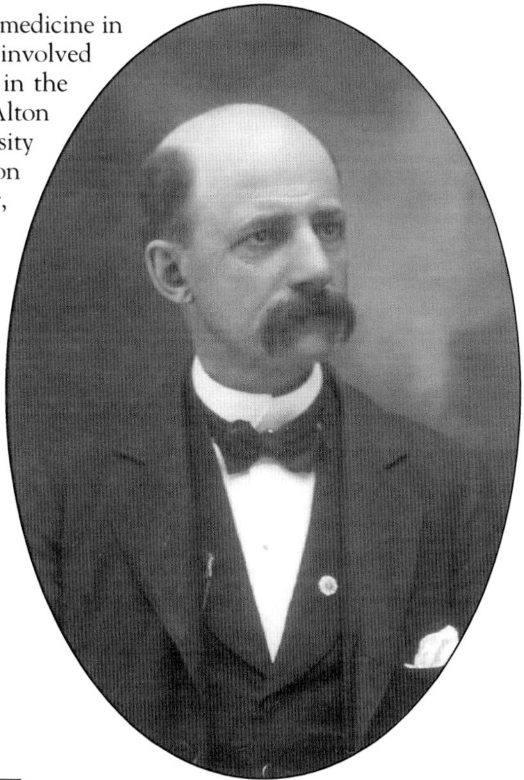

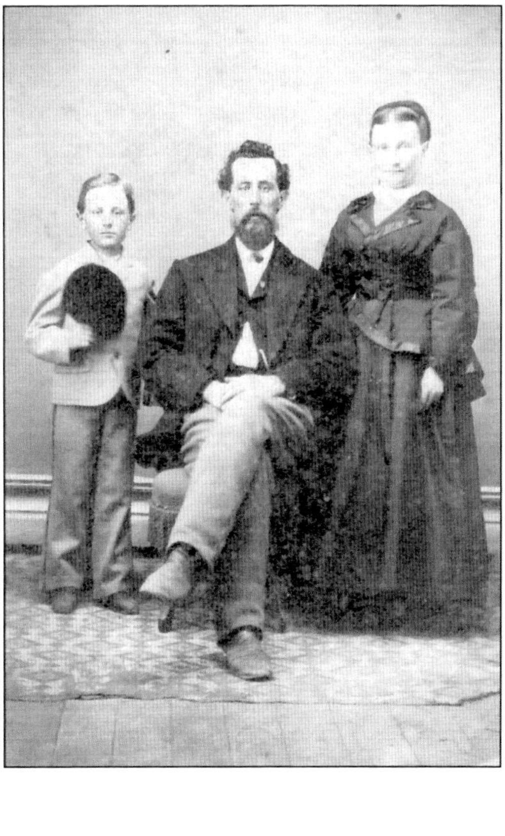

Dr. B.F. Willey and Family. Dr. Willey was born c. 1830 in Ohio. His wife was named Ordelia and their son, Guy, was born in 1858. The Willey family lived in Orleans Township. This photograph was taken for a *carte de visite*. These photographic calling cards reached a peak of popularity in the 1860s and 1870s. The *carte de visite* process was developed in France in the middle of the 19th century. It allowed for multiple cardboard prints to be produced and made the daguerreotype obsolete. (Courtesy of the Portland Area Historical Society.)

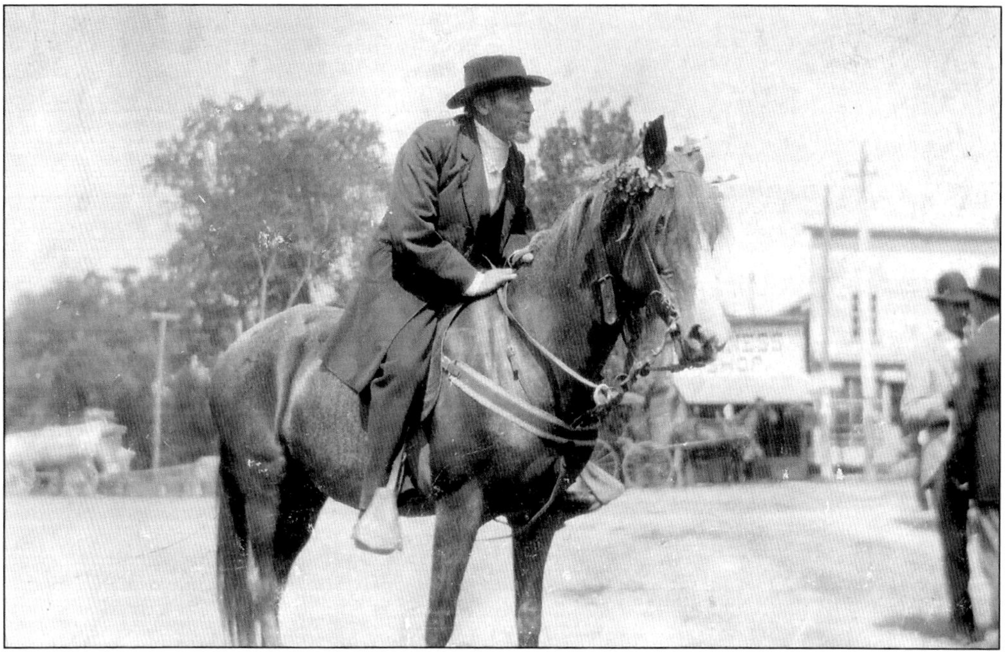

HENRY CONKLIN. Conklin was born in 1825 and, like many of Portland's early pioneers, was a native of New York State. He was purported to have been a soldier in the Mexican War. In this photograph, Conklin is riding on his roan mare, Betty, on the occasion of Decoration Day. Conklin spent his civilian years as a farmer and died in 1896. (Courtesy of the Portland Area Historical Society.)

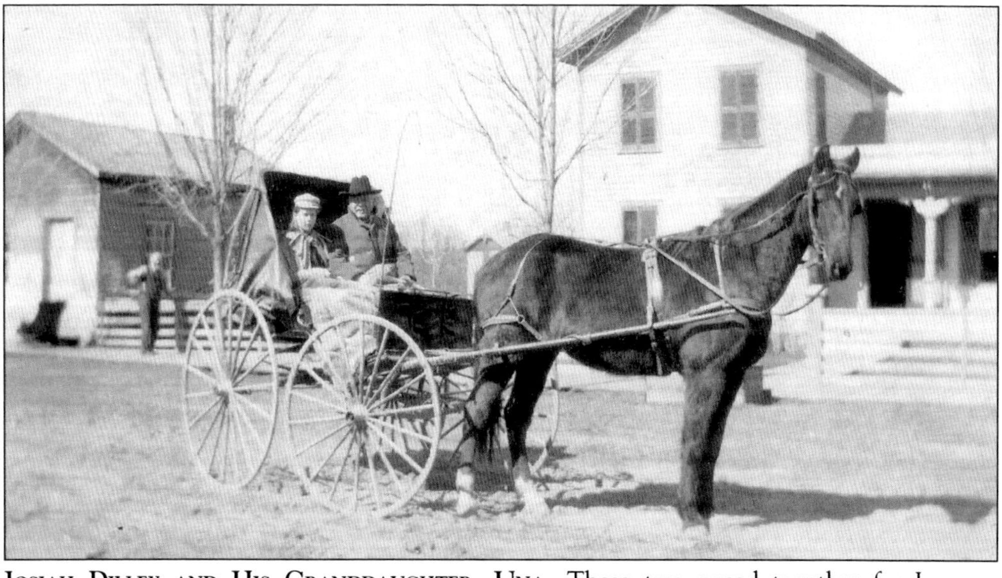

JOSIAH DILLEY AND HIS GRANDDAUGHTER, UNA. These two posed together for Lorenzo Webber's camera in April 1895. Josiah Dilley was born in England and arrived in the United States at age 20. He was a prosperous farmer whose farm and homestead were located at the corner of Broad Street (now known as West Bridge Street) and Market Street. Dilley and his wife Catherine had six children: John, Sarah, Franklin, Mary, Charles, and Josiah. (Courtesy of the Portland Area Historical Society.)

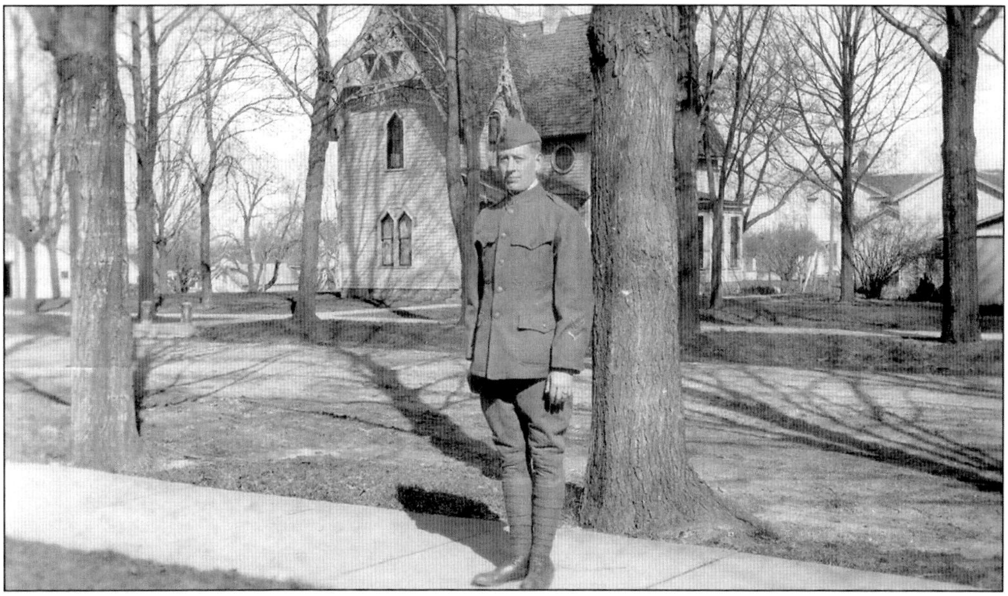

Two Veterans of World War I. Herman Lehman (above) had recently arrived home from military service when this picture was taken by his brother, Leo, on Easter Sunday 1919. John Leslie (below, right) was born in Canada. As a boy, he came to the United States with his mother Mary. After World War I, Leslie operated a garage and for a time served as Commander of Portland's American Legion post. (Courtesy of the Portland Area Historical Society.)

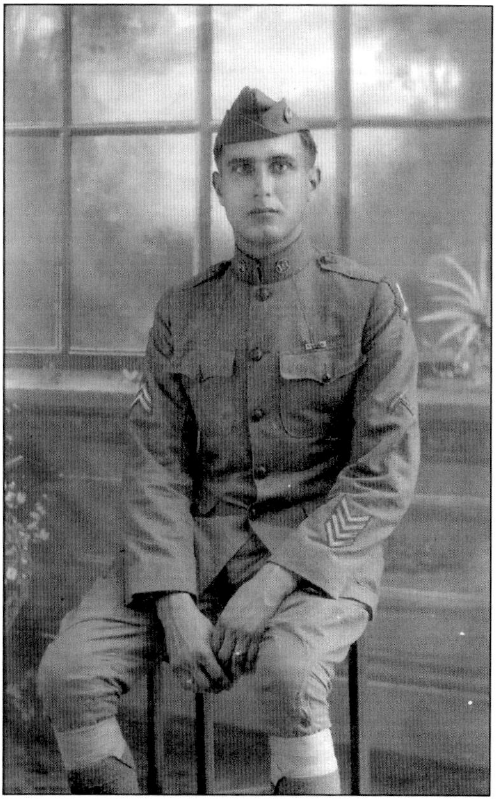

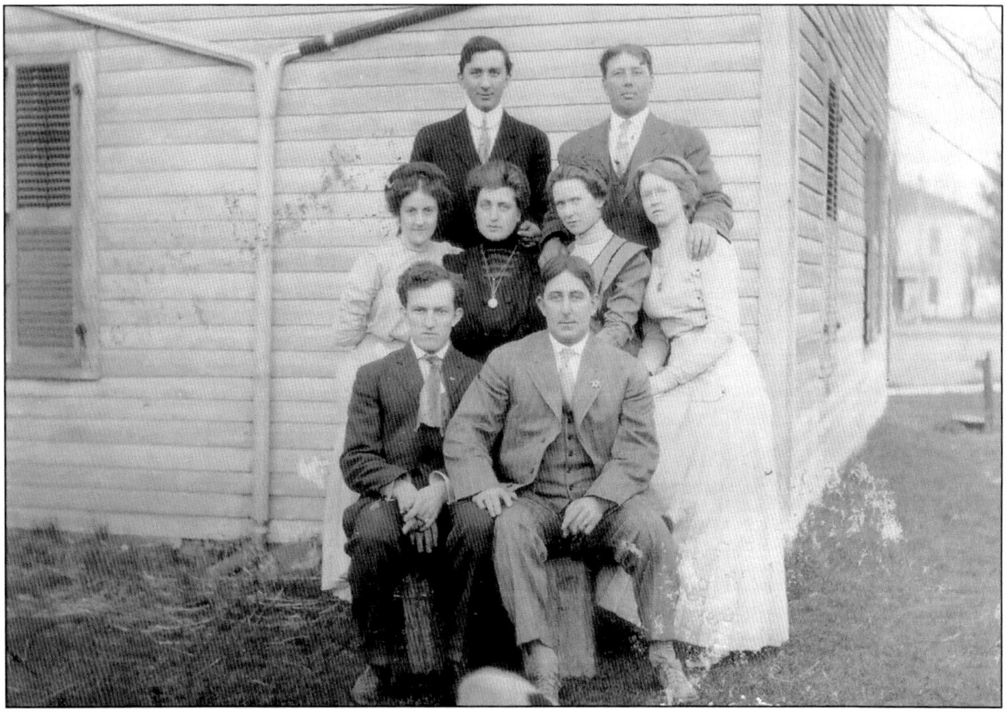

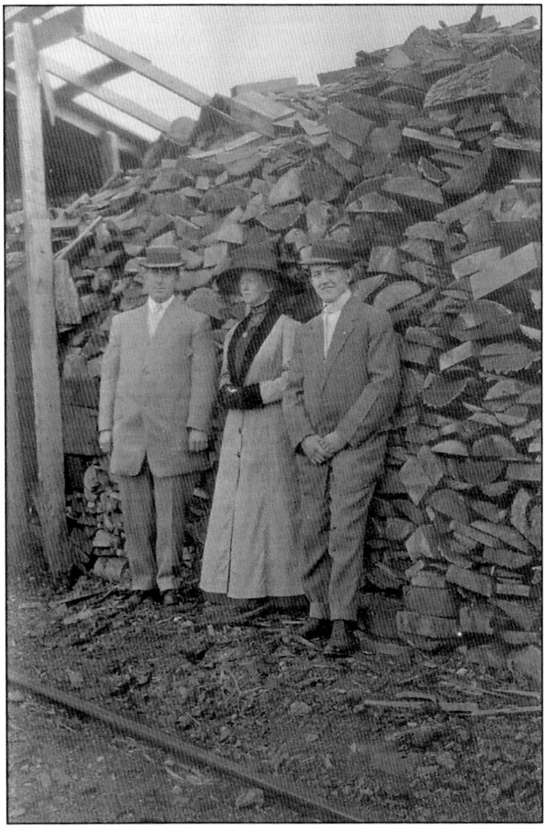

A Group of Friends. Pictured above are, from left to right, as follows: (front row) Oscar Rice and Jay Clark; (middle row) Bessie Lehman, Mable Clark, Helen Fineis, and Sara Rice; (top row) Leo Lehman and Peter Fineis. The nattily dressed trio to the left are: (from left) Jay Clark, Sara Rice, and Oscar Rice. (Courtesy of the Portland Area Historical Society.)

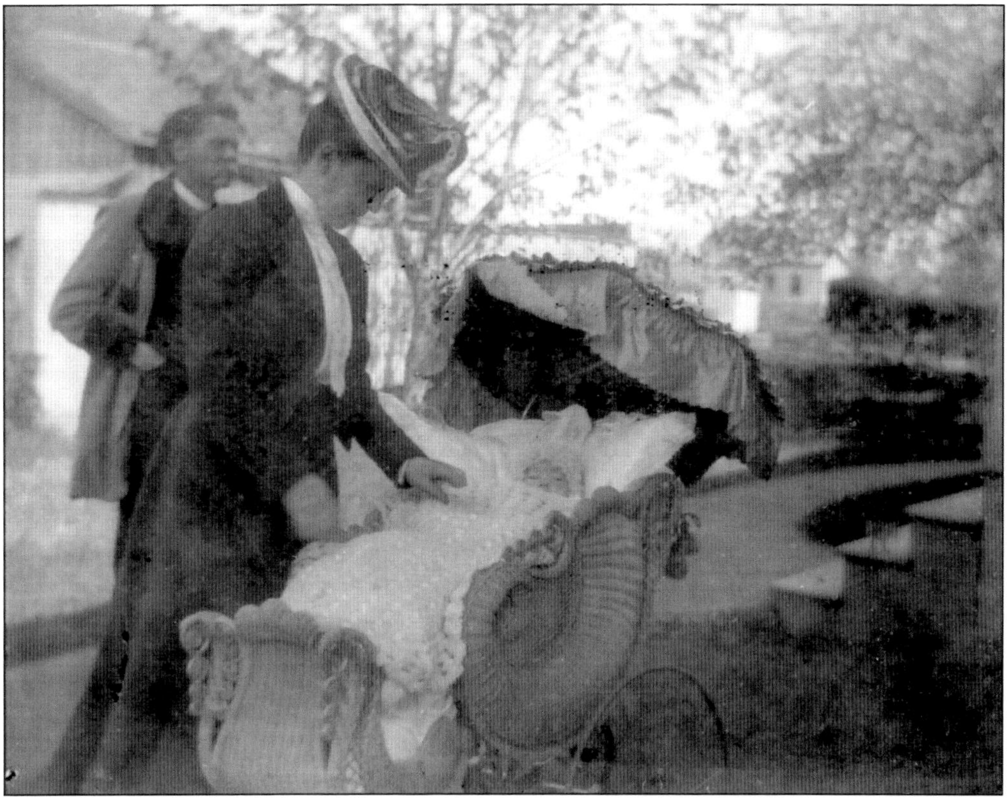

Dora Webber with Her Daughter. Lorenzo Webber's wife, Dora, is pictured with her daughter, Charlotte. Dora's father, W.H. Stone, stands in the background. (Courtesy of the Portland Area Historical Society.)

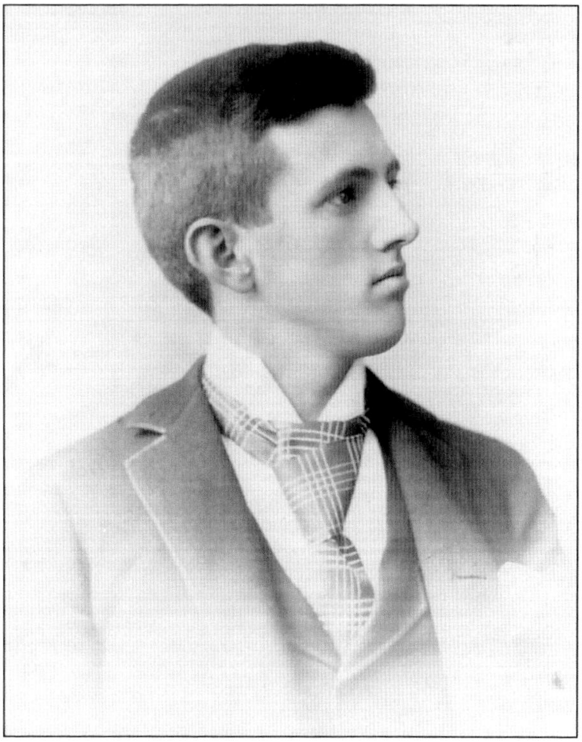

George Webber. George was the younger brother of Lorenzo Webber and assisted their father John at the Webber Bank. When George died tragically at the tender age of 19, Lorenzo returned to Portland from his studies at Harvard University to replace George as his father's assistant. He worked in the bank business for the next 40 years. (Courtesy of the Portland Area Historical Society.)

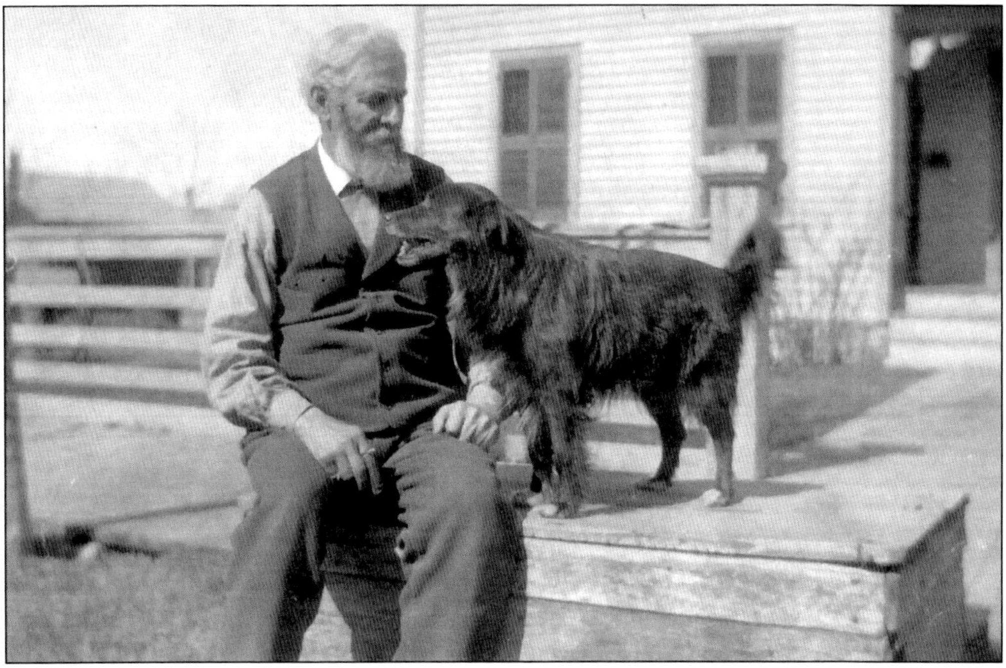

WILLIAM H. WHITE WITH HIS DOG, JIM, APRIL 1895. William H. White was another early pioneer of the Portland area and lived an extremely full life. He was born in Easton, Pennsylvania, April 23, 1828, and came to Portland with his parents in September 1842. His parents settled on a farm northwest of the village. White was not fond of farming and as a young man he worked in manufacturing and as a painter. He also served as village clerk, village marshal, and Portland Township treasurer. He died in 1919 at the age of 91. (Courtesy of the Portland Area Historical Society.)

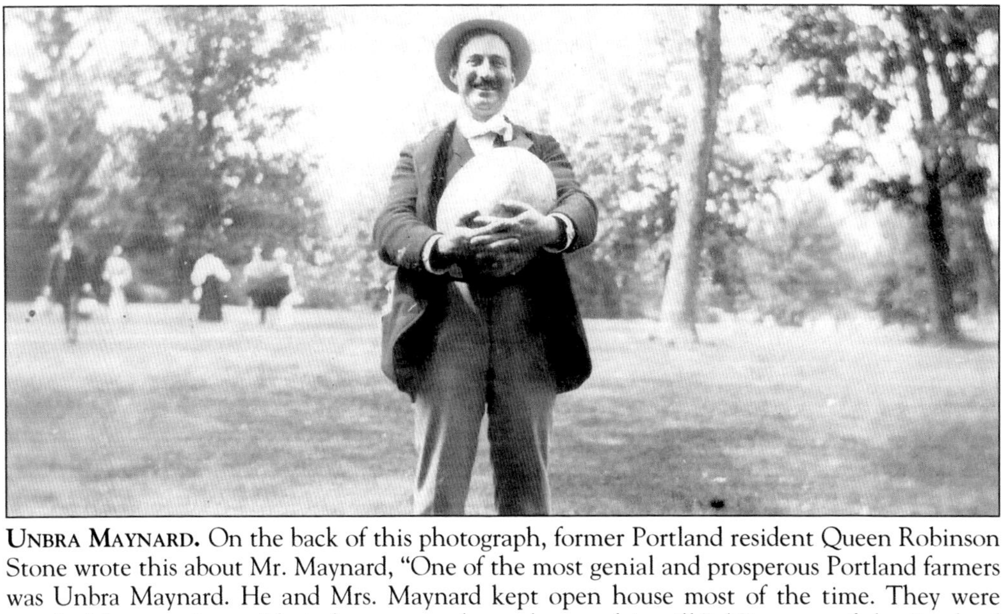

UNBRA MAYNARD. On the back of this photograph, former Portland resident Queen Robinson Stone wrote this about Mr. Maynard, "One of the most genial and prosperous Portland farmers was Unbra Maynard. He and Mrs. Maynard kept open house most of the time. They were wonderful entertainers. Their farm was a show place and is still." (Courtesy of the Portland Area Historical Society.)

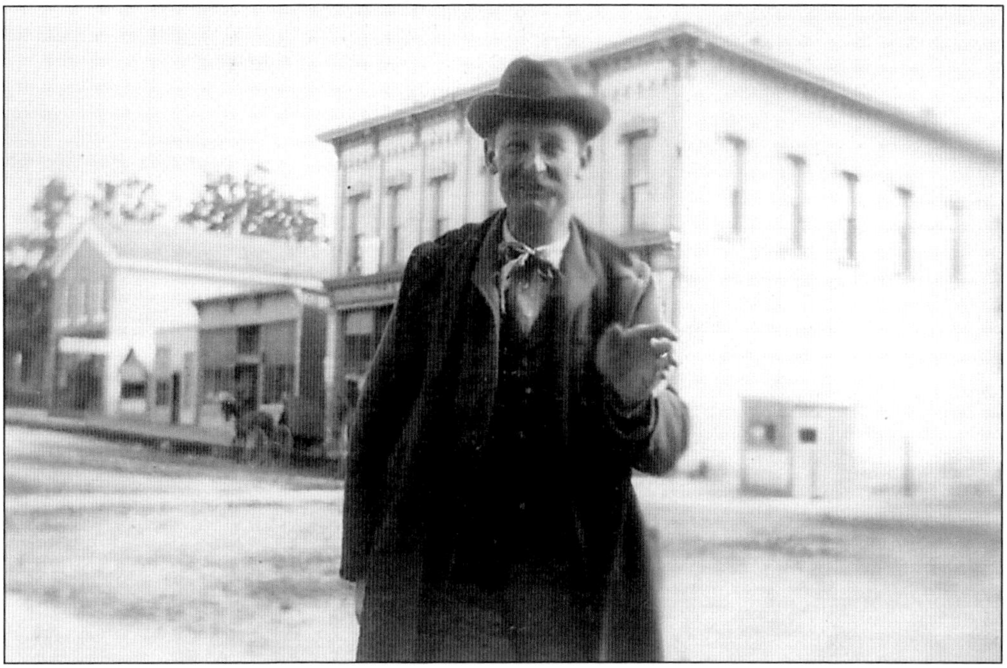

George Buck. George Buck was captured on camera by Portland banker Lorenzo Webber in 1895. Visible in the background is the McClelland Block (currently known as the Peake Building), which in 1895 was home to the Woodbury and Churchill store on the left and John McClelland's general store on the right. (Courtesy of the Portland Area Historical Society.)

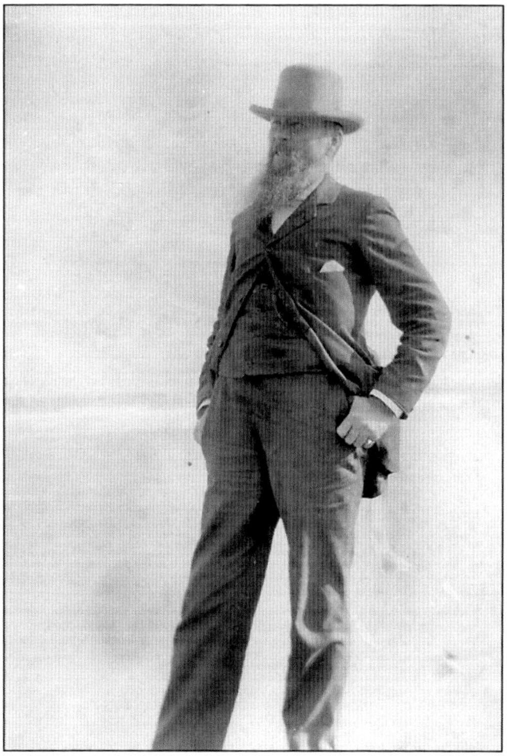

George H. Doane. Doane was vice president of the Portland Milling Company and came to Portland from Detroit in 1893. When the Newman & Rice flour mill burned down in February of that year, the firm was reorganized and renamed the Portland Milling Company. George Doane, who had considerable milling experience, arrived in the village at this time. He assumed the position of vice president before construction began on the new plant in April 1893. (Courtesy of the Portland Area Historical Society.)

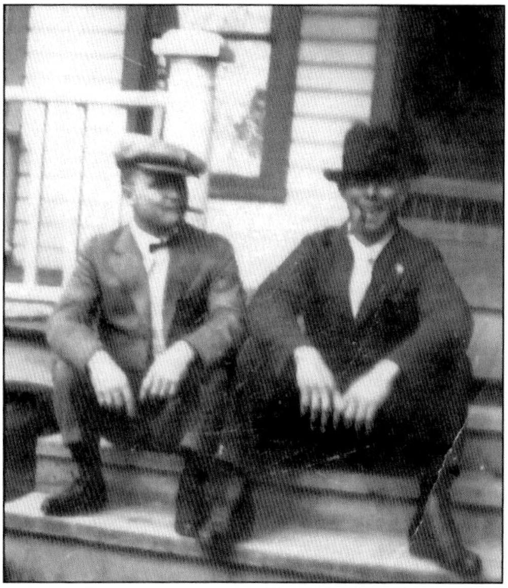

Harry High and Ward Merrifield Share a Laugh. Harry High was born in 1885. He and his wife Iva lived on Kent Street in Portland. Ward Merrifield was a farmer who, with his wife Mable, lived in Sebewa township. (Courtesy of the Portland Area Historical Society.)

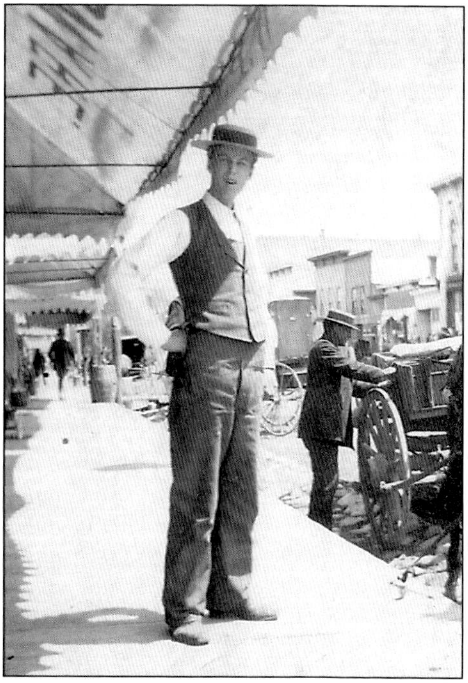

Bert Reynolds. Bert Reynolds was a clerk at the hardware store next door to the Webber Bank on Kent Street. This is another of the many photographs Lorenzo Webber took of average Portland townspeople. (Courtesy of the Portland Area Historical Society.)

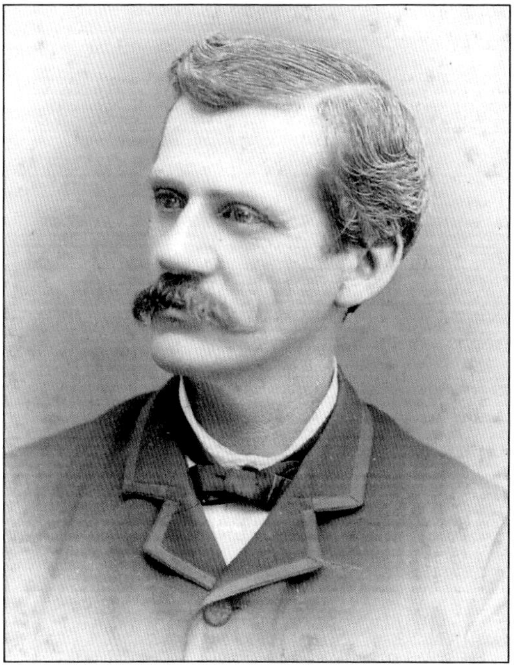

George Allen. Earlier in this chapter is a photograph of an elderly Dr. Allen in his horse buggy. This is a portrait of Allen taken by the L.K. Showman studio in Portland, *c.* 1880. As a testament to Dr. Allen's reputation as the "baby doctor," the anonymous caption written on the back of the photograph reads, "He brought me in the world, am now 75 years old. September 26, 1947." (Courtesy of the Portland Area Historical Society.)

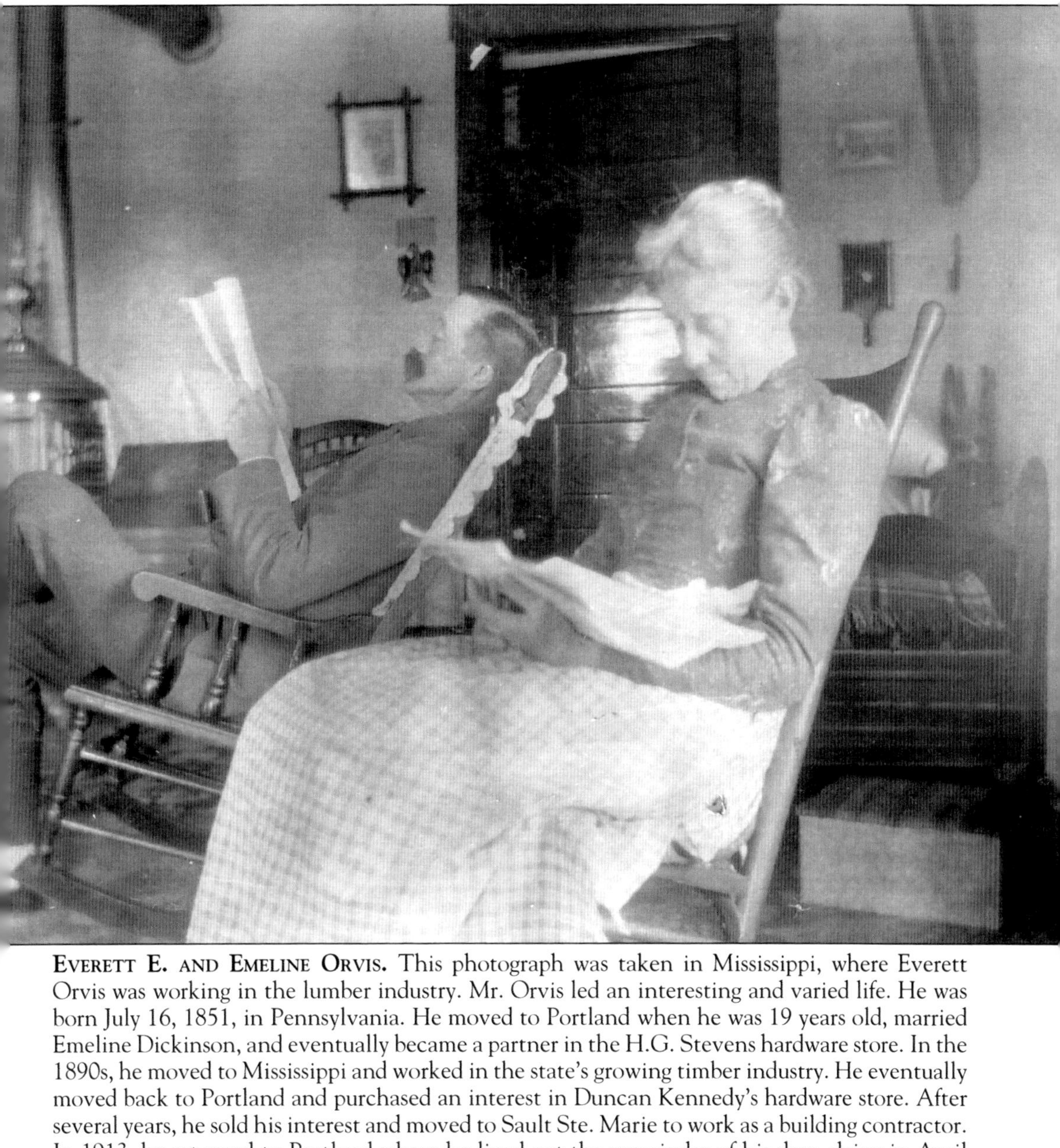

Everett E. and Emeline Orvis. This photograph was taken in Mississippi, where Everett Orvis was working in the lumber industry. Mr. Orvis led an interesting and varied life. He was born July 16, 1851, in Pennsylvania. He moved to Portland when he was 19 years old, married Emeline Dickinson, and eventually became a partner in the H.G. Stevens hardware store. In the 1890s, he moved to Mississippi and worked in the state's growing timber industry. He eventually moved back to Portland and purchased an interest in Duncan Kennedy's hardware store. After several years, he sold his interest and moved to Sault Ste. Marie to work as a building contractor. In 1913, he returned to Portland where he lived out the remainder of his days, dying in April 1935. His wife Emeline died in 1927. (Courtesy of the Portland Area Historical Society.)

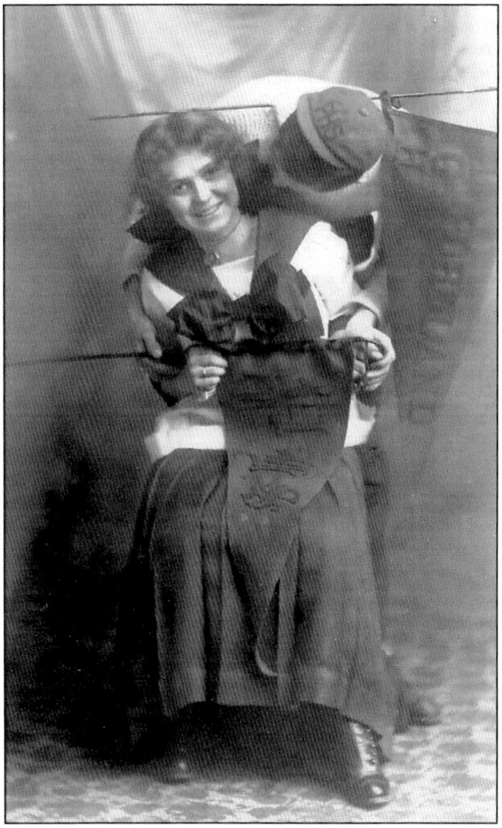

Two Lighthearted Van Horn Postcards. These two postcards depict youthful Portland residents in carefree and lighthearted scenes. In the photo on the left, high school students Mary Smith and Max Cook clown for the camera. In the photo below, Leo Matthews, Jack Hill, and Basil Lowry look like they can barely contain their giddiness. (Courtesy of the Portland Area Historical Society.)

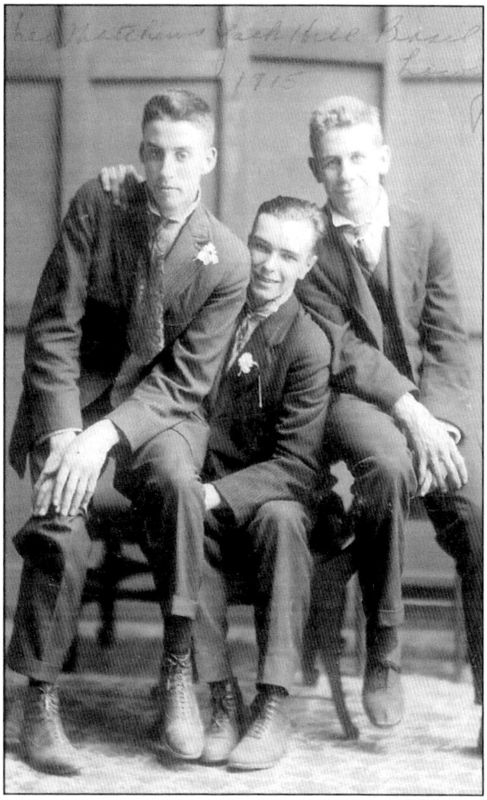

Ten

Recreation, Leisure, and Events

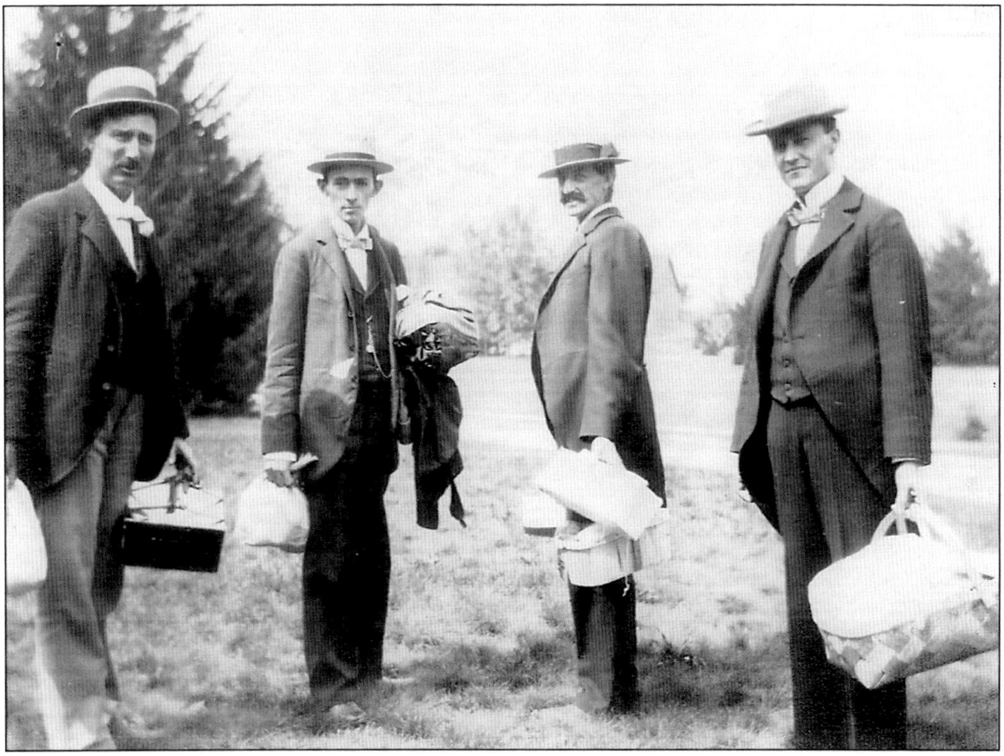

Off on a Picnic. From left to right are Unbra Maynard, Lorenzo Webber, and two men identified as dentists, Dr. Smith and Dr. John Green. (Courtesy of the Portland Area Historical Society.)

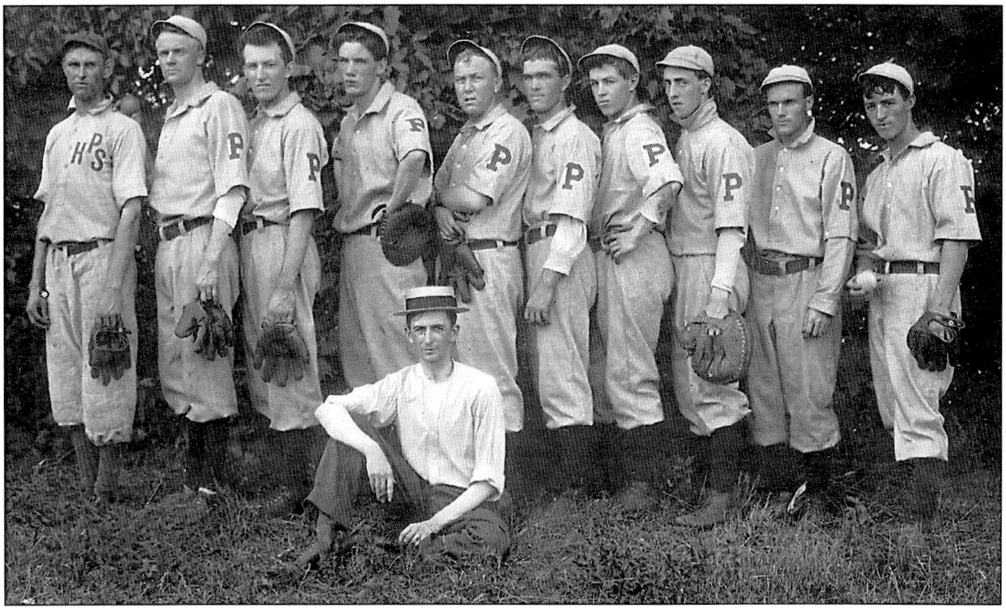

BASEBALL TEAM, C. 1910S. Baseball has always been a popular pastime in Portland. Early village baseball teams were comprised of skilled and serious-minded local ballplayers who took on all comers. Some of Portland's opponents included the REO team, McGraw's Tigers of Detroit, Ramona of Grand Rapids, and the Oldsmobiles. This edition of the Portland team includes, from left to right: unidentified, James Webster, Oscar Rice, Claude Plant Sr., Roy Dawdy, Lester Russell, Tom Bates, Chester Divine, Bill Young, and Bill Bates. Seated in front is Neil Tomy. (Chester Divine owned and operated the Hotel Divine.) (Courtesy of the Portland Area Historical Society.)

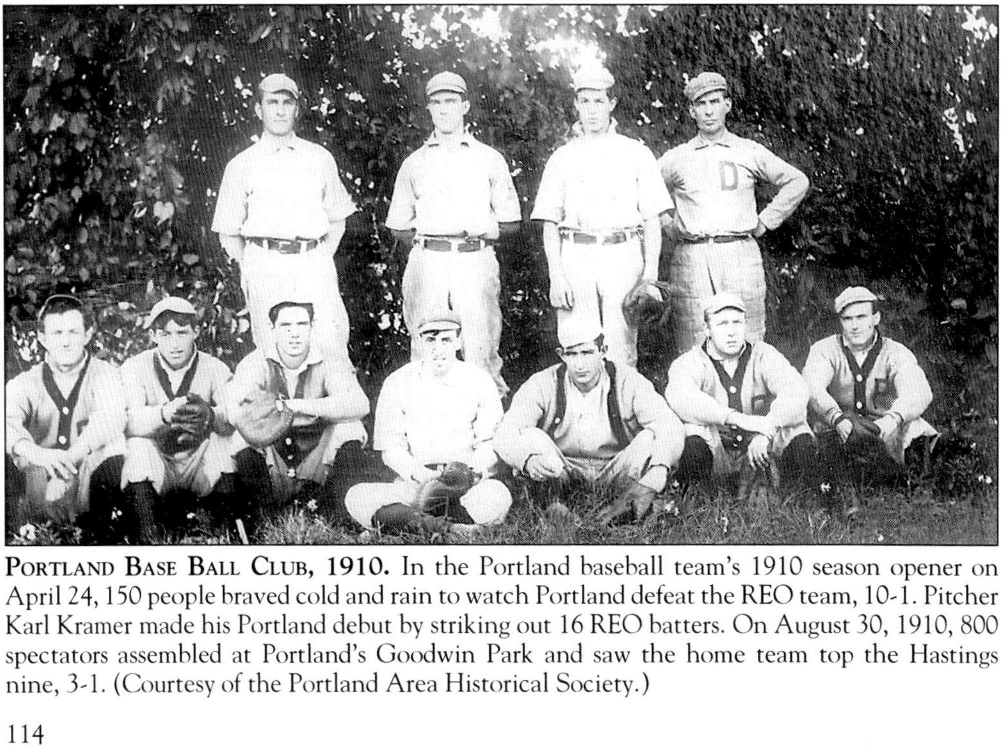

PORTLAND BASE BALL CLUB, 1910. In the Portland baseball team's 1910 season opener on April 24, 150 people braved cold and rain to watch Portland defeat the REO team, 10-1. Pitcher Karl Kramer made his Portland debut by striking out 16 REO batters. On August 30, 1910, 800 spectators assembled at Portland's Goodwin Park and saw the home team top the Hastings nine, 3-1. (Courtesy of the Portland Area Historical Society.)

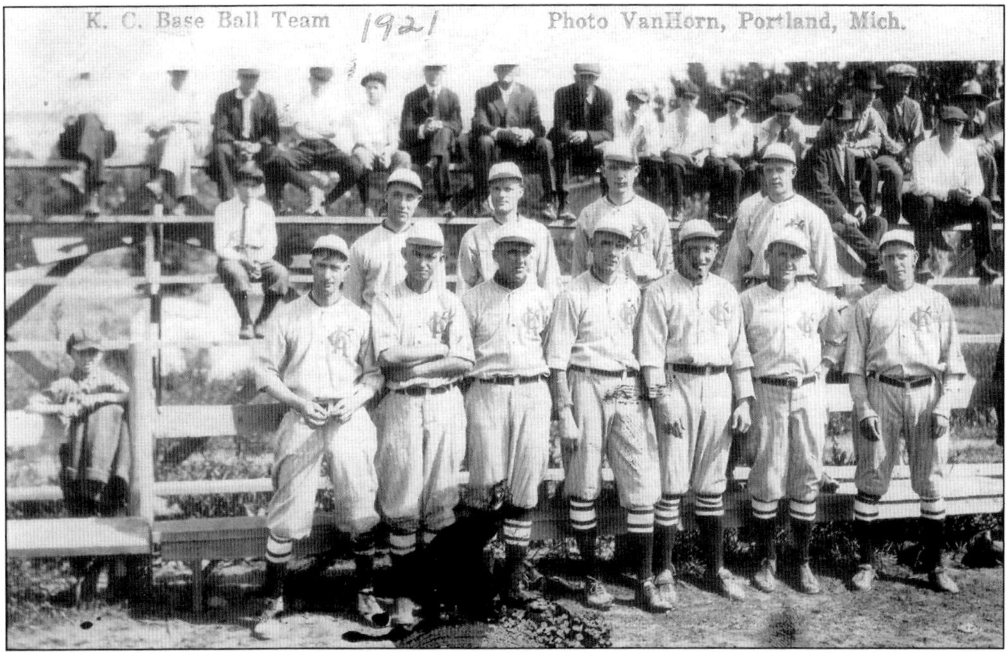

KNIGHTS OF COLUMBUS BASEBALL TEAM, 1921. (Courtesy of the Portland Area Historical Society.)

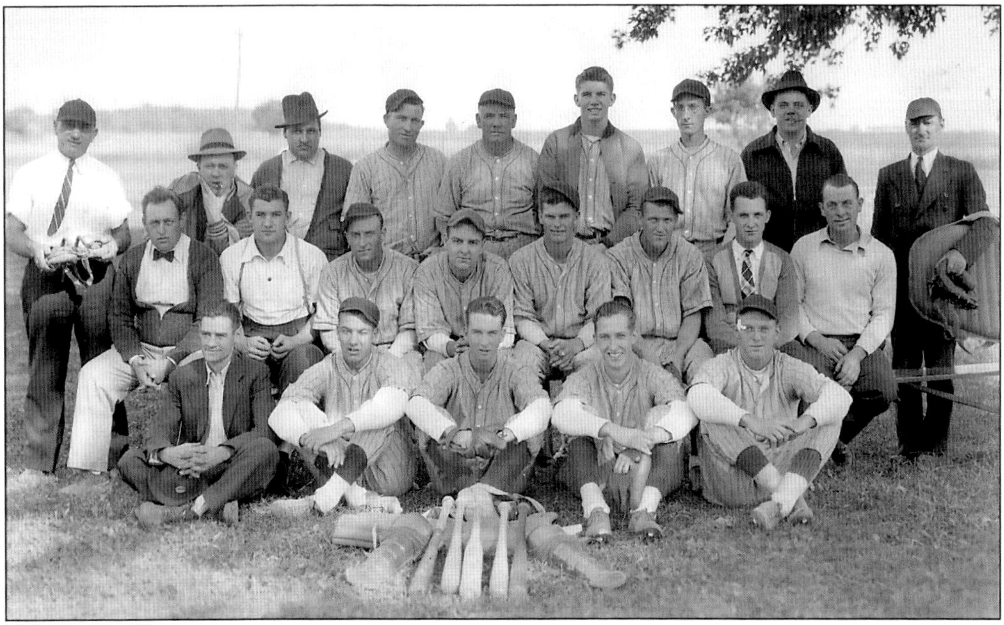

PORTLAND CITY BASEBALL TEAM. Some of the players on this team include Howard Kortes, Herbert (Unk) Schaefer, Art Baker, Buster Graft, Clare Graft, Harold Sandborn, Tom Esch, George Sandborn, John Watkins, Ford Esch, and Claude Plant. Art Baker is fourth from left in the middle row and Clare Graft is sixth from left in the same row. Both were catchers on the team. Harold Sandborn, pitcher, is seated between Art Baker and Clare Graft. Claude Plant, the manager, is standing fifth from left in the top row. (Courtesy of the Portland Area Historical Society.)

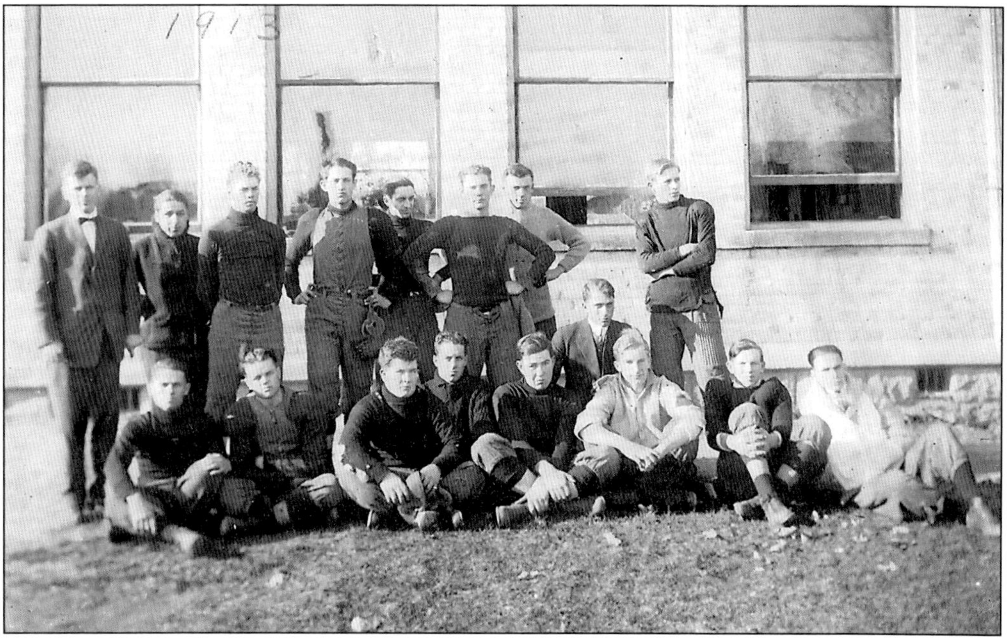

PORTLAND HIGH SCHOOL FOOTBALL TEAMS, 1913 AND 1914. Portland High School lost only two games on the gridiron during the autumn of 1913, both came at the hands of Ionia. On October 11, Grand Ledge had apparently defeated Portland, 13-7. However, after the contest, a referee acknowledged that he had made a mistake on the field and declared the game a 13-13 tie. Other noteworthy wins were a 3-0 victory over Belding and a 41-0 decision over Lake Odessa. The 1914 squad won the Ionia County championship. The team claimed the crown when they defeated Belding 19-0 on November 26. When they returned to Portland that evening, a bonfire was set up near John McClelland & Son's store where "enthusiasts gathered to expel several lusty shouts for the heroes." (Courtesy of the Portland Area Historical Society.)

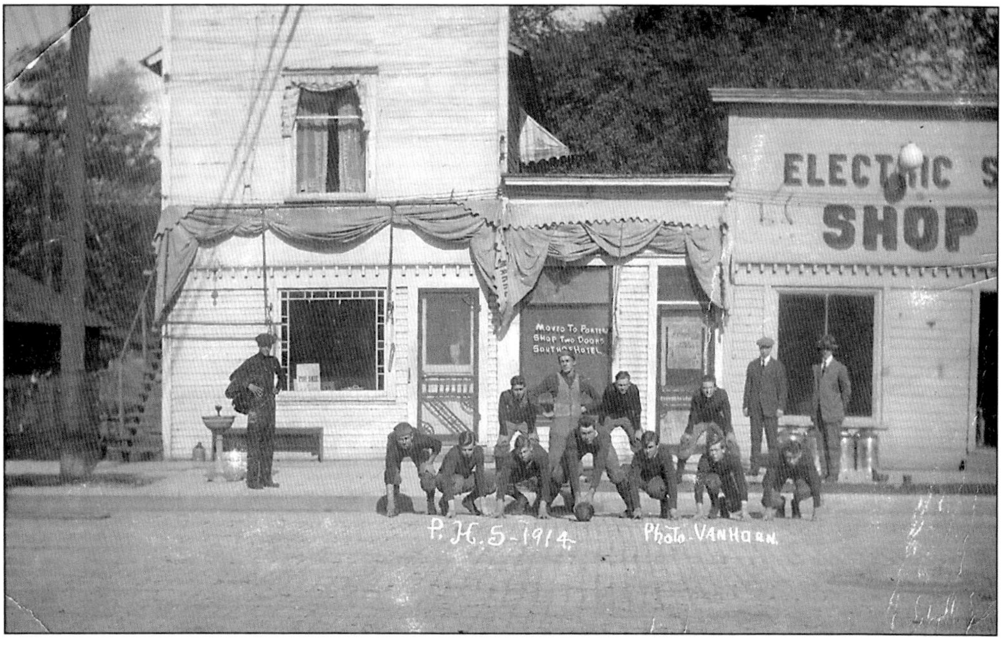

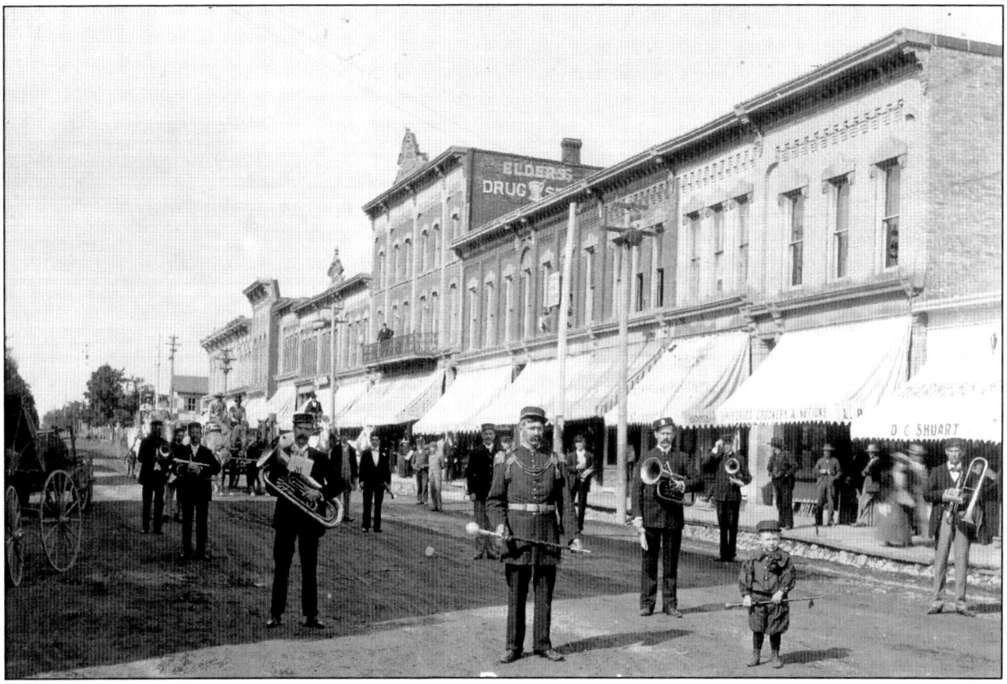

PORTLAND CORNET BAND. In the photograph above, the band is pictured before embarking on the train to Lowell for the 1897 Central Michigan Band Association contest and parade. The parade was scheduled to begin at 10:30 in the morning and 25 bands from around the area were expected to perform. Below, the band is captured in a more casual pose. (Courtesy of the Portland Area Historical Society.)

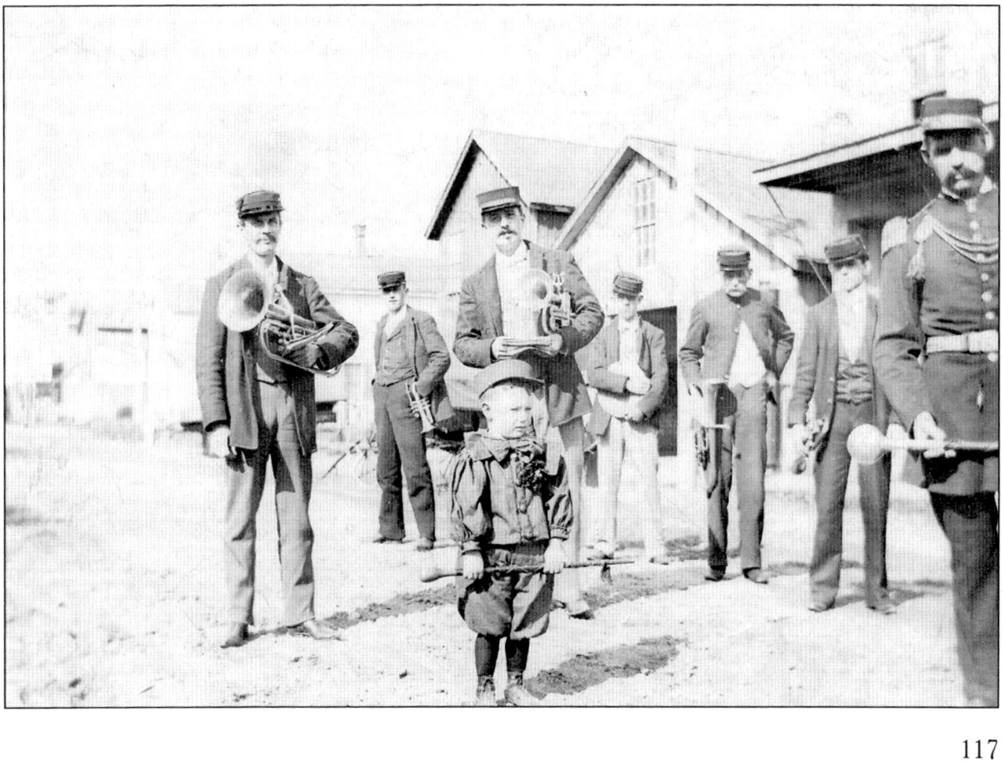

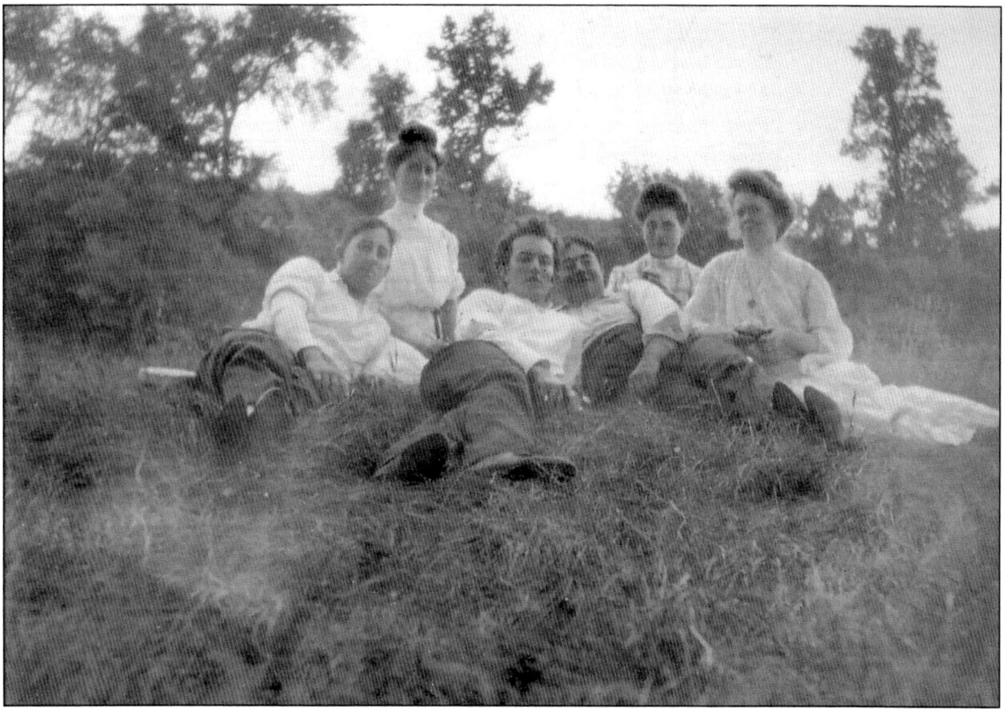

A LEISURELY COUNTRY OUTING. On the next two pages are George Van Horn postcards that show the various leisurely activities available in Portland. Pictured in the above photograph are, from left to right: Jay Clark, Grace Bates, Oscar Rice, Dick Bates, Mabel Clark, and Sara Rice. Pictured below are, from left to right: unidentified, Leo Lehman, Oscar Rice, Sara Rice, unidentified, unidentified, and Grace Bates. (Courtesy of the Portland Area Historical Society.)

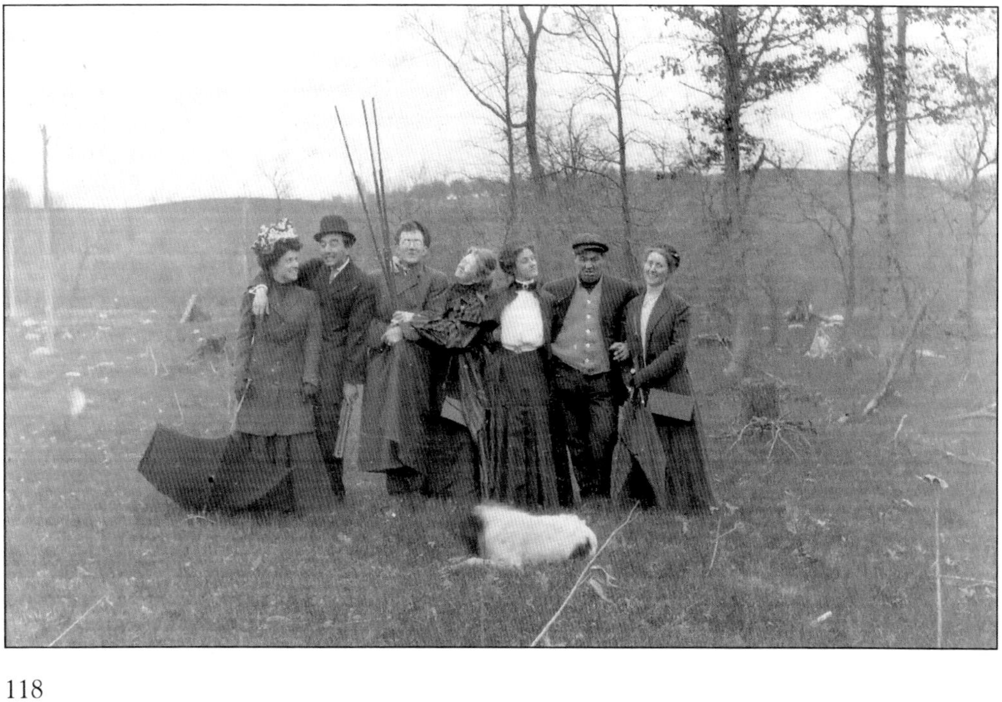

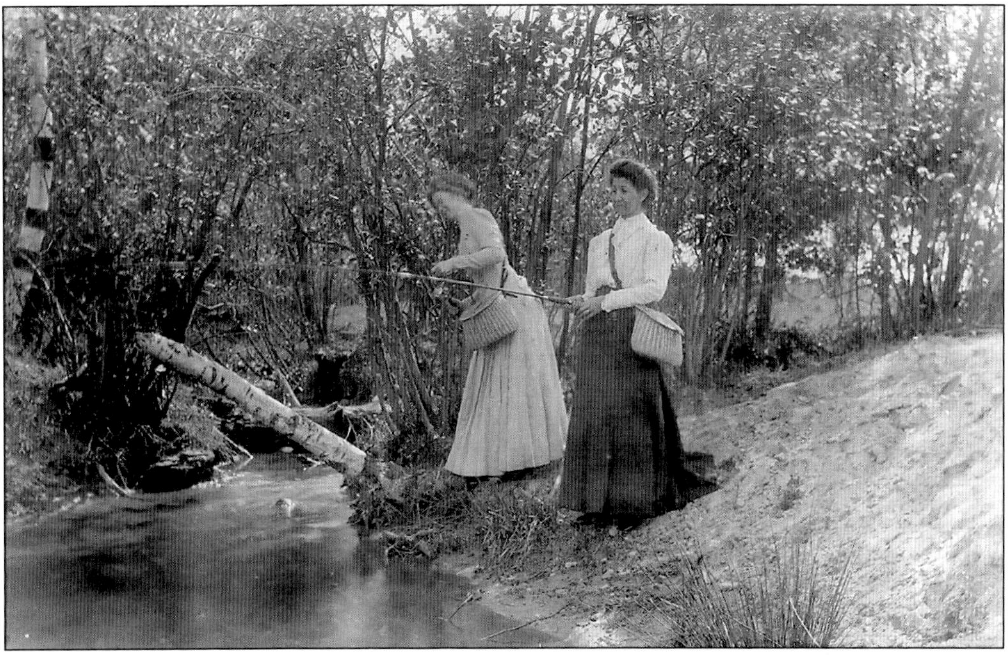

Sara Rice and Unidentified Woman Fishing. (Courtesy of the Portland Area Historical Society.)

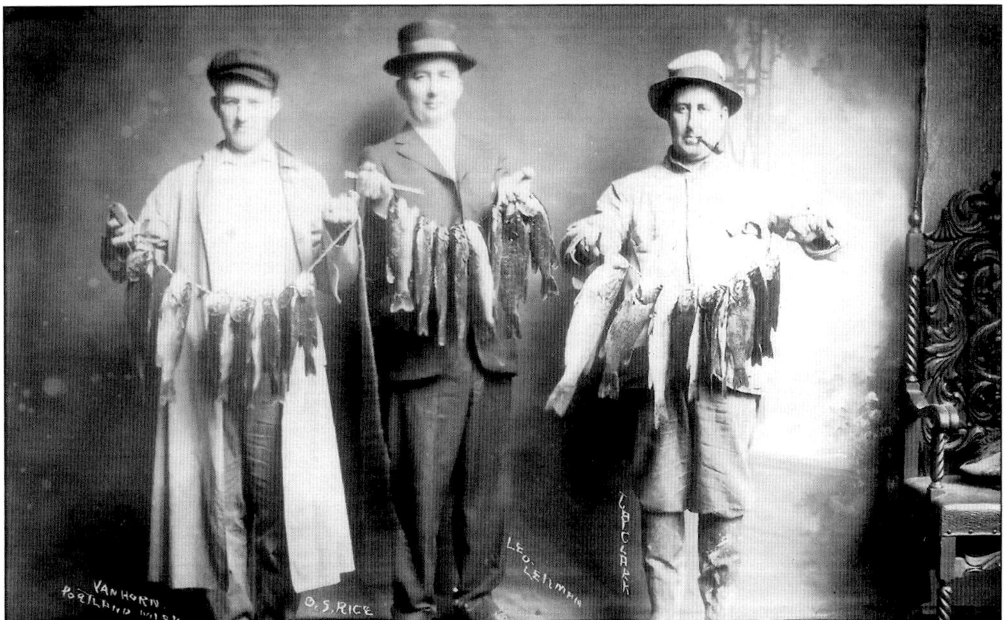

Successful Fishing Trip. Oscar Rice, Leo Lehman, and Jay Clark proudly display the bounty of a fishing expedition. Since Portland is located at the confluence of two rivers, fishing has always been a popular local activity. (Courtesy of the Portland Area Historical Society.)

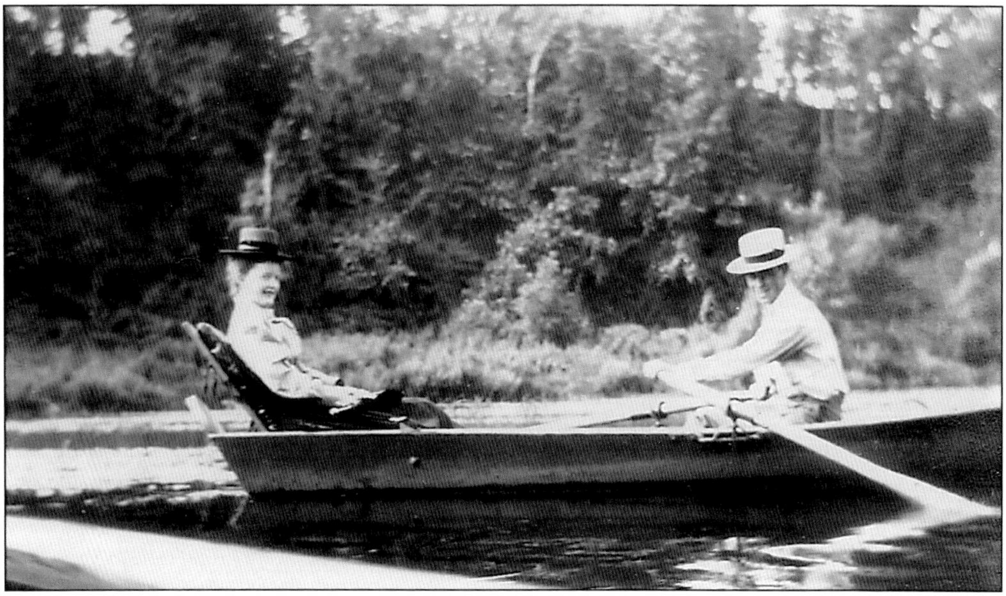

BOATING ON THE GRAND RIVER, C. 1890S. Lulu McClelland Richards relaxes in the back of the boat as Ethol Stone paddles. Boating has also, over the years, been a popular activity in the Portland area. (Courtesy of the Portland Area Historical Society.)

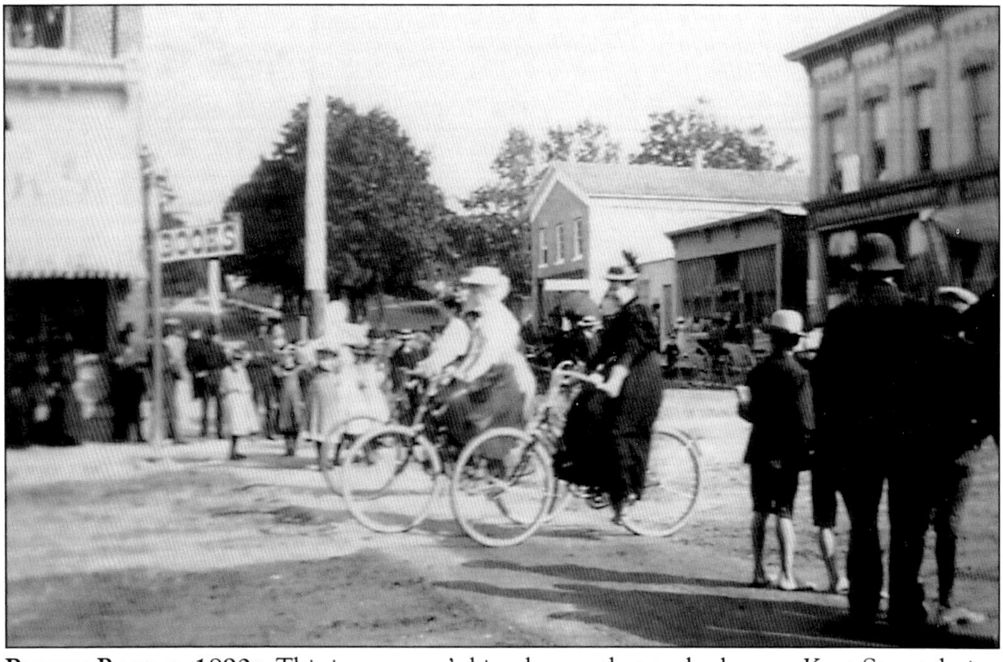

BICYCLE RACE, C. 1890S. This is a women's bicycle race that took place on Kent Street during a farmer's picnic. The early "high-wheeler" bicycles of the 1870s were almost impossible for women to ride because female clothing tended to get in the way. The 1884 introduction of the "safety" bicycle, a machine with two wheels of equal size, opened up the sport to many more people. In 1887, a safety bicycle for women was manufactured for the first time. The "Victor" featured a dropped frame and no cross bar. By 1890, close to 100,000 men and women were cycling in the United States. (Courtesy of the Portland Area Historical Society.)

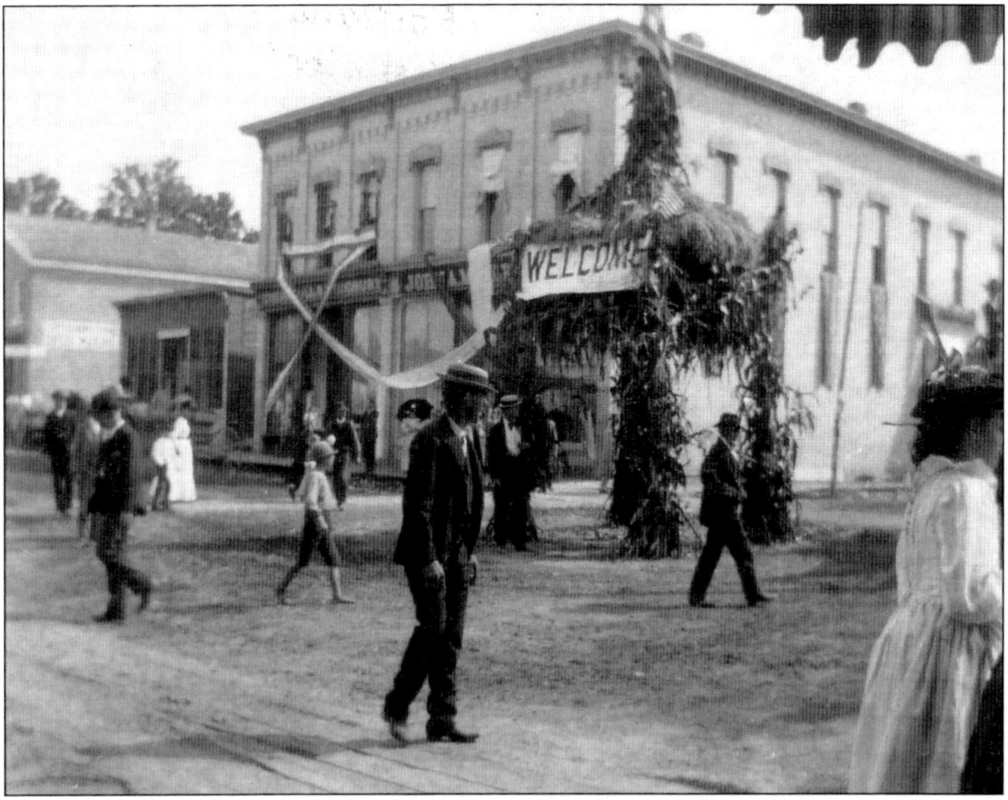

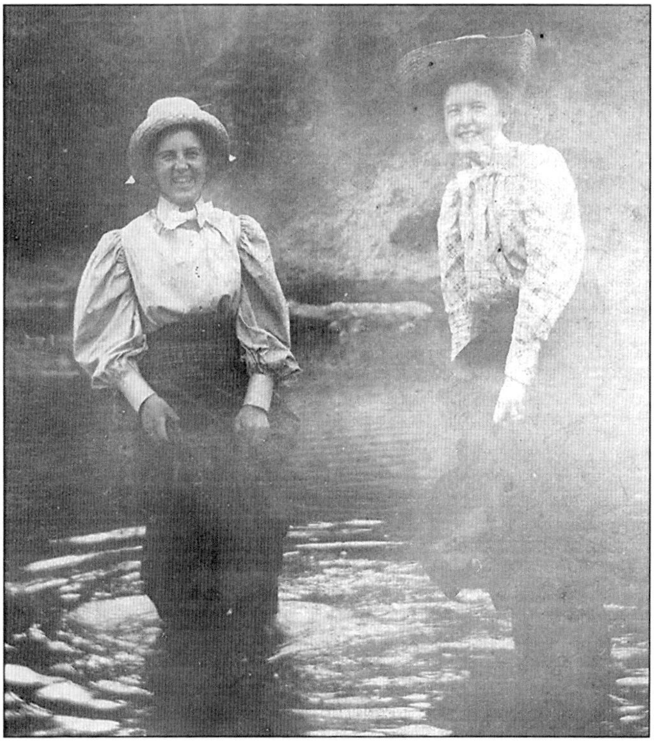

Farmer's Picnic, c. 1890s. Farmer's picnics have long been a tradition in agricultural areas around the United States. In this photograph, the Churchill & Woodbury and John A. McClelland stores are elaborately decorated with banners and ribbons. In the center of the Bridge and Kent Street intersection is an ornate welcome "pavilion." (Courtesy of the Portland Area Historical Society.)

Wading in the Grand River. Lorenzo Webber snapped this carefree shot of his wife, Dora, and Lulu McClelland enjoying the refreshing waters of the Grand River. (Courtesy of the Portland Area Historical Society.)

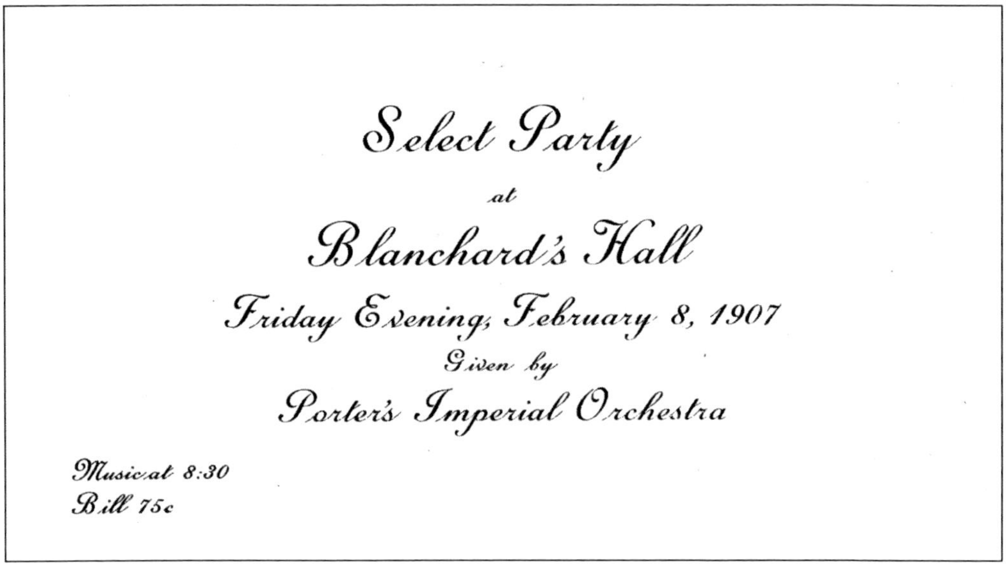

Select Party
at
Blanchard's Hall
Friday Evening, February 8, 1907
Given by
Porter's Imperial Orchestra

Music at 8:30
Bill 75c

INVITATION TO A PARTY. This postcard invitation was sent to Portland resident Charles Gilden and postmarked February 2, 1907. This event was held at the Opera House, which, for a time, was operated by David Blanchard. Porter's Imperial Orchestra was a local musical ensemble led by Bill Porter. Members of the group included Jay Clark, Roy Dawdy, Leon Hixson, Leo Lehman, Will McClelland, Lorenzo Webber, and John Webster. (Courtesy of Robert Torp-Smith.)

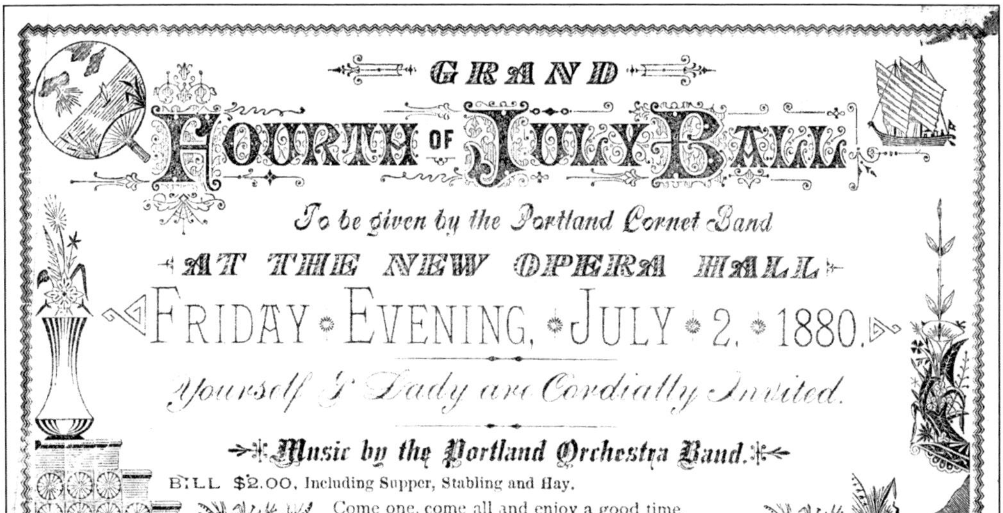

GRAND
FOURTH OF JULY BALL
To be given by the Portland Cornet Band
AT THE NEW OPERA HALL
FRIDAY EVENING, JULY 2, 1880.
Yourself & Lady are Cordially Invited.
Music by the Portland Orchestra Band.
BILL $2.00, Including Supper, Stabling and Hay.
Come one, come all and enjoy a good time.

FOURTH OF JULY BALL INVITATION, 1880. This Fourth of July Ball was one of the very first events to take place at Portland's sparkling new opera house. The following week, the *Portland Observer* reported, "The Cornet Band had a very pleasant party at the Opera House Friday evening, but they did not make any money out of it." The opera house's interior featured the Great Seal of Michigan decorating the center of the rounded proscenium arch in front of the inclined stage and an elaborate garden scene painted on the upstage wall. (Courtesy of the Portland Area Historical Society.)

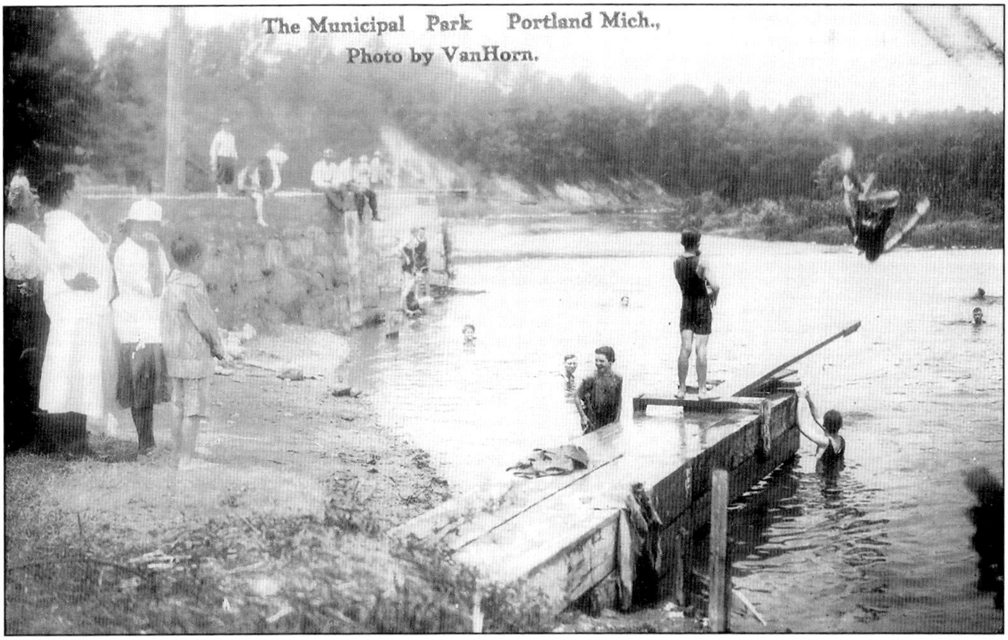

Water Wonderland. All of these people are clearly enjoying the cool relaxation of the waters around the Portland area. The municipal park was probably upriver on the Grand, near the location of the old municipal dam. (Top photograph courtesy of the Portland Area Historical Society. Bottom photograph courtesy of Anne Rademacher.)

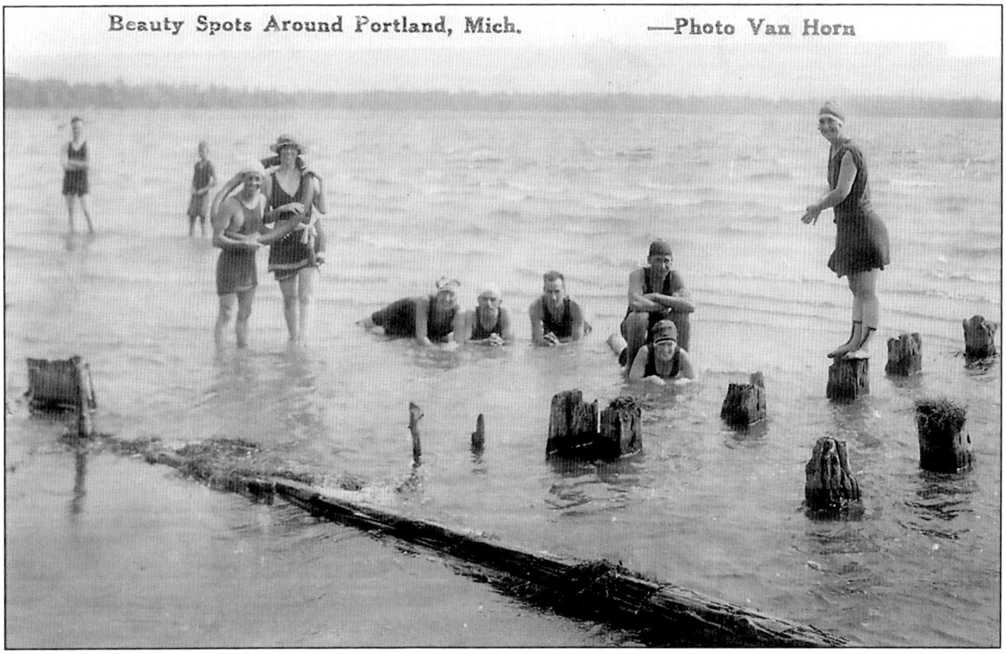

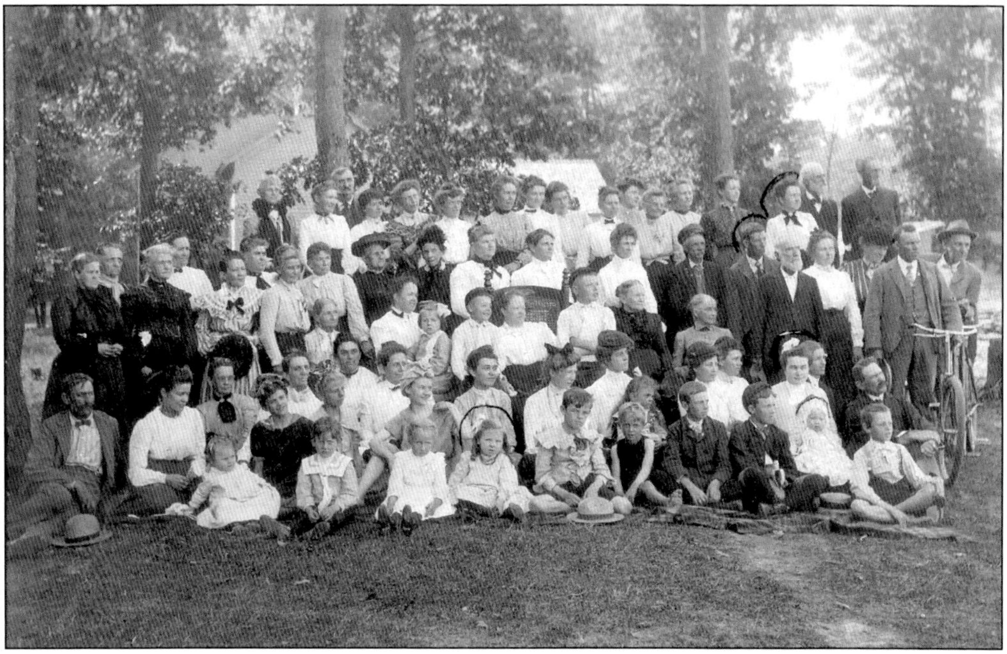

PICNIC AT THE MUNICIPAL DAM. Some of the many people pictured include: George Buck, Mary Buck, Mary Rice, Charles C. Rice, Belle Ramsey, Rose Powell, Amelia Howe, Jennie Rice, and Maude Dilley. (Courtesy of the Portland Area Historical Society.)

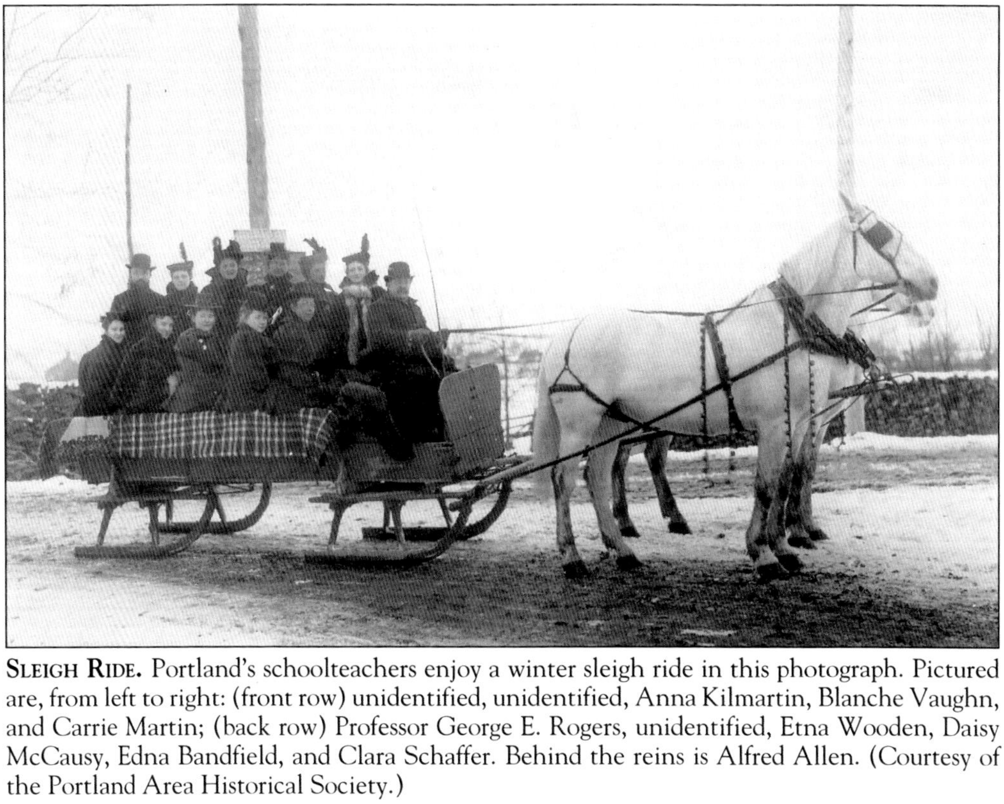

SLEIGH RIDE. Portland's schoolteachers enjoy a winter sleigh ride in this photograph. Pictured are, from left to right: (front row) unidentified, unidentified, Anna Kilmartin, Blanche Vaughn, and Carrie Martin; (back row) Professor George E. Rogers, unidentified, Etna Wooden, Daisy McCausy, Edna Bandfield, and Clara Schaffer. Behind the reins is Alfred Allen. (Courtesy of the Portland Area Historical Society.)

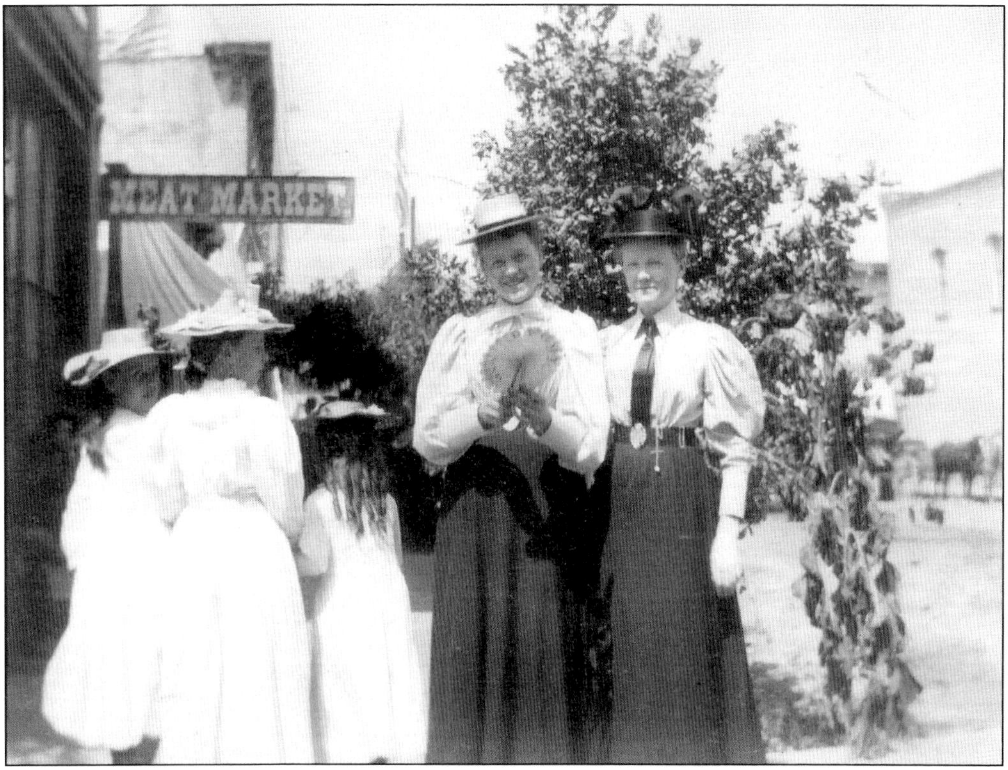

Farmers' Picnic. Above, Etola and Lucy Whitlock pose on Bridge Street during the festivities of a farmers' picnic. The business behind them is Frank Sprout's Meat Market. Below, William Gibbs' buggy is decorated with cornstalks and straw. (Courtesy of the Portland Area Historical Society.)

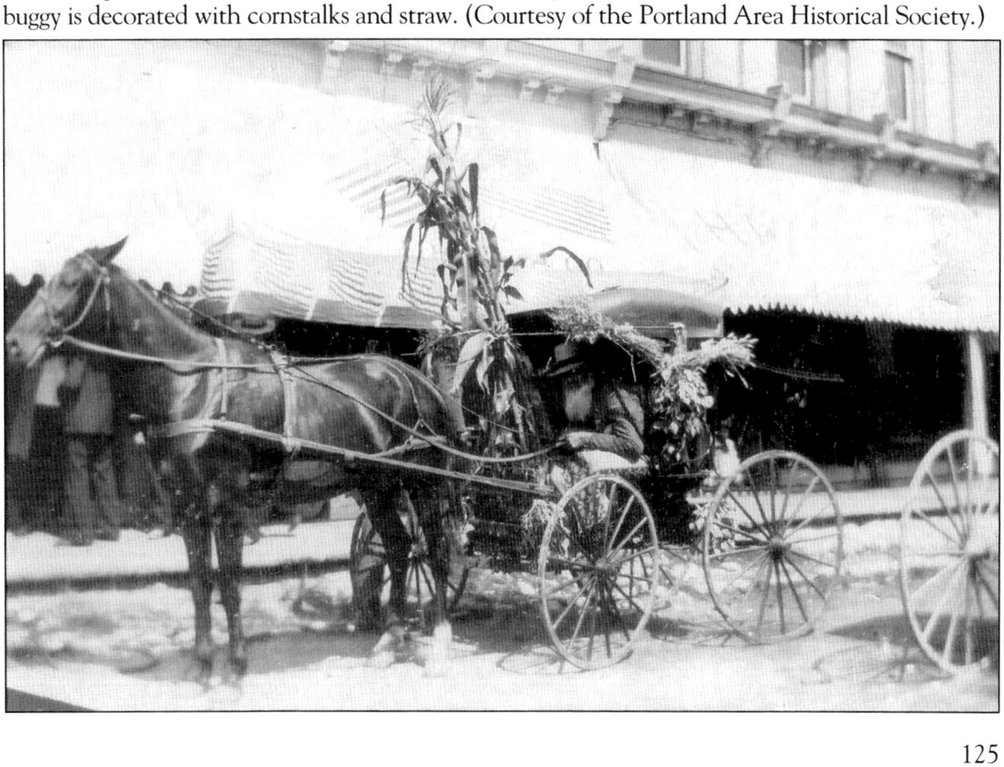

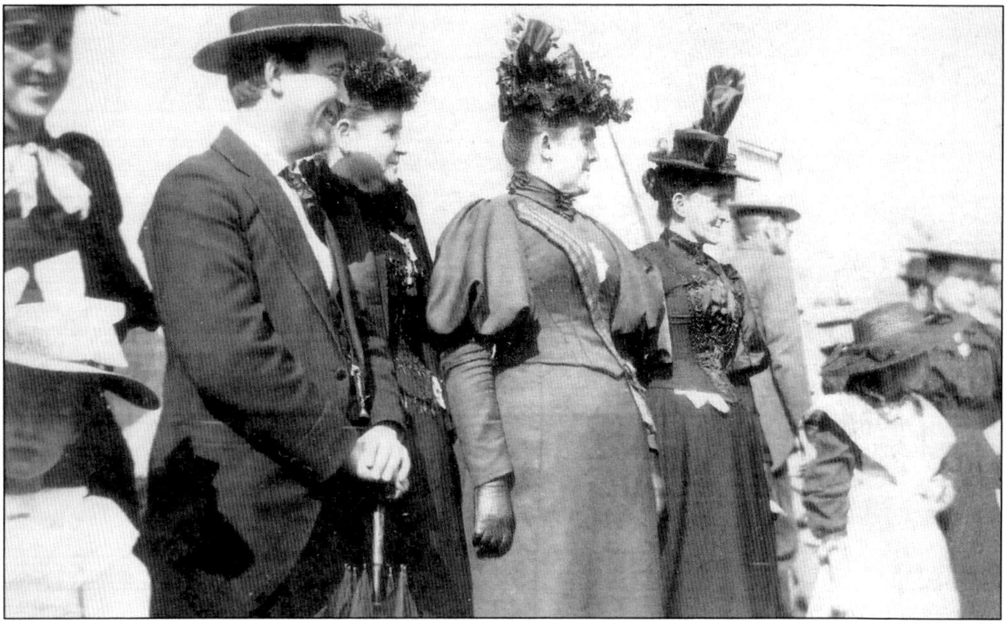

MEMORIAL DAY, c. 1906. Some of the people in this photograph are, from left to right: Fred Cornell (in straw boater), Mrs. Eddie Kennedy, Mrs. Olin E. Robinson, Queen Robinson Stone, and Bessie Adams (little girl). (Courtesy of the Portland Area Historical Society.)

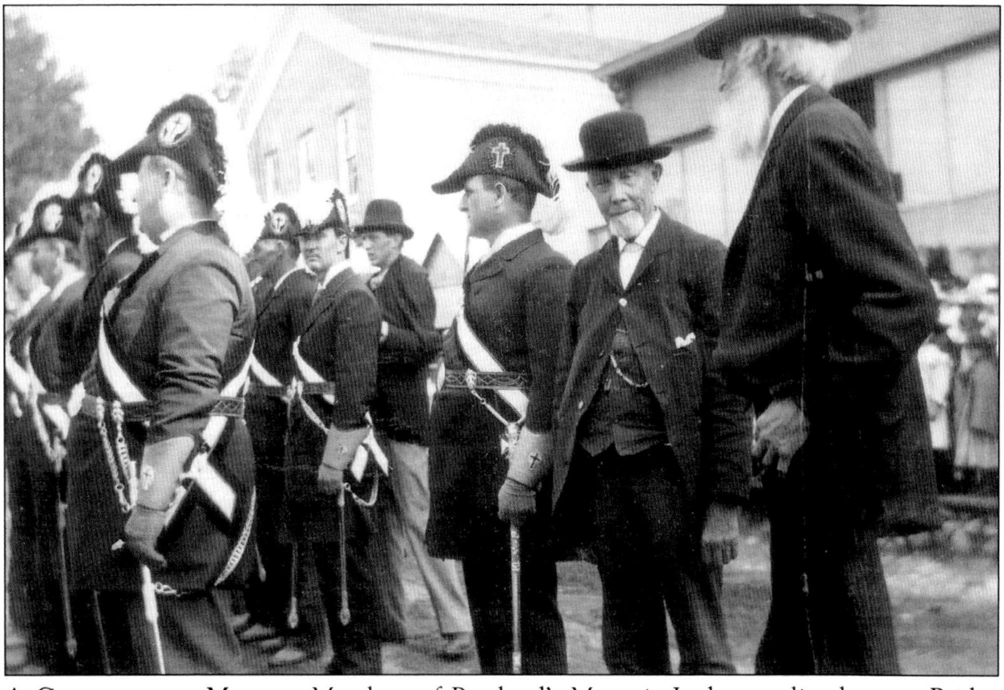

A GATHERING OF MASONS. Members of Portland's Masonic Lodge are lined up on Bridge Street. Portland Lodge #31 Free and Accepted Masons was chartered on January 10, 1849. The lodge met at various locations until 1925, when it moved into the Masonic Temple that still stands at the southwest corner of Bridge and Maple Street. (Courtesy of the Portland Area Historical Society.)

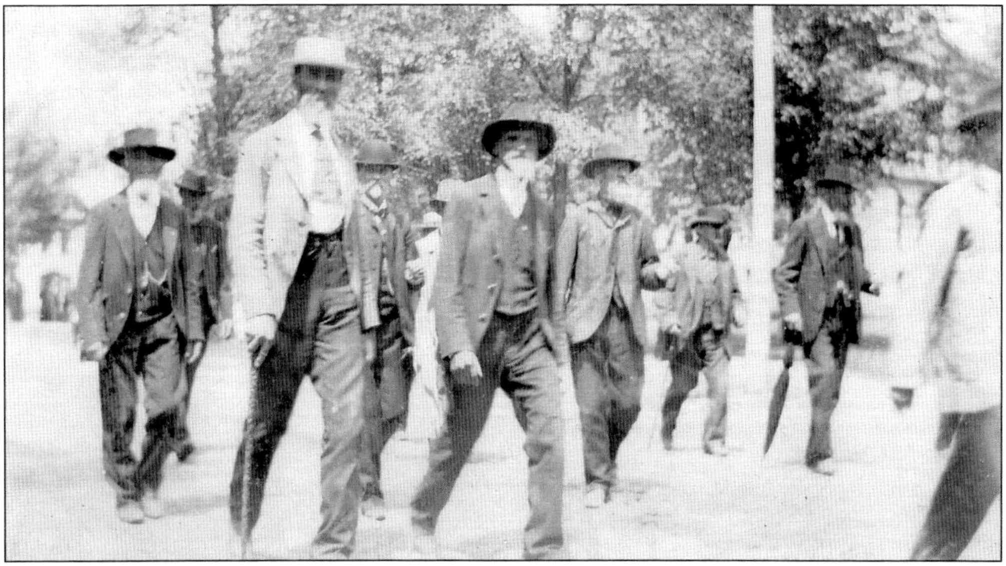

Parade of Civil War Veterans, c. 1895. This photograph was taken on Memorial Day, a holiday that was originally called Decoration Day because it was designated as a day to honor the nation's Civil War dead by decorating their graves. The tall man with the cane is Harrison Outwater. Outwater served as a private with the 1st New York Light Artillery during the Civil War. (Courtesy of the Portland Area Historical Society.)

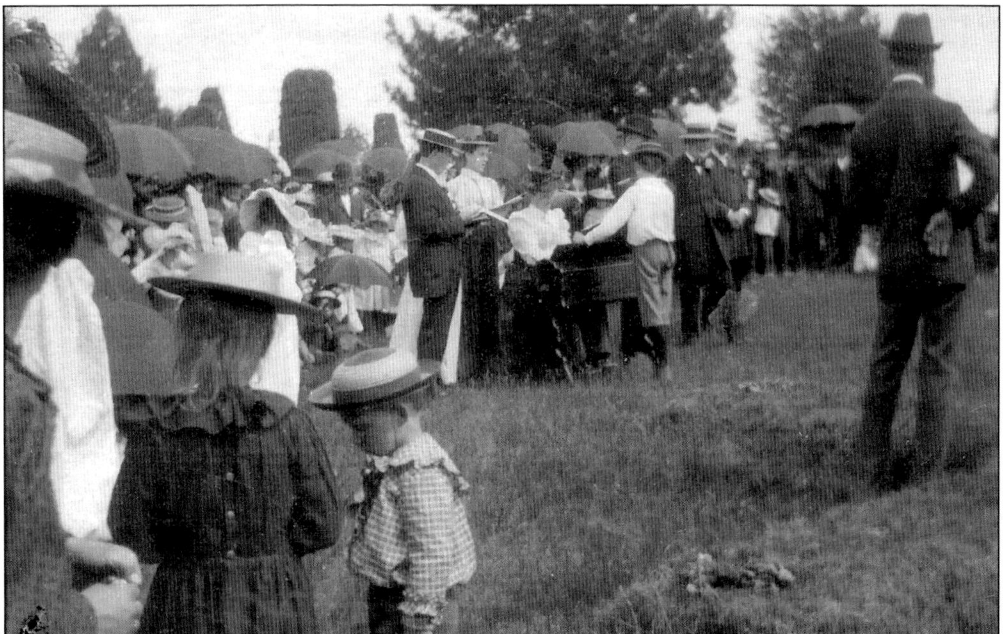

Memorial Day Commemoration, c. 1895. Musicians perform at a Memorial Day ceremony at the Portland Cemetery. The organist is identified as Mrs. Olin E. Robinson. The two singers are identified as Fred Cornell and Meredith Smith. Visible in the background are the tall sculpted shrubs that flanked the cemetery entrance on Bridge Street. (Courtesy of the Portland Area Historical Society.)

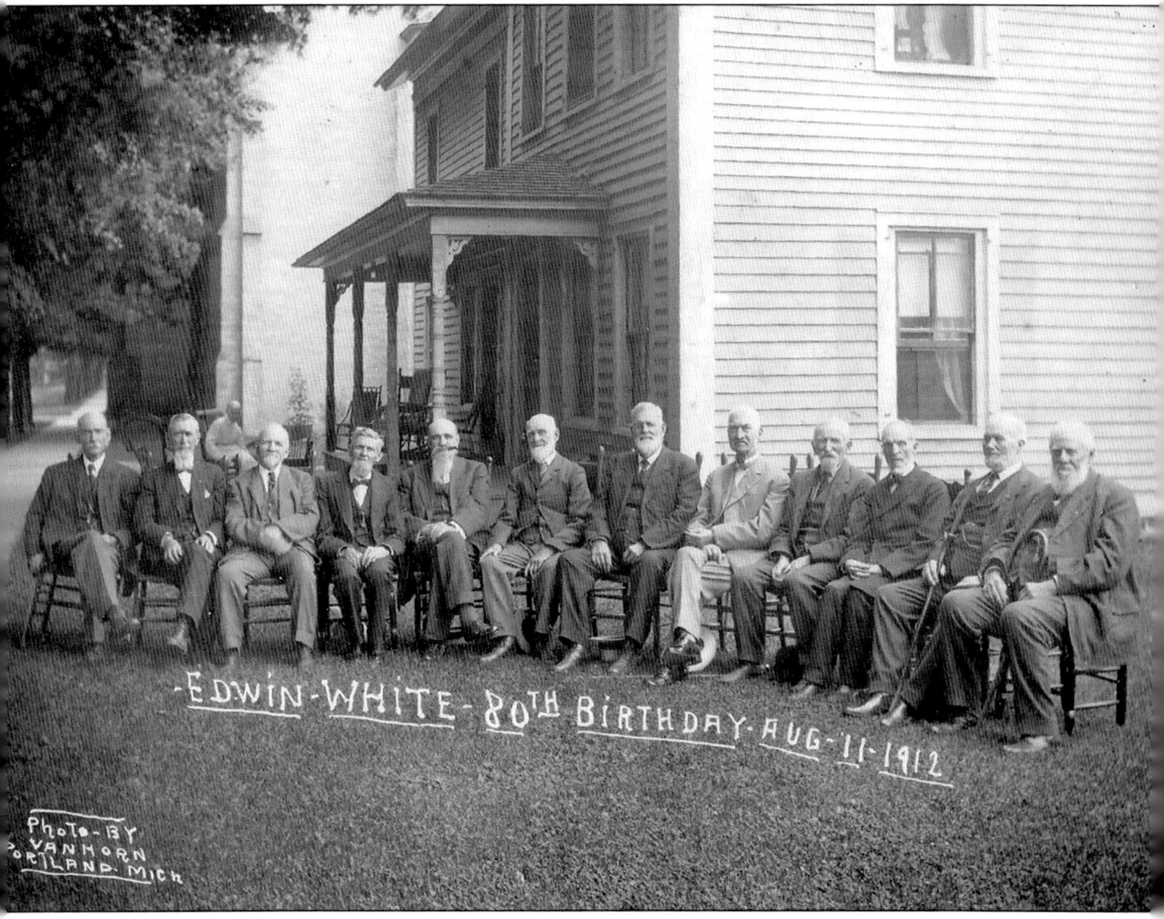

GATHERING OF PIONEERS. On Saturday, August 10, 1912, eleven of Portland's venerable pioneers gathered at the home of Mr. and Mrs. George Buck to celebrate Edwin White's birthday, which happened to fall on August 11. Edwin White was the father of Mrs. Buck. Dinner was served at noon, and in the afternoon the elderly gentlemen chatted. Photographer George Van Horn paid the men a visit in the afternoon and took this photograph. He arranged them in the order of their ages. From left to right are: William White (75), Dr. Charles C. Dellenbaugh (78), W.A. Staley (78), Edwin White (80), Isaac Perrigo (80), H.G. Stevens (80), Samuel Gibbs (80), Charles H. Maynard (81), Lester LaSalle (81), Rev. D.E. Millard (84), and William Towner (84). Mrs. Edwin White is the woman seated in the background. (Courtesy of the Portland Area Historical Society.)